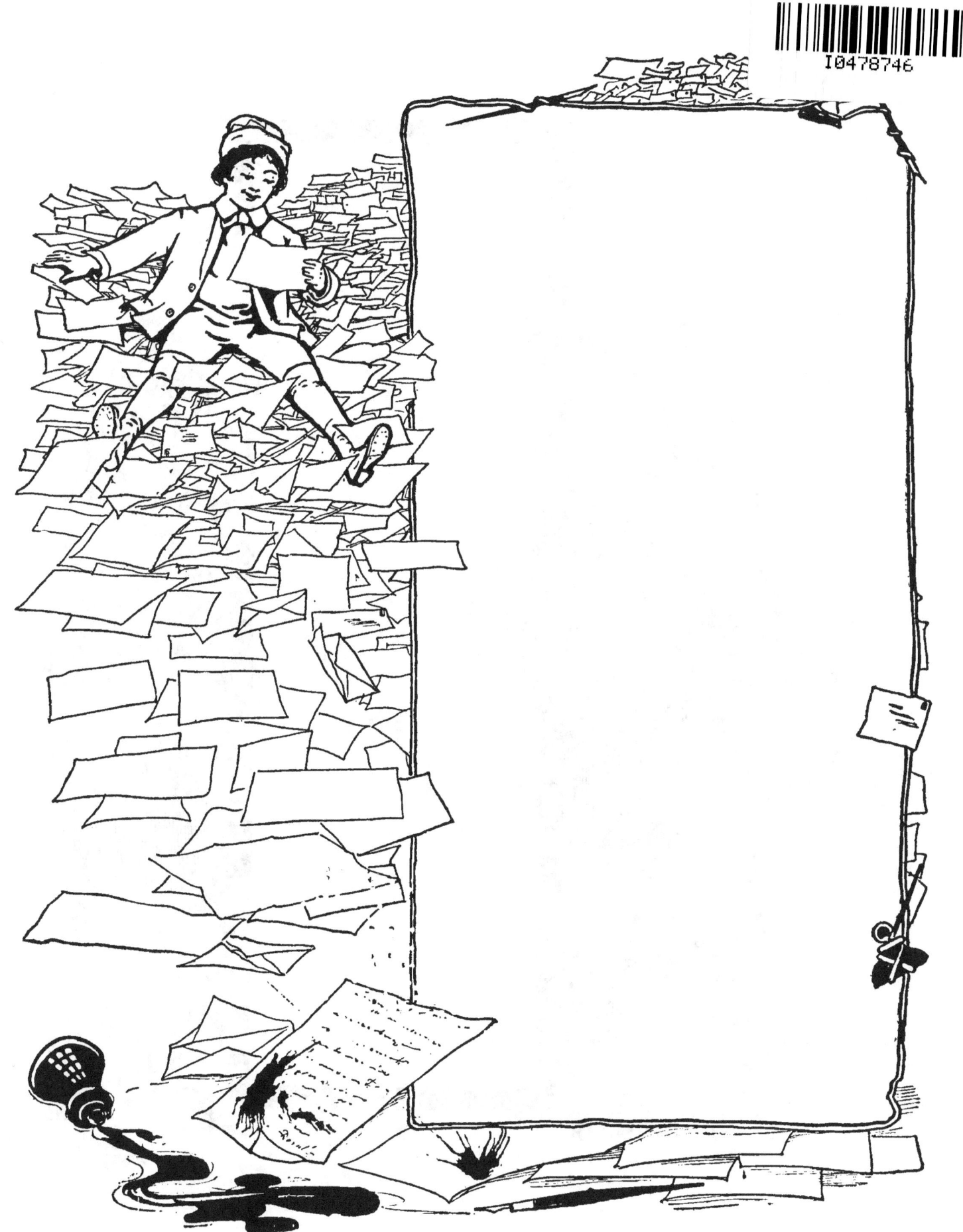

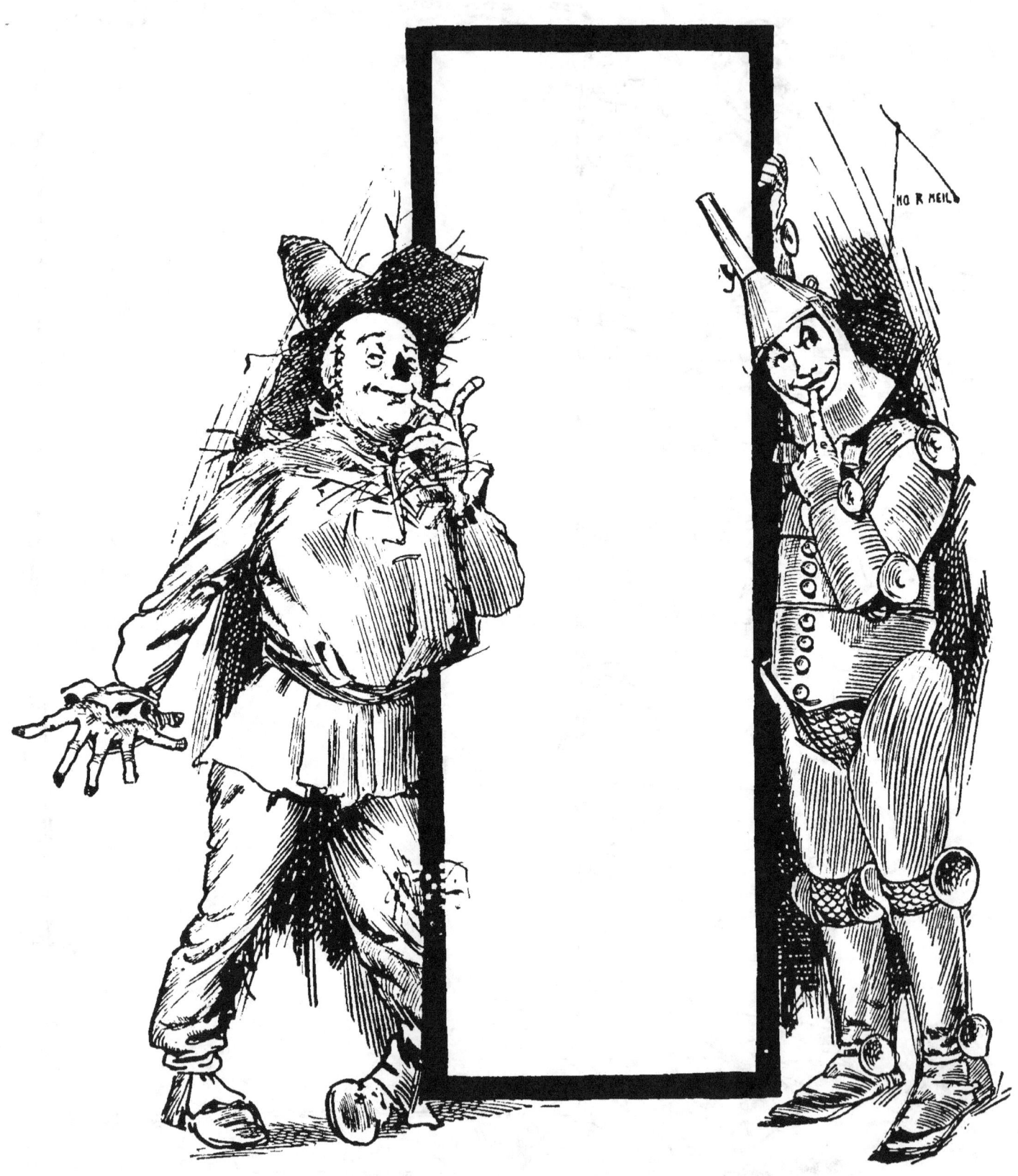

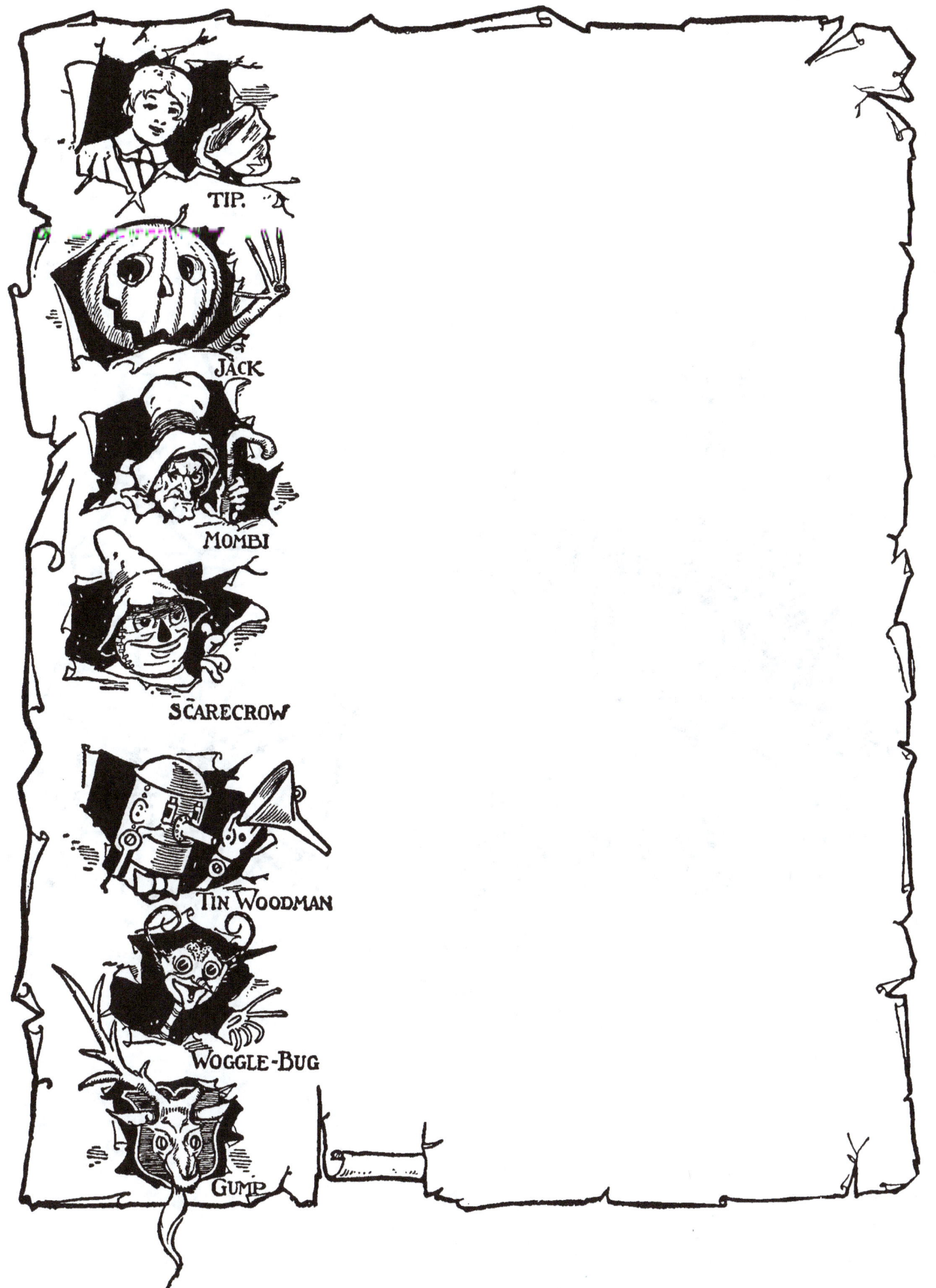

TIP.

JACK

MOMBI

SCARECROW

TIN WOODMAN

WOGGLE-BUG

GUMP

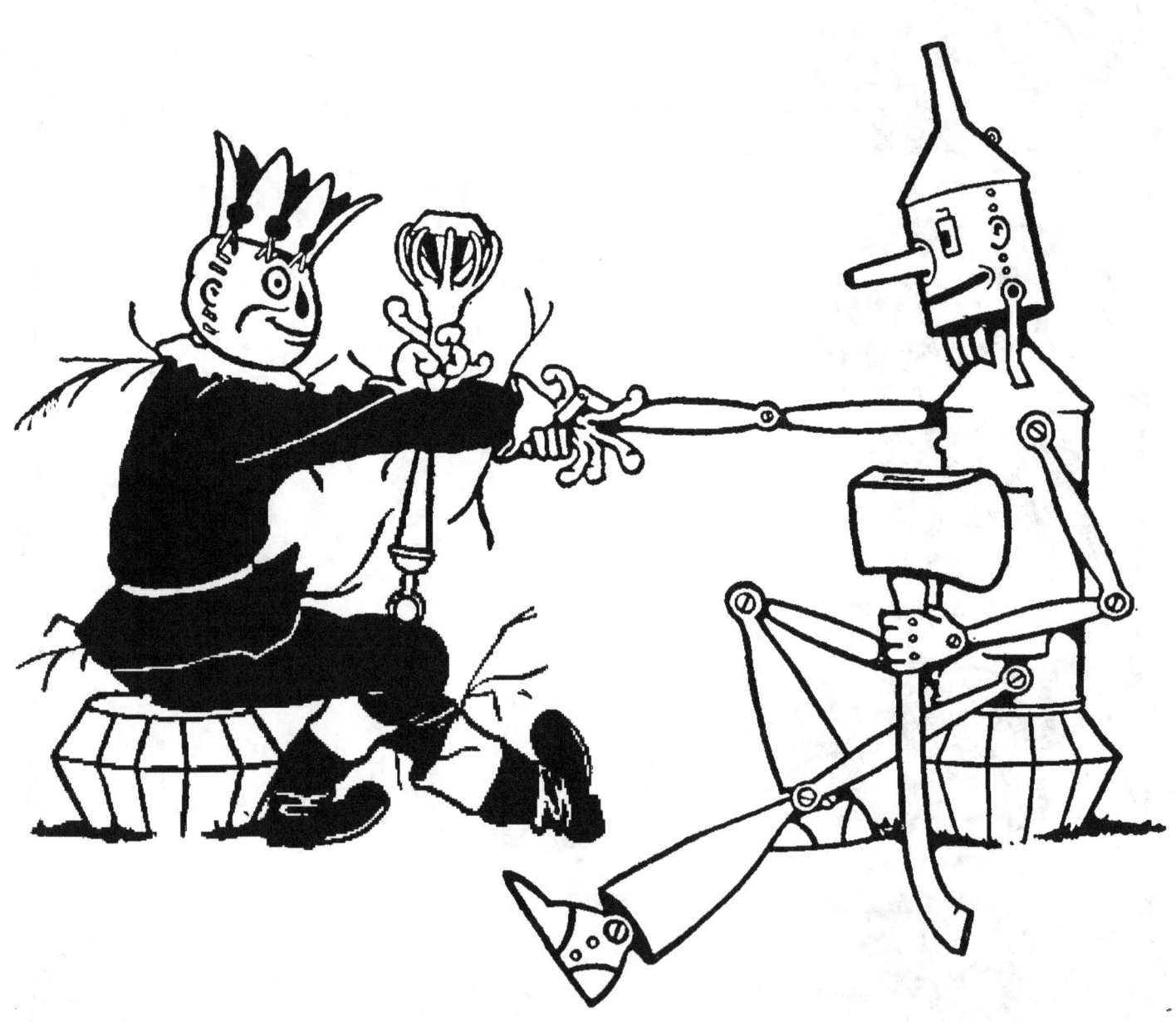

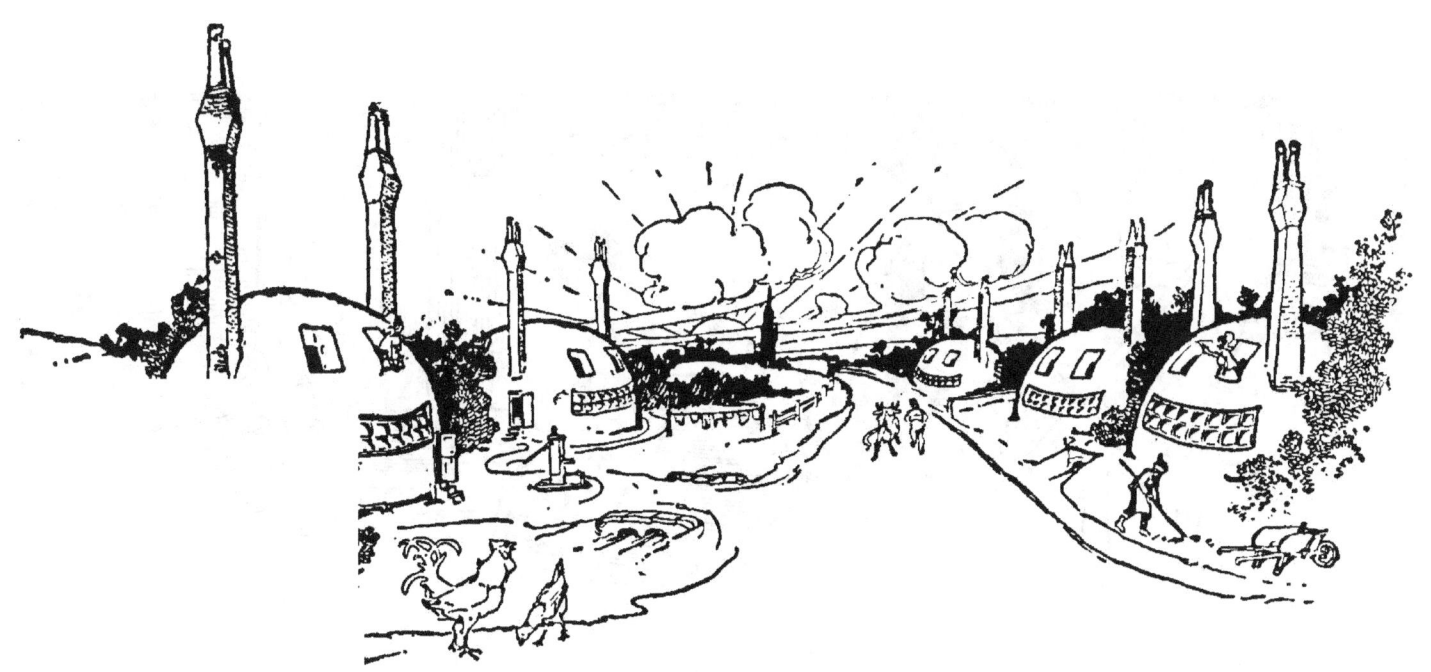

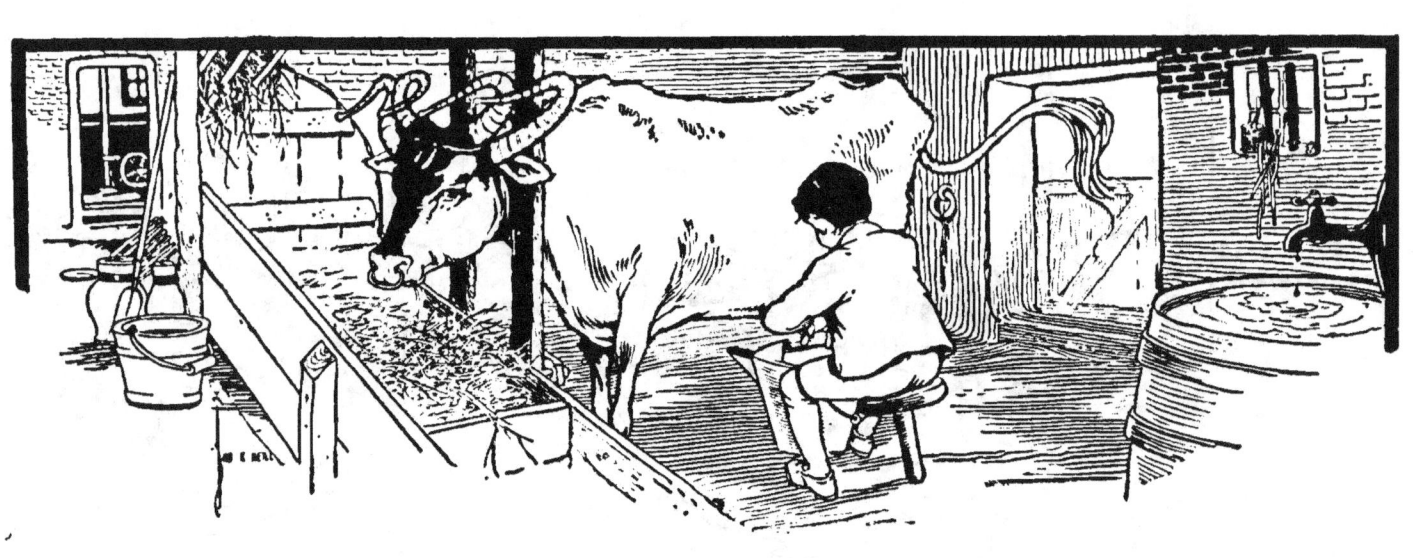

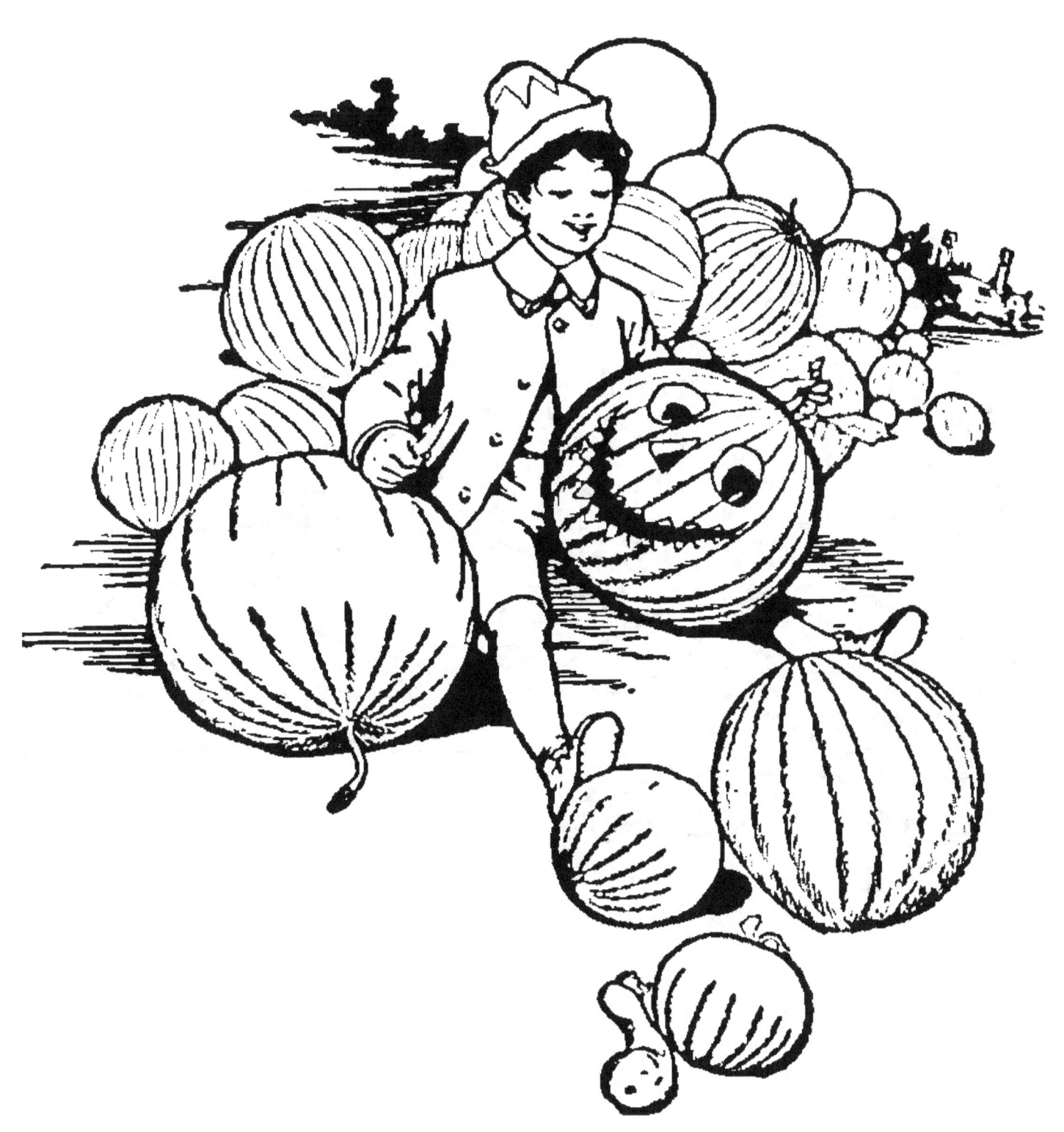

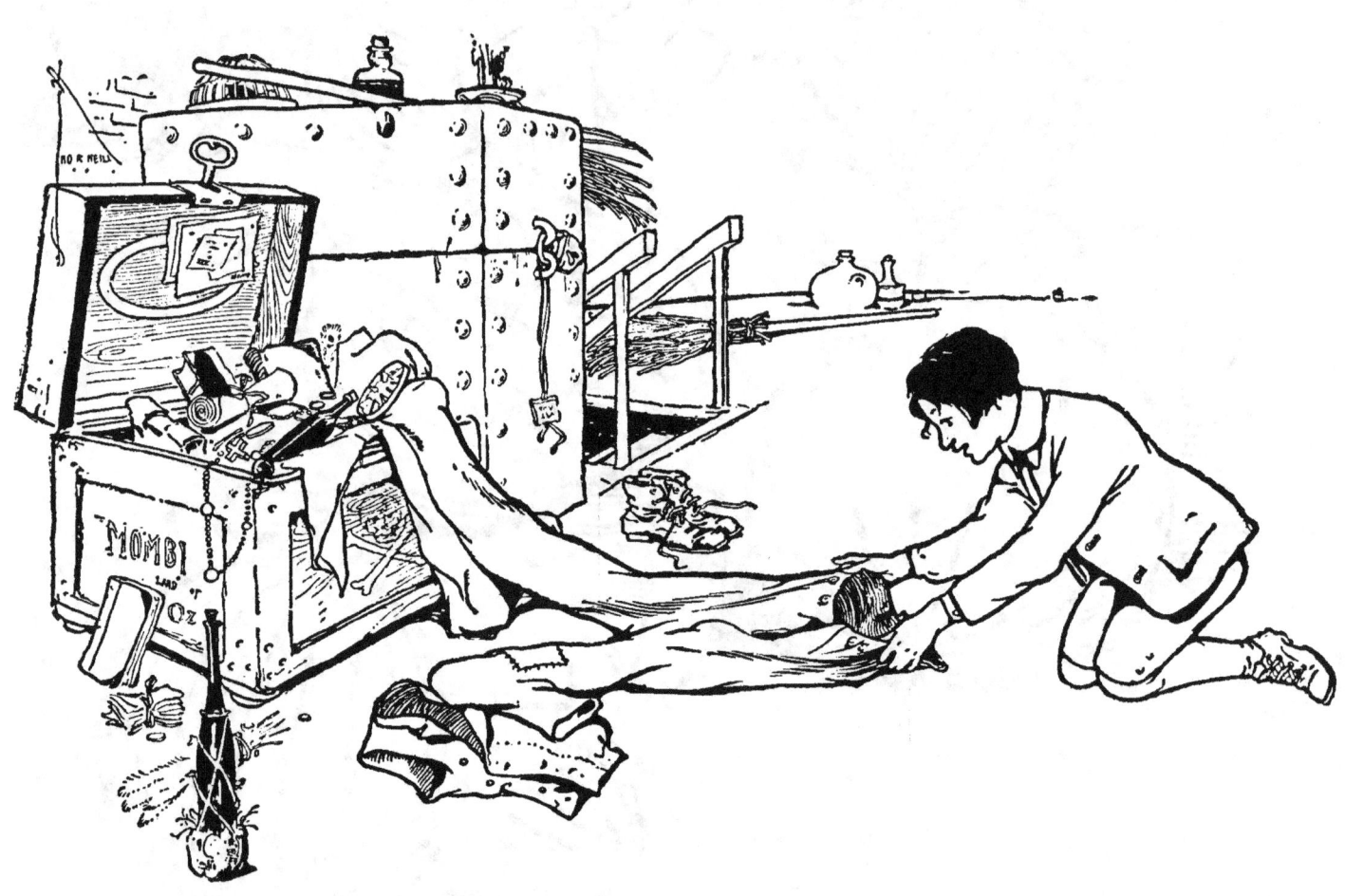

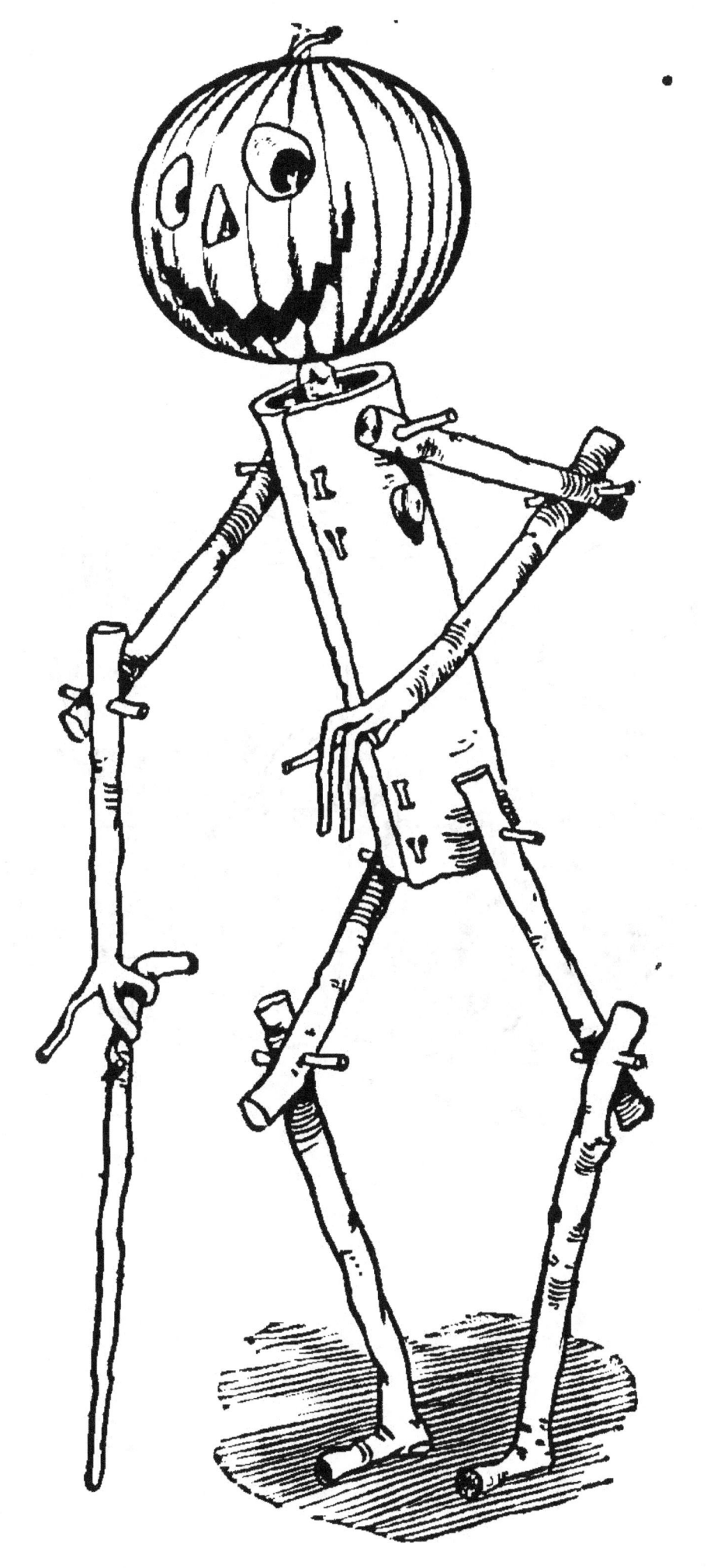

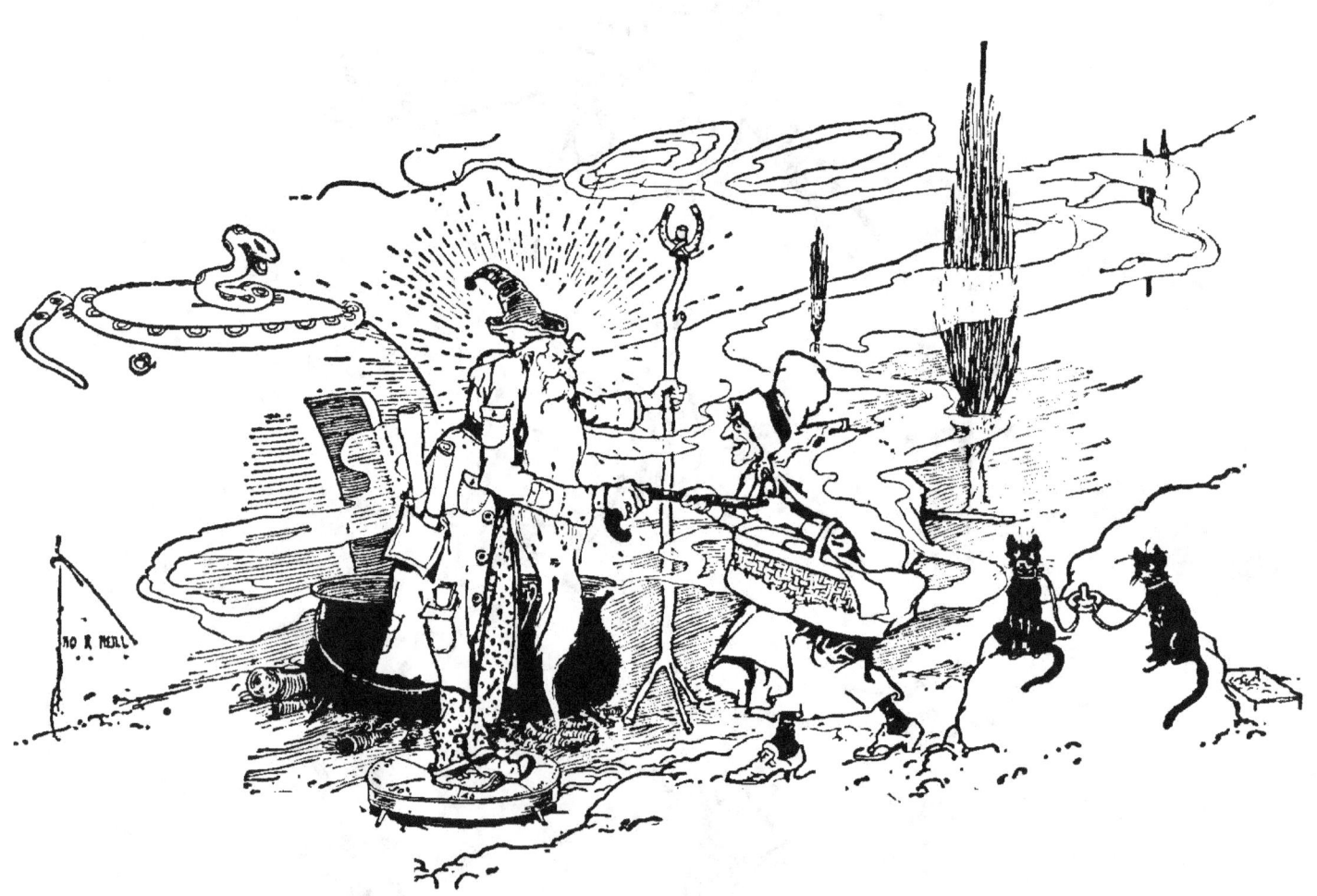

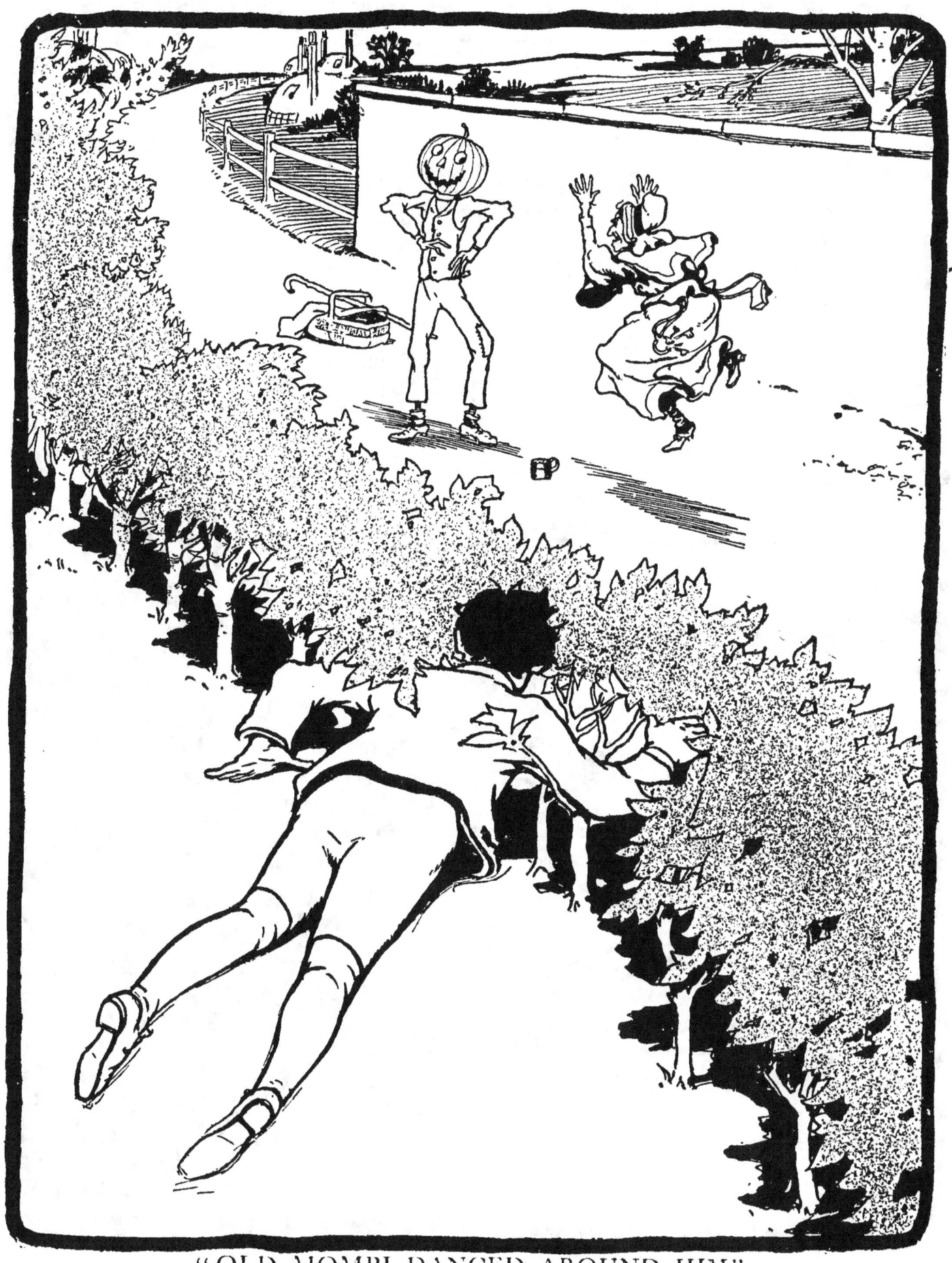

"OLD MOMBI DANCED AROUND HIM"

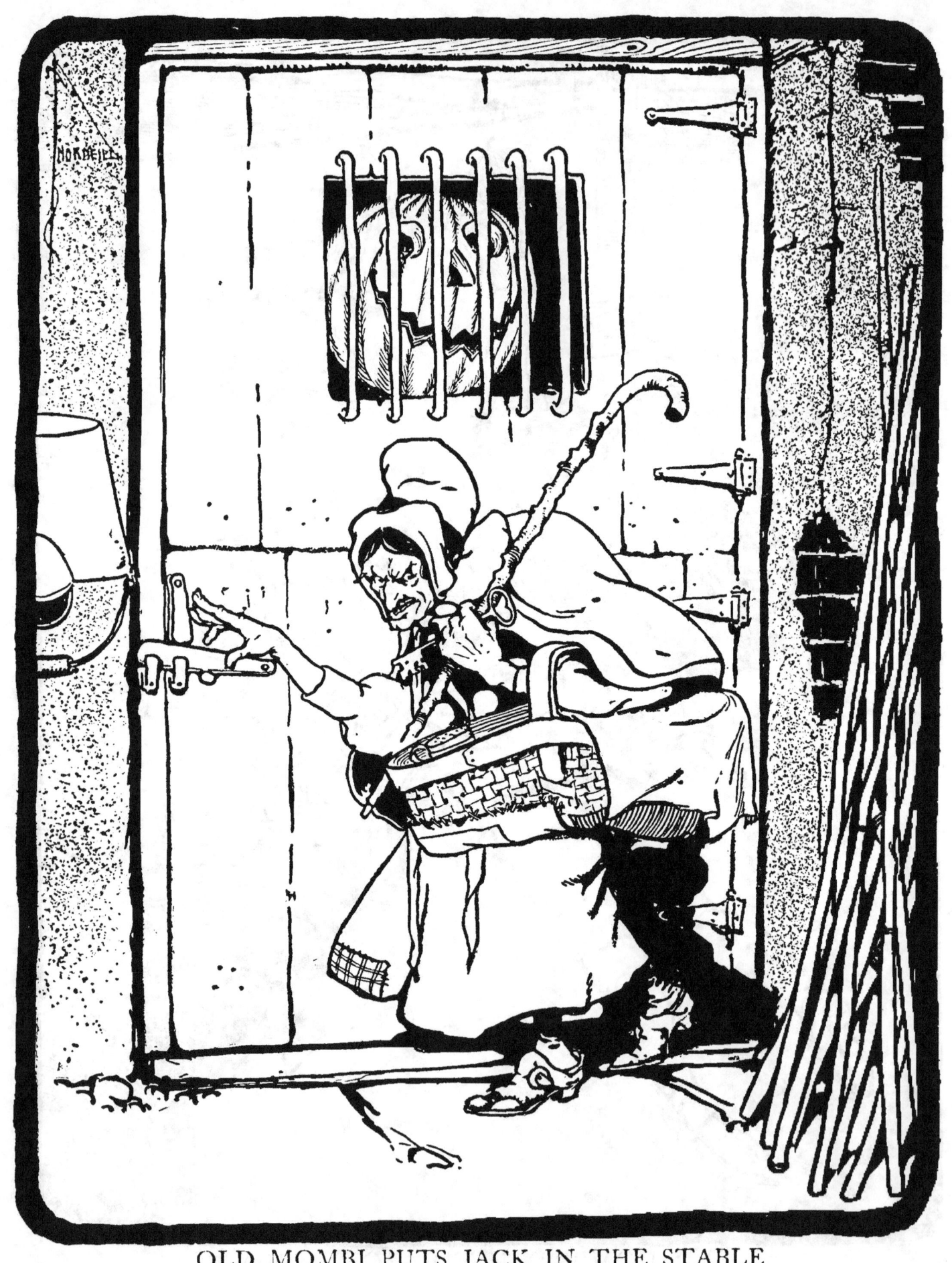

OLD MOMBI PUTS JACK IN THE STABLE

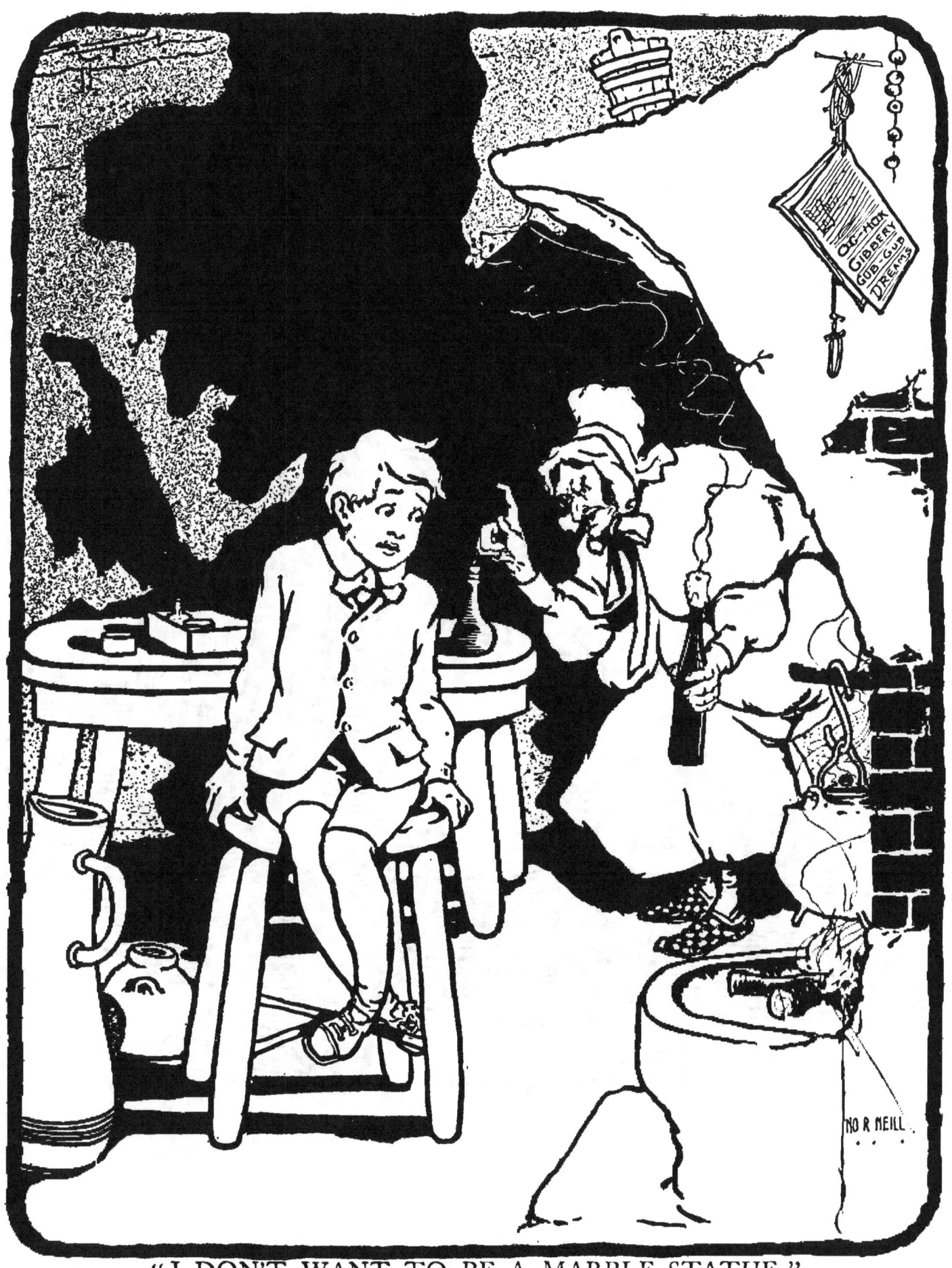

"I DON'T WANT TO BE A MARBLE STATUE."

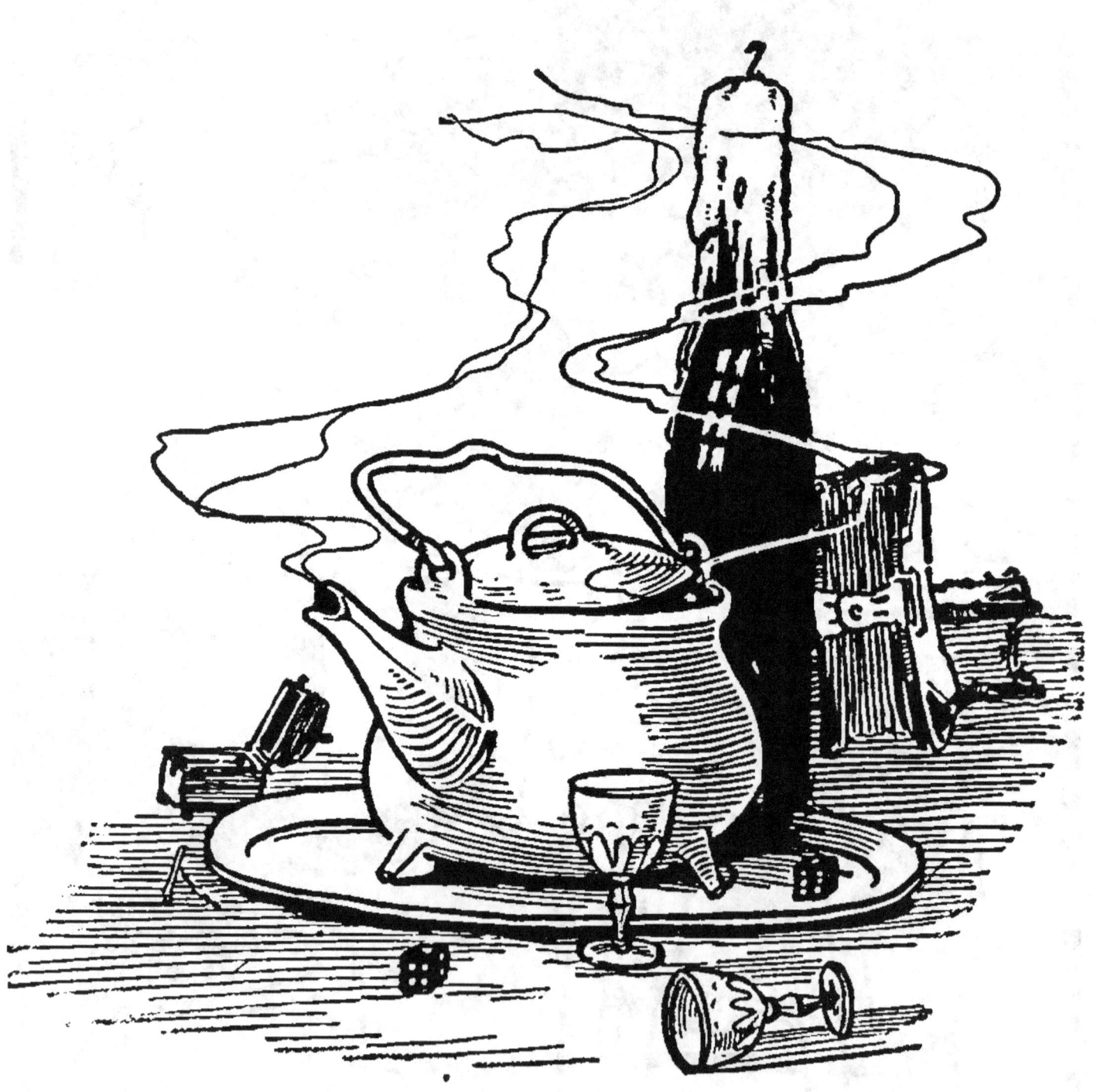

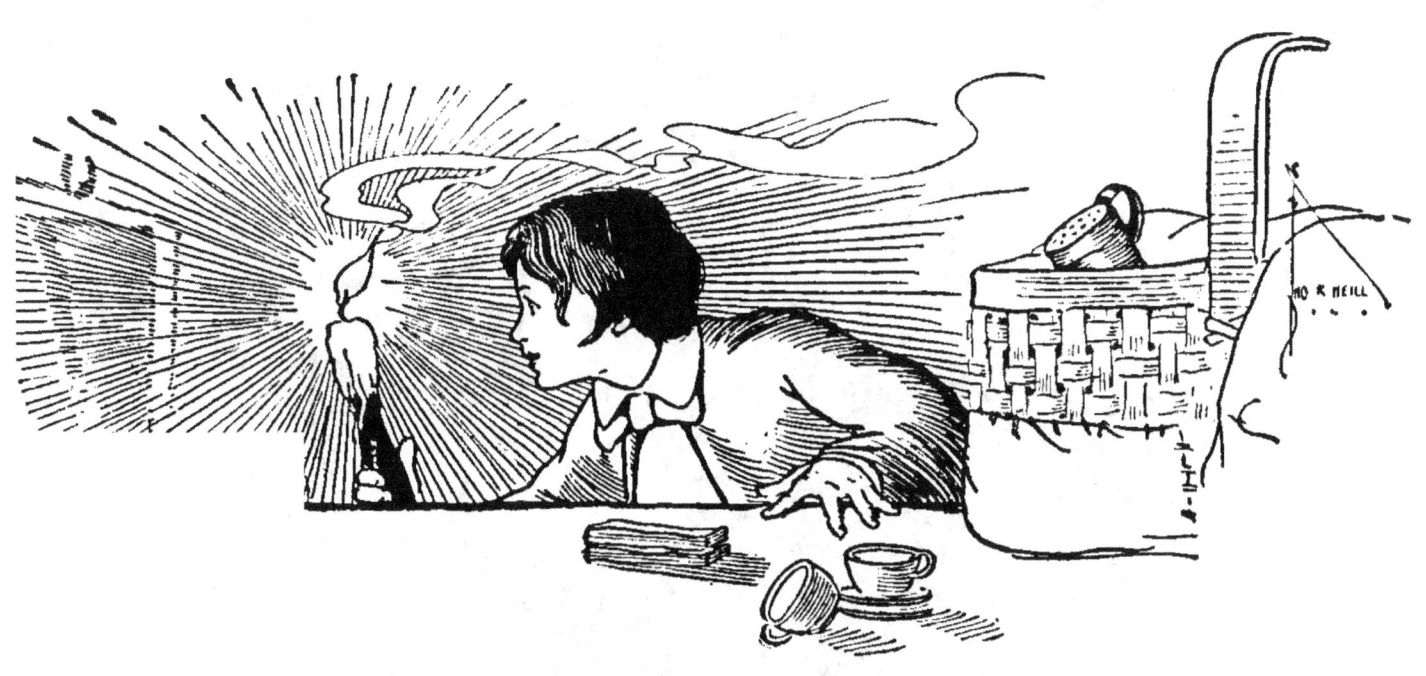

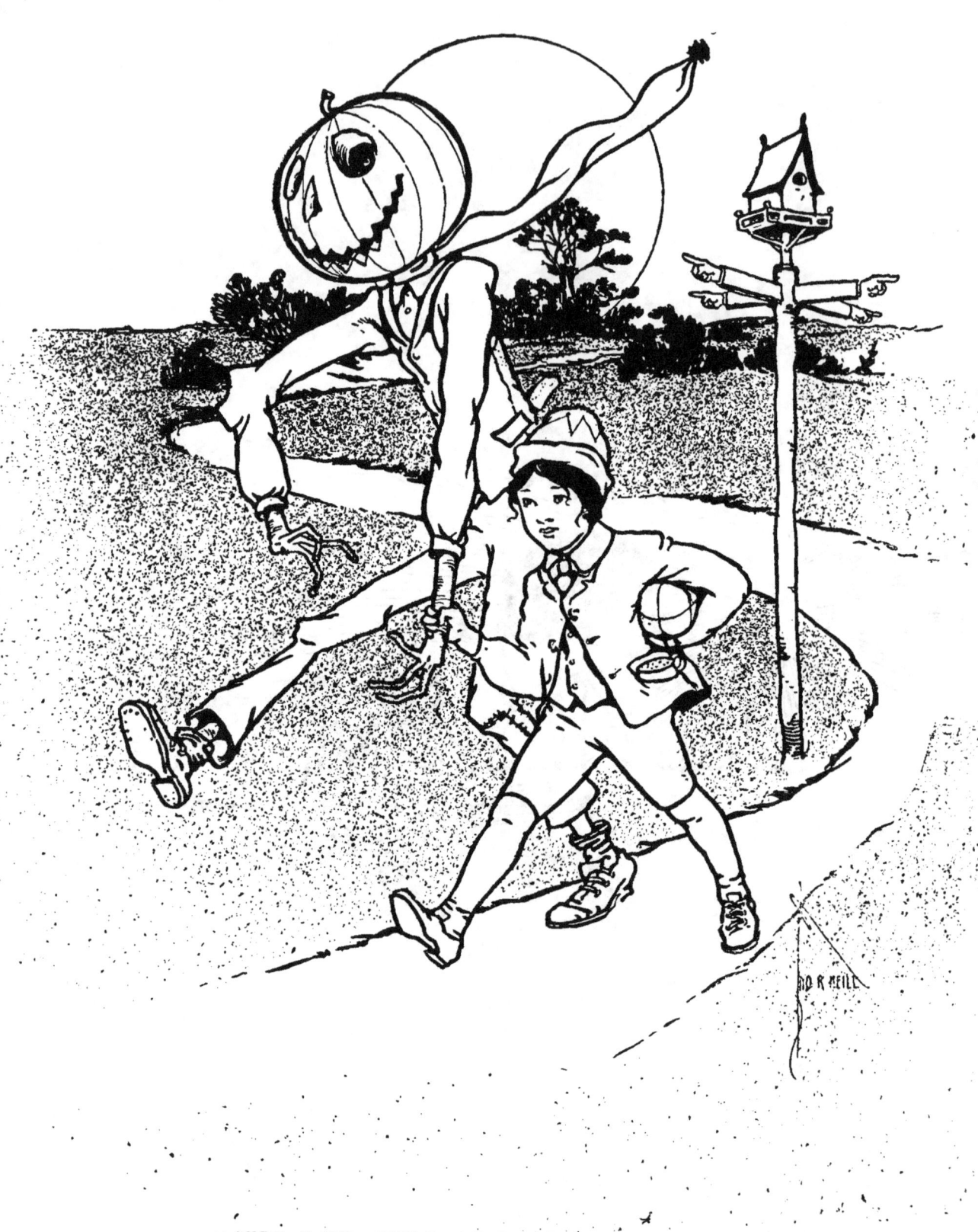

"TIP LED HIM ALONG THE PATH."

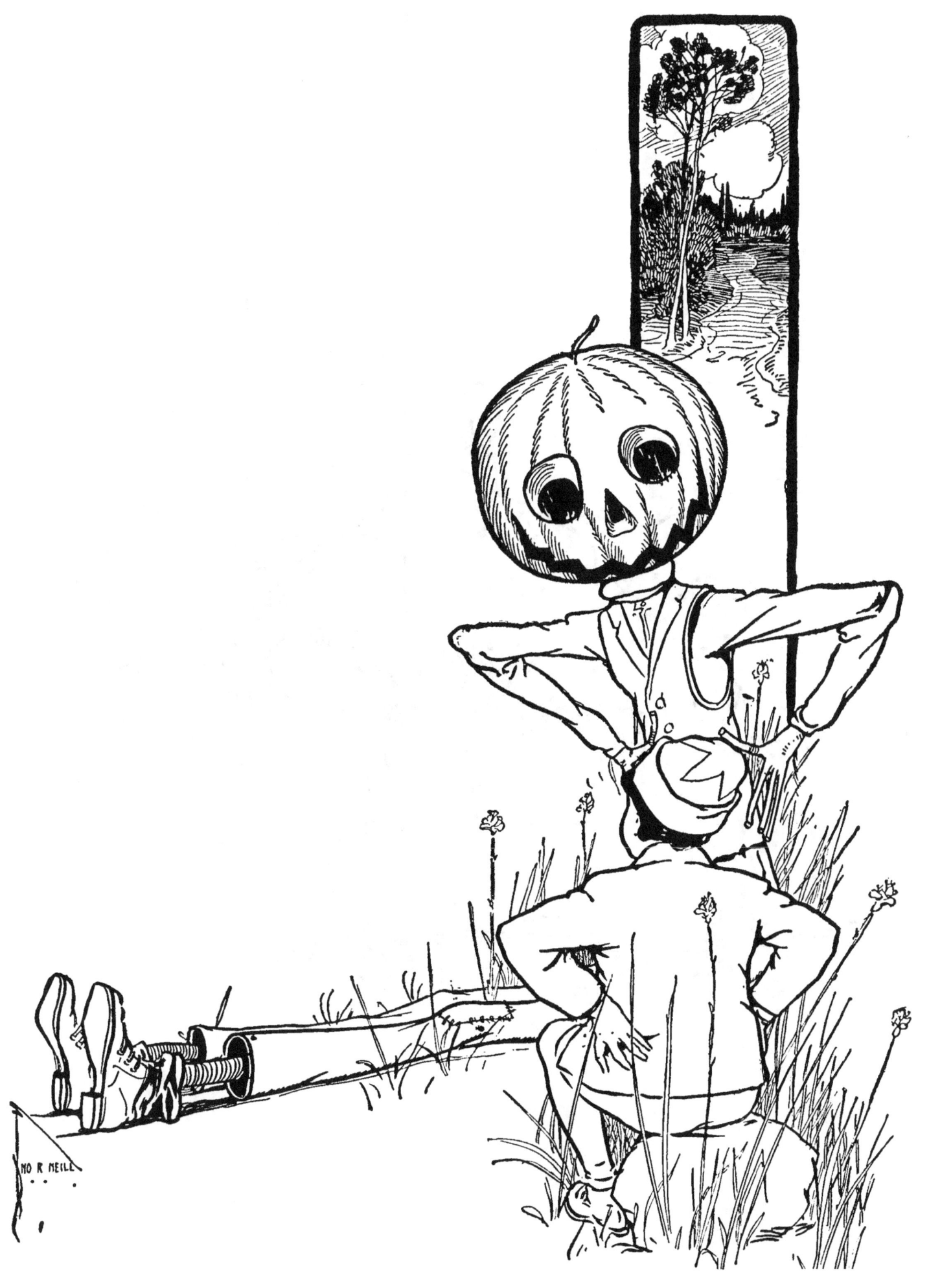

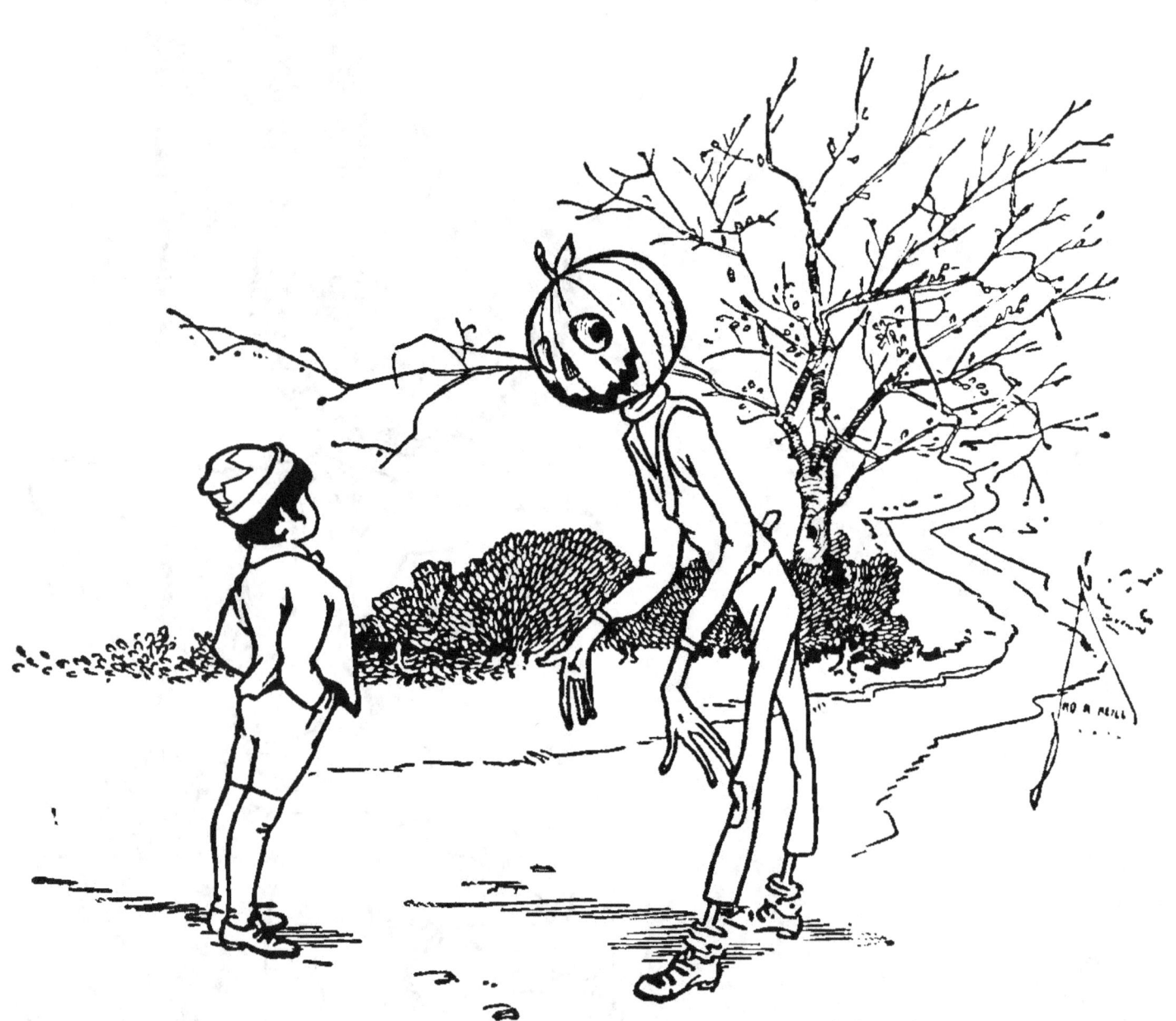

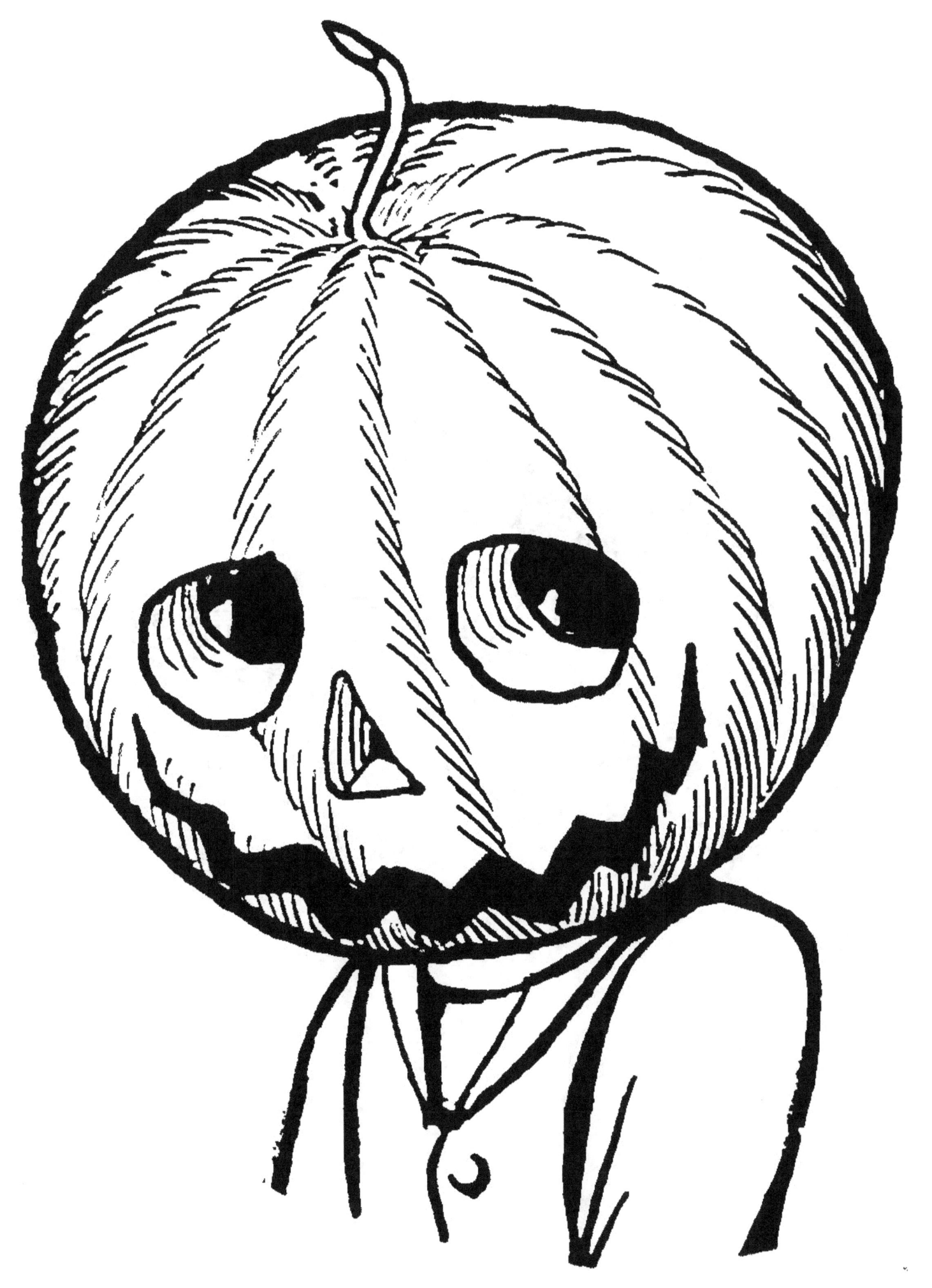

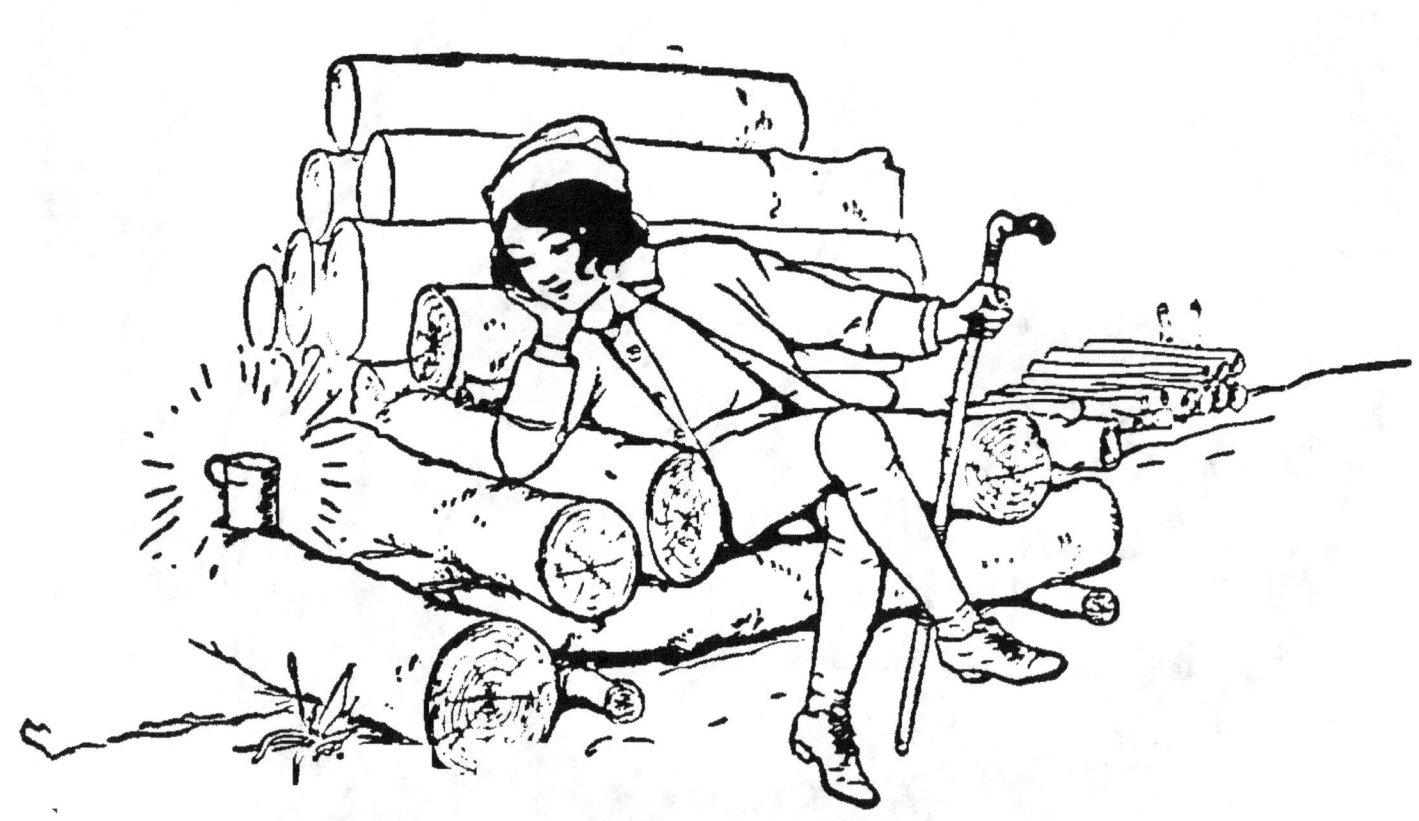

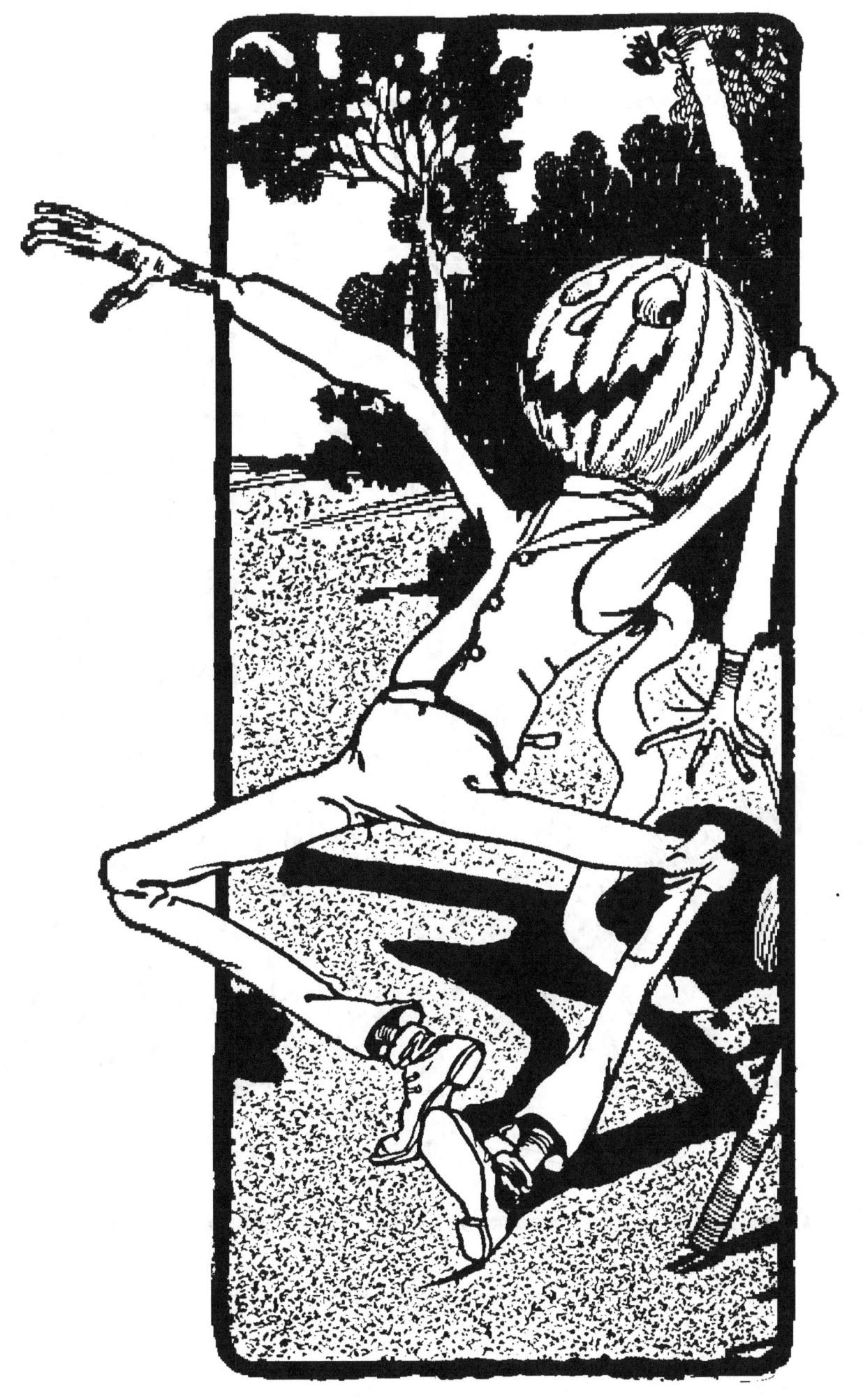

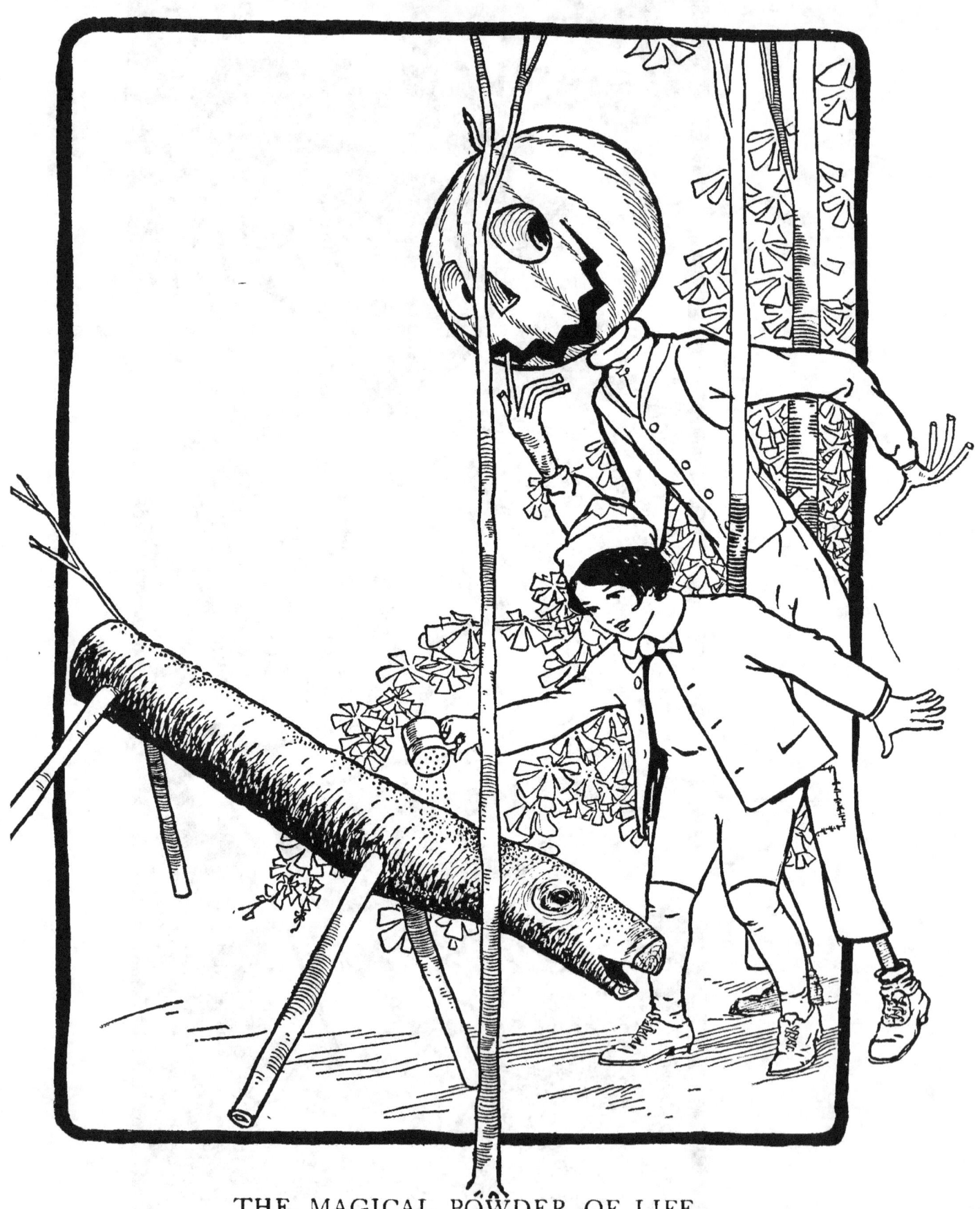

THE MAGICAL POWDER OF LIFE

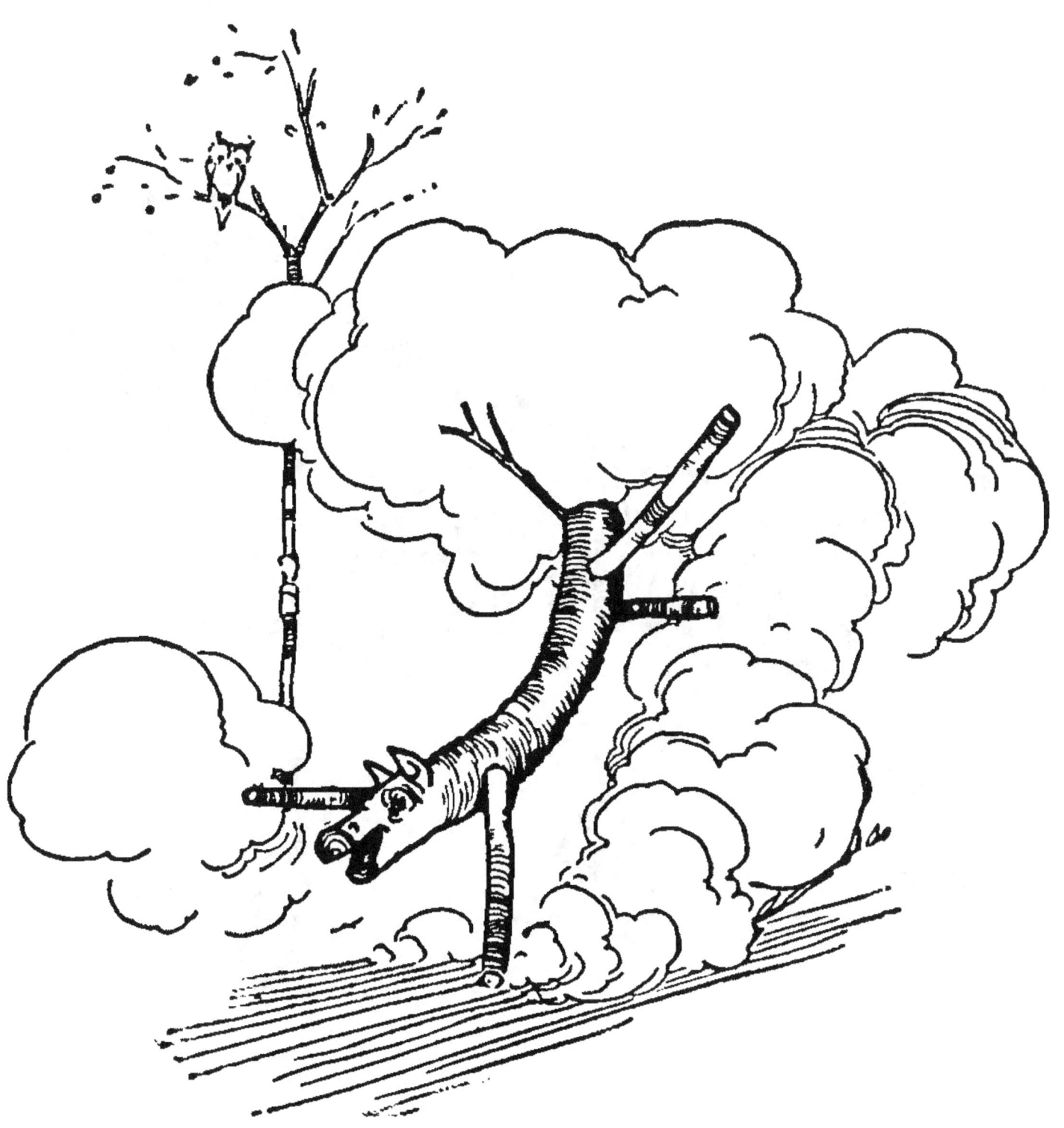

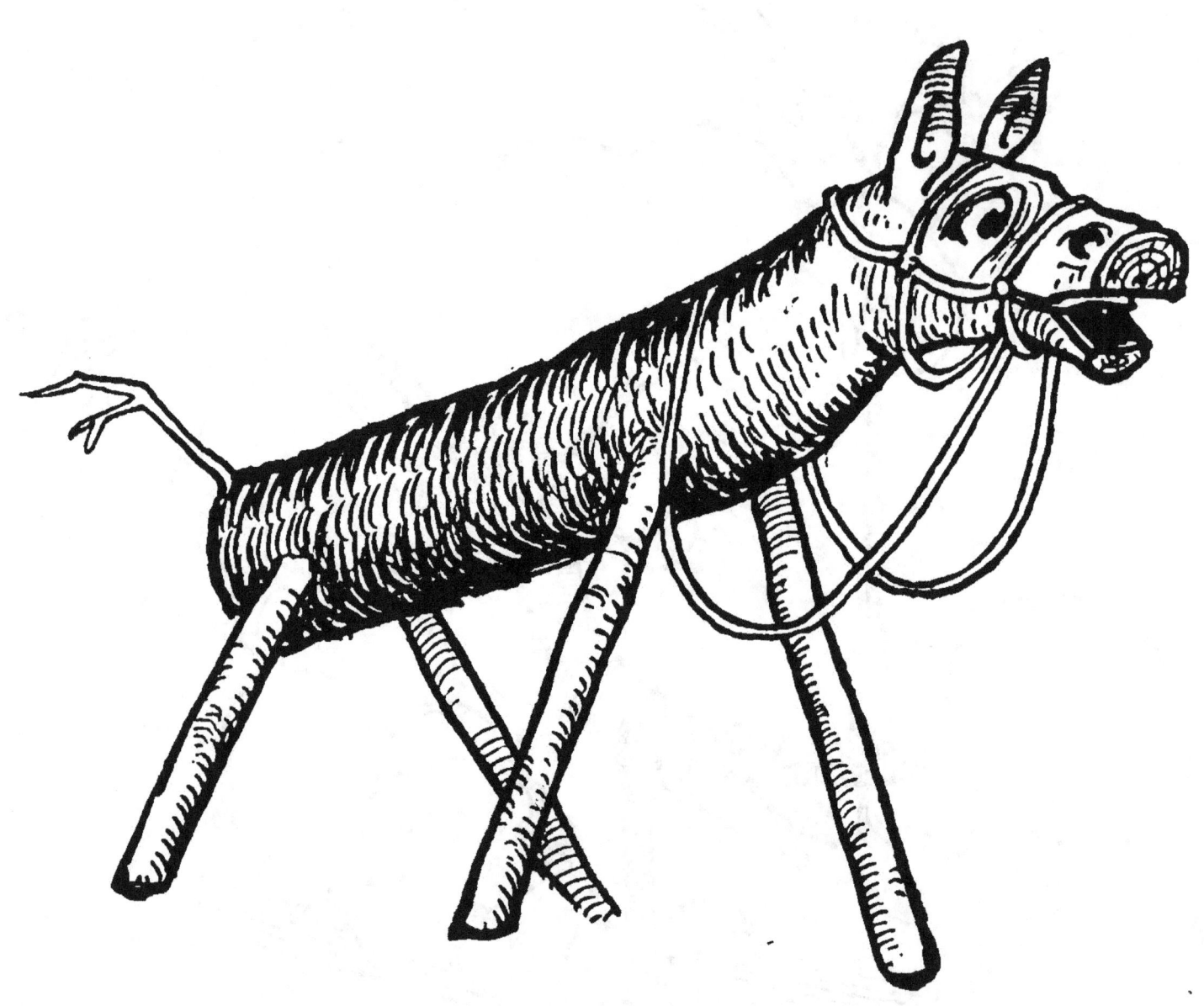

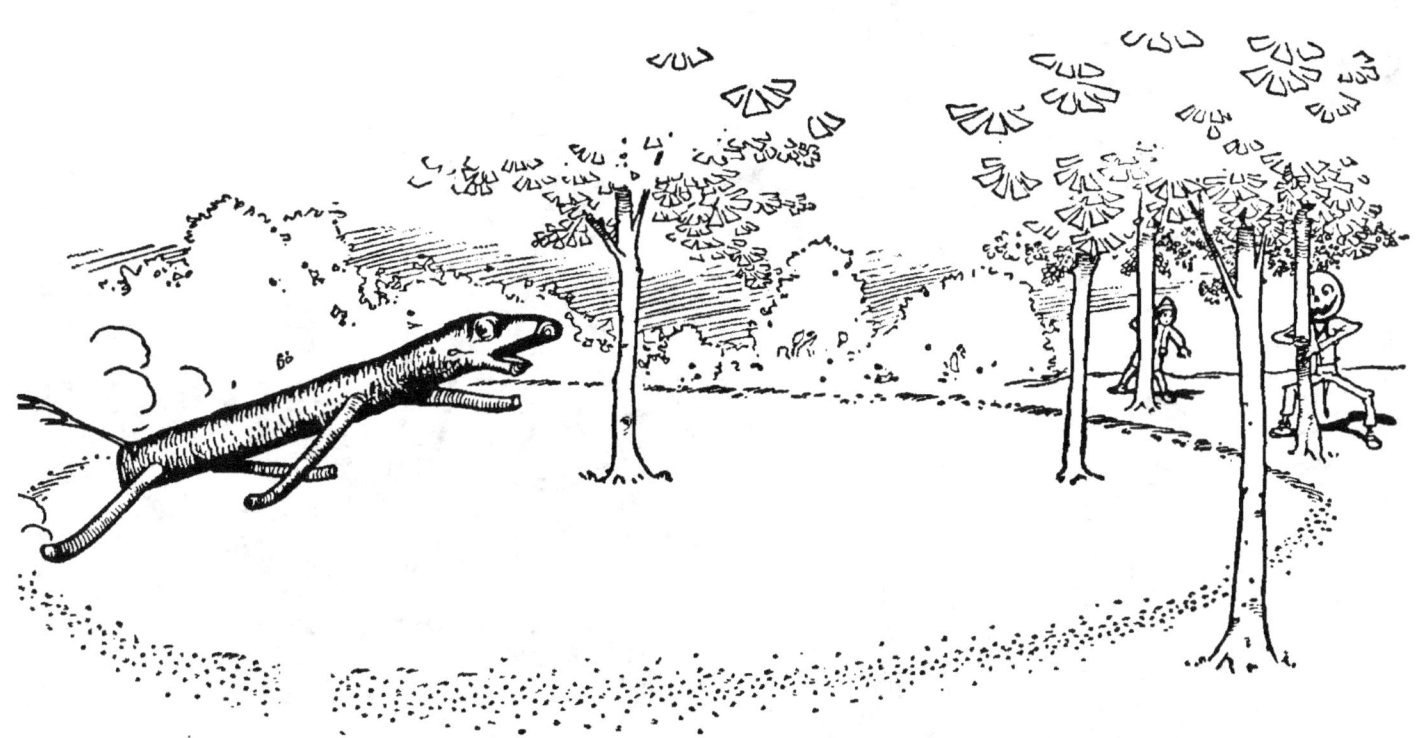

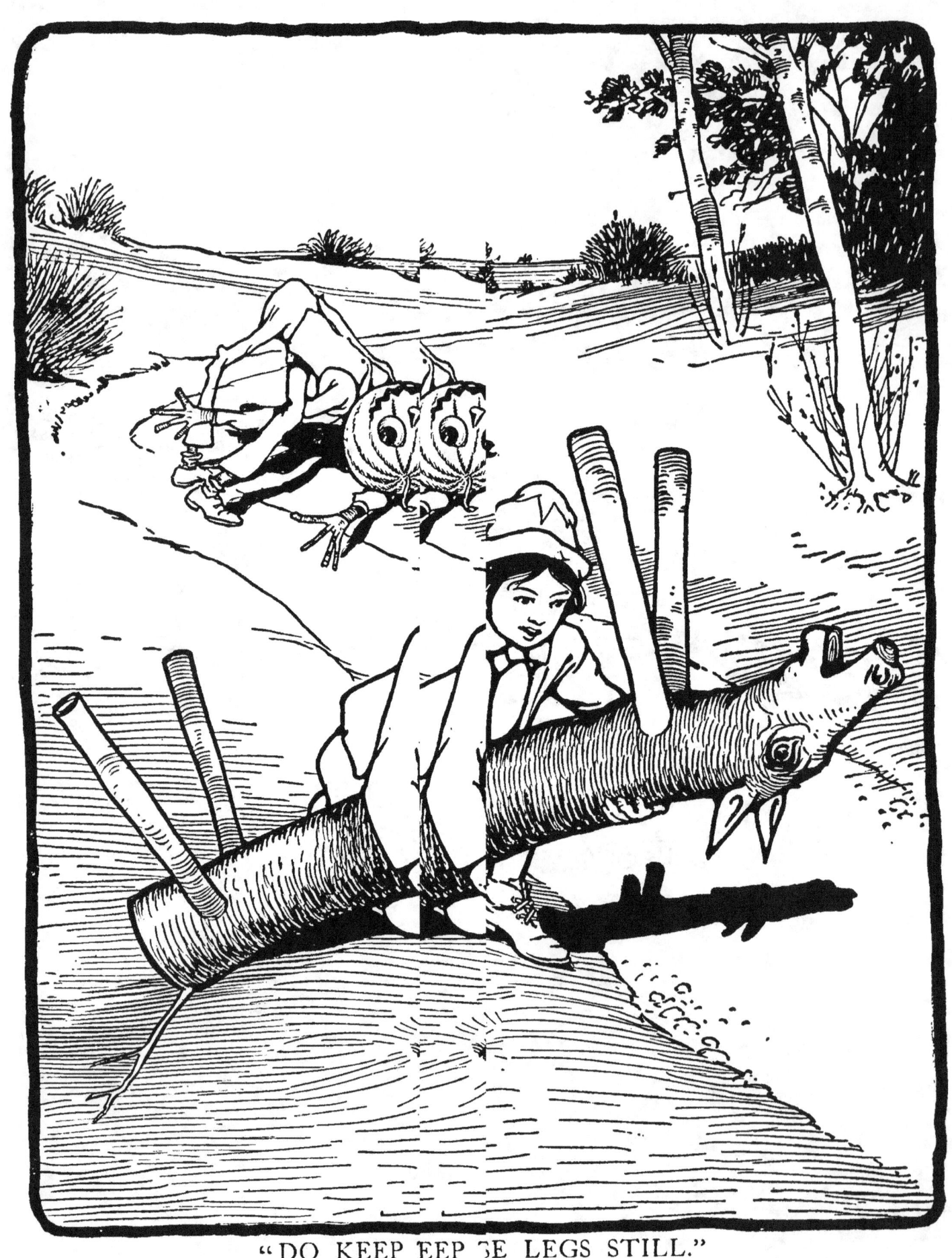

"DO KEEP EEP 3E LEGS STILL."

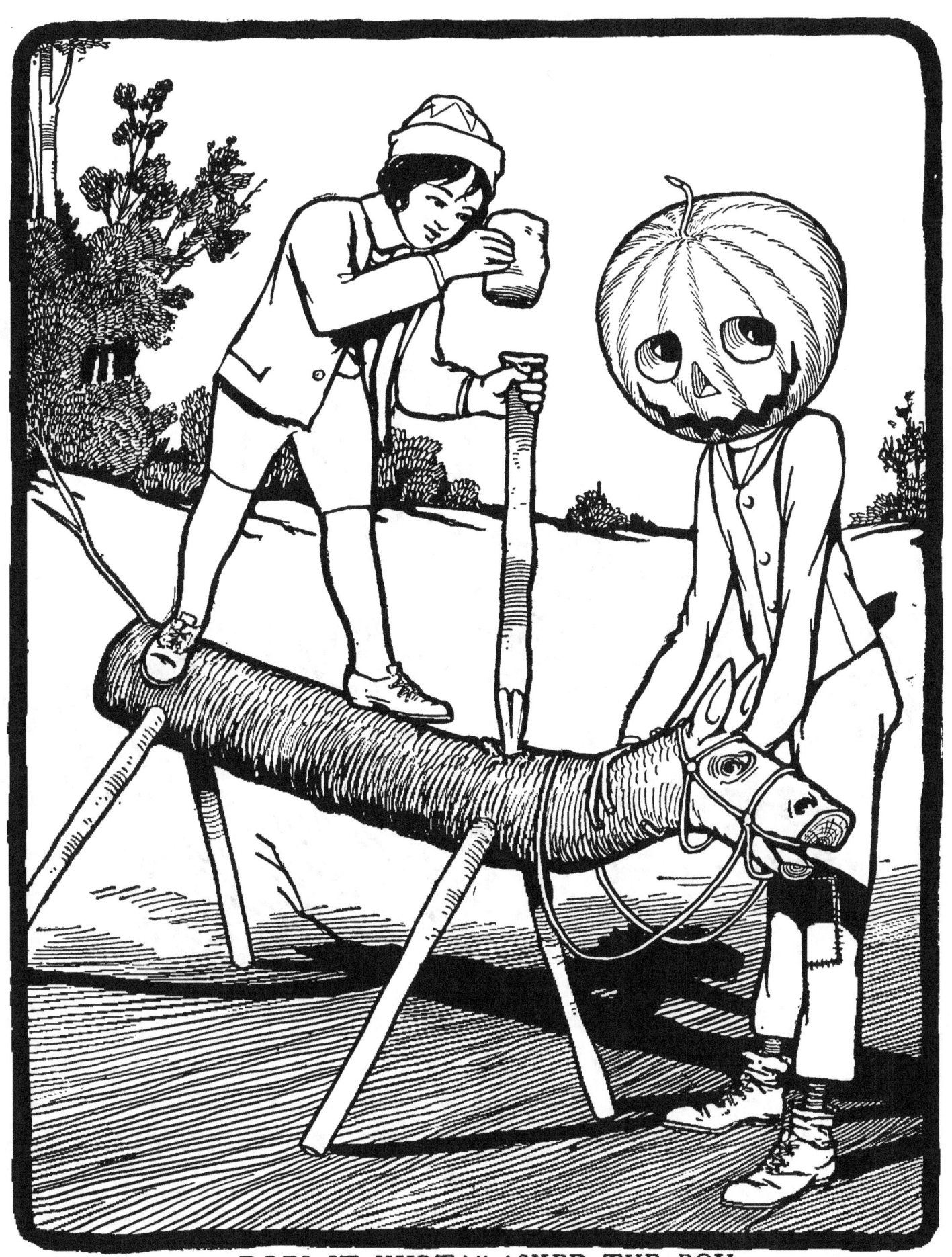

"DOES IT HURT?" ASKED THE BOY.

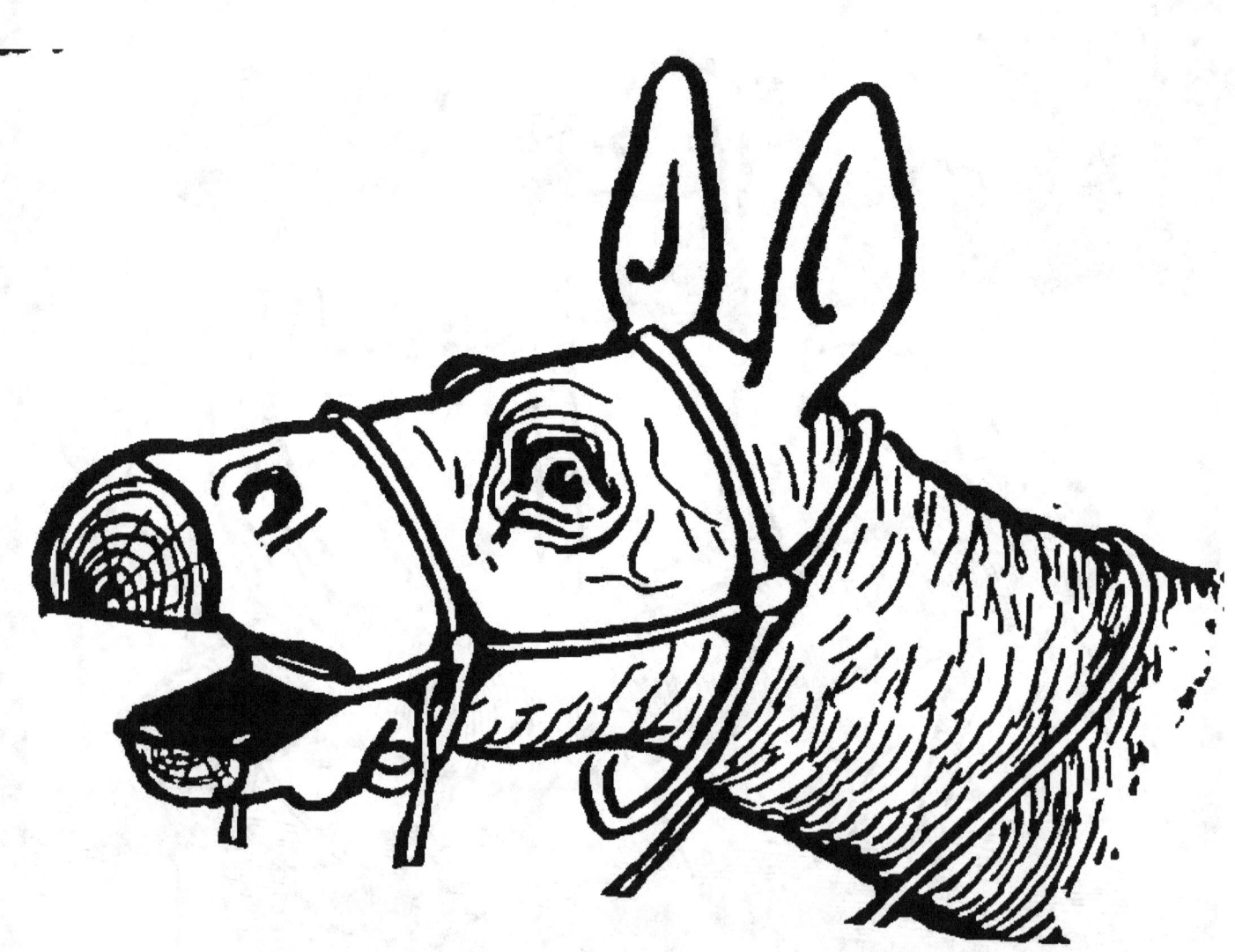

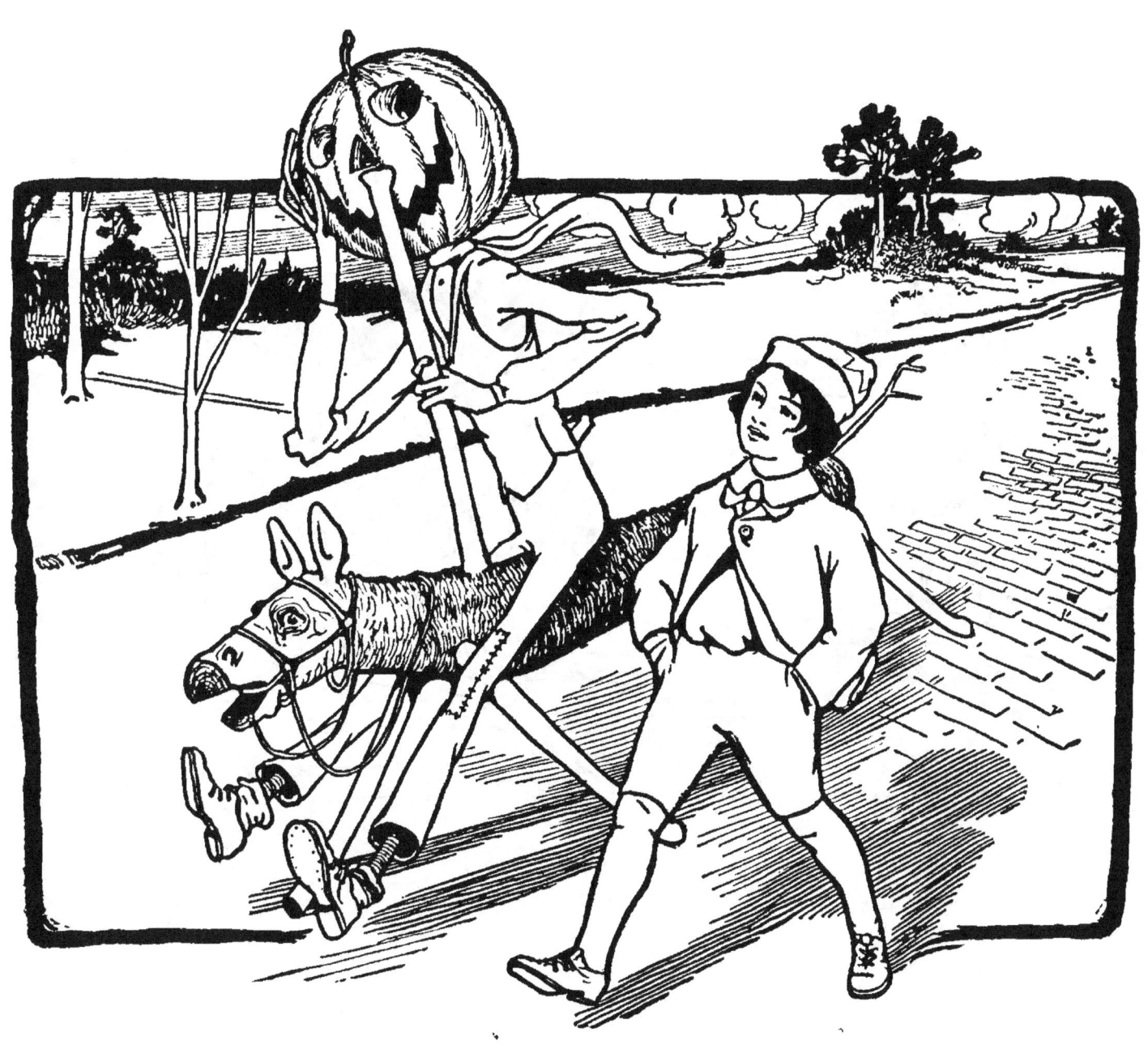

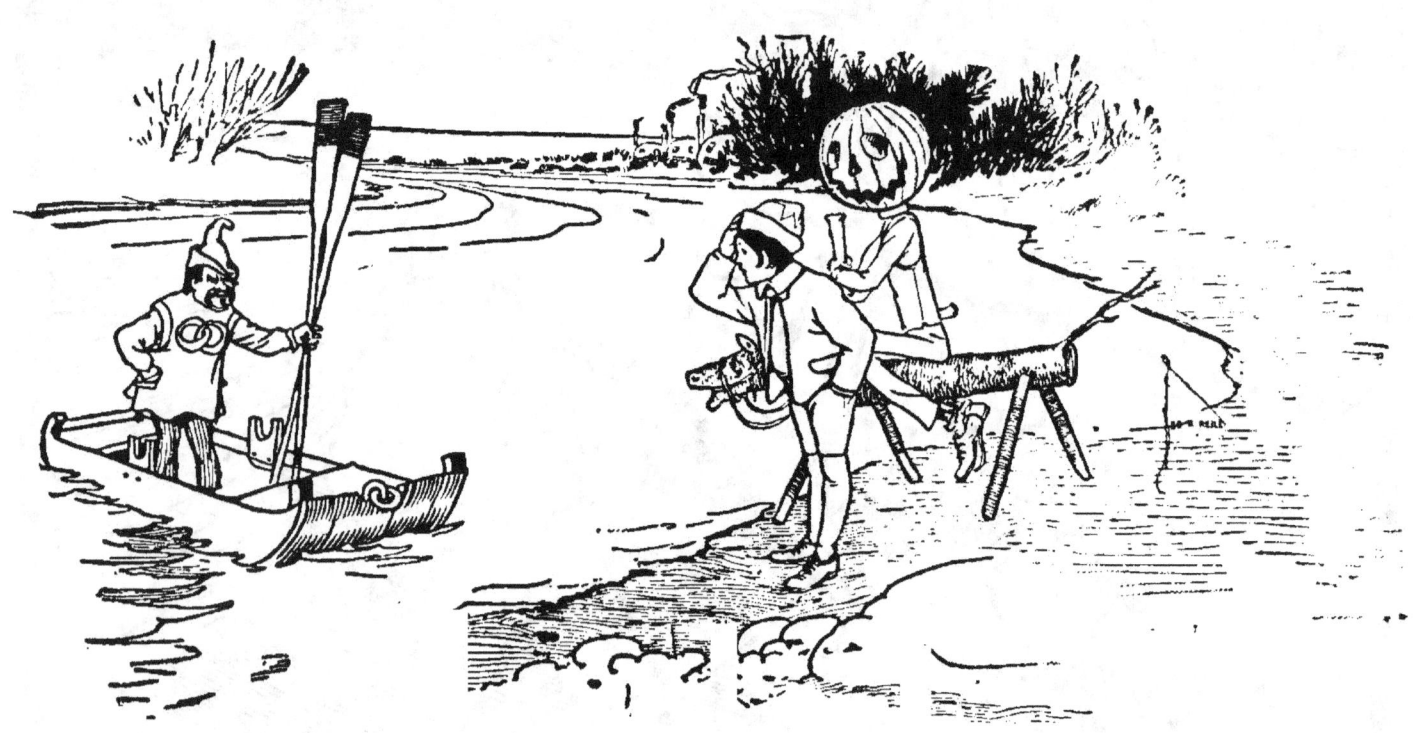

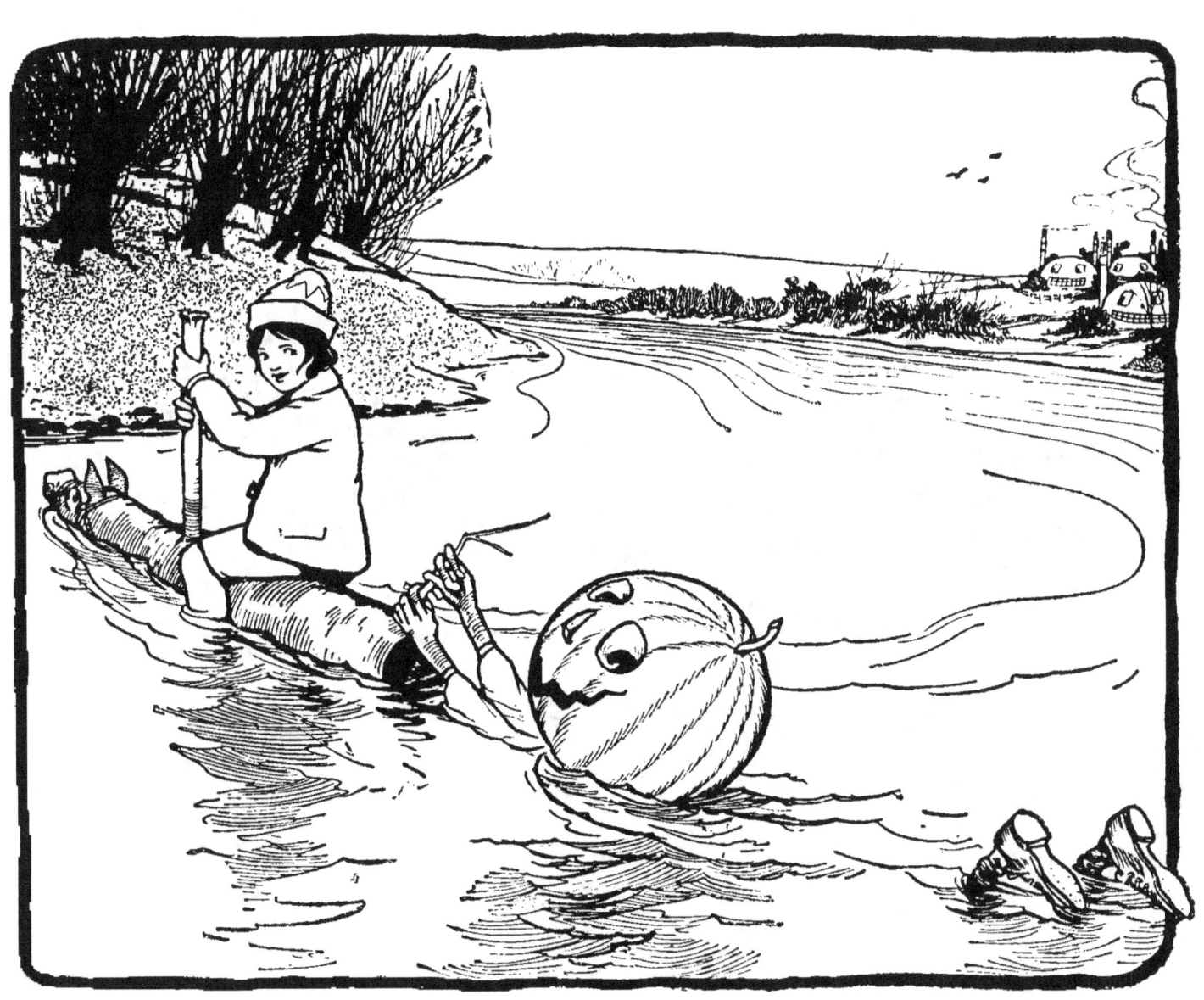

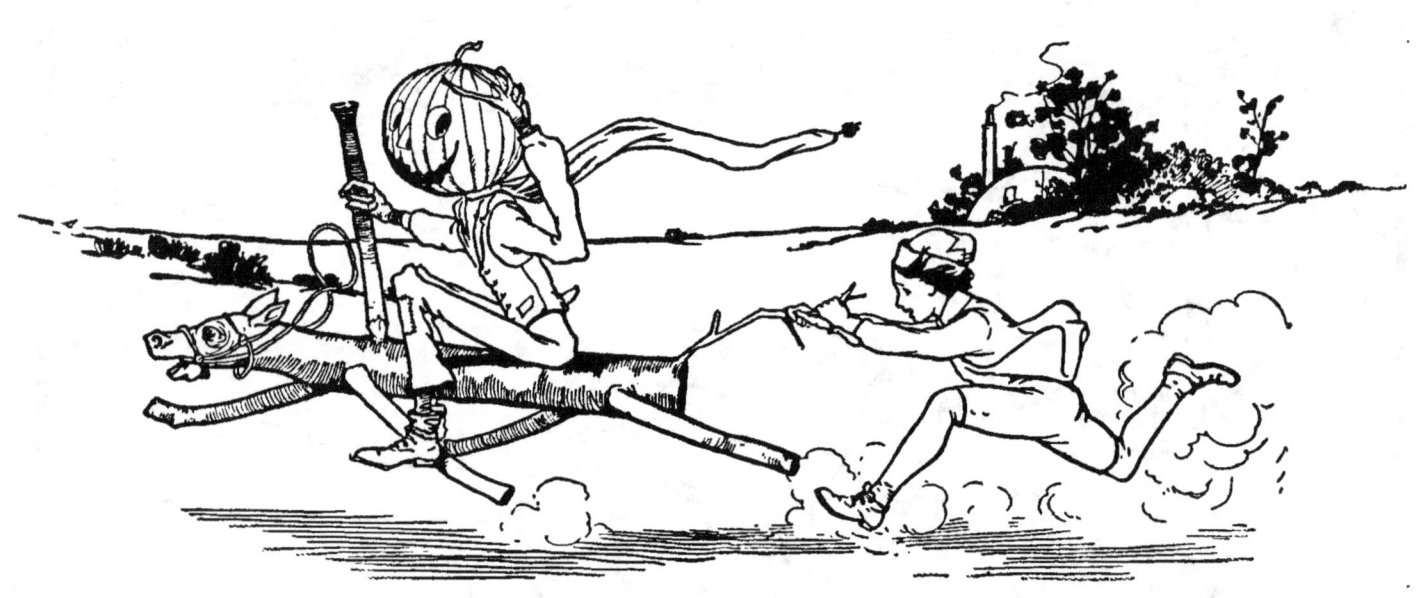

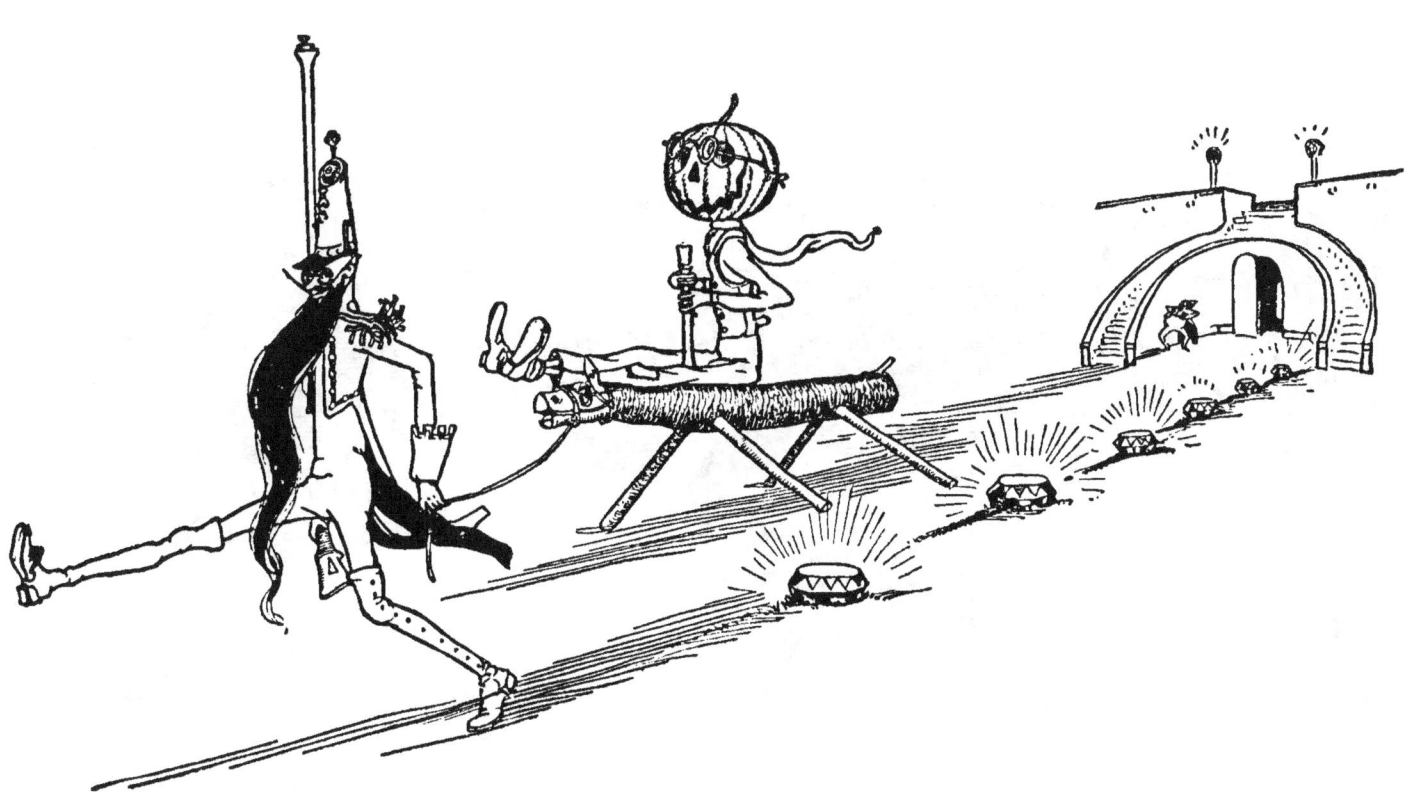

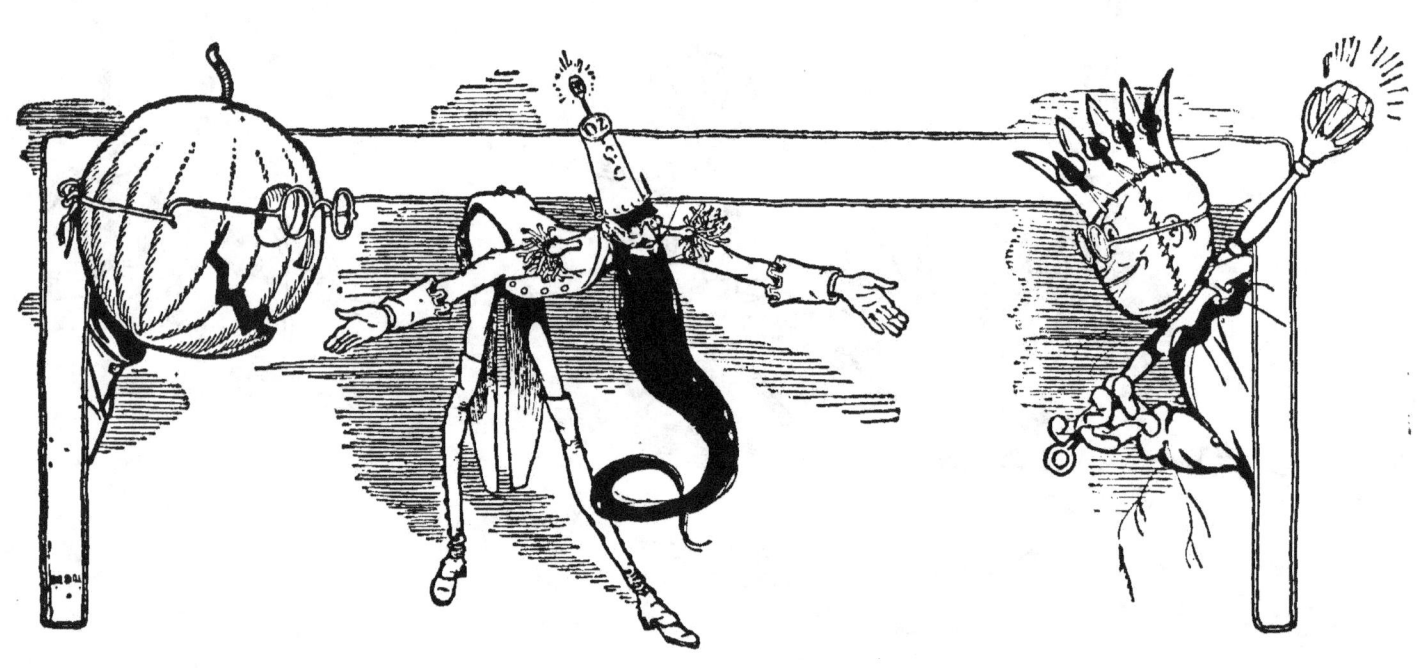

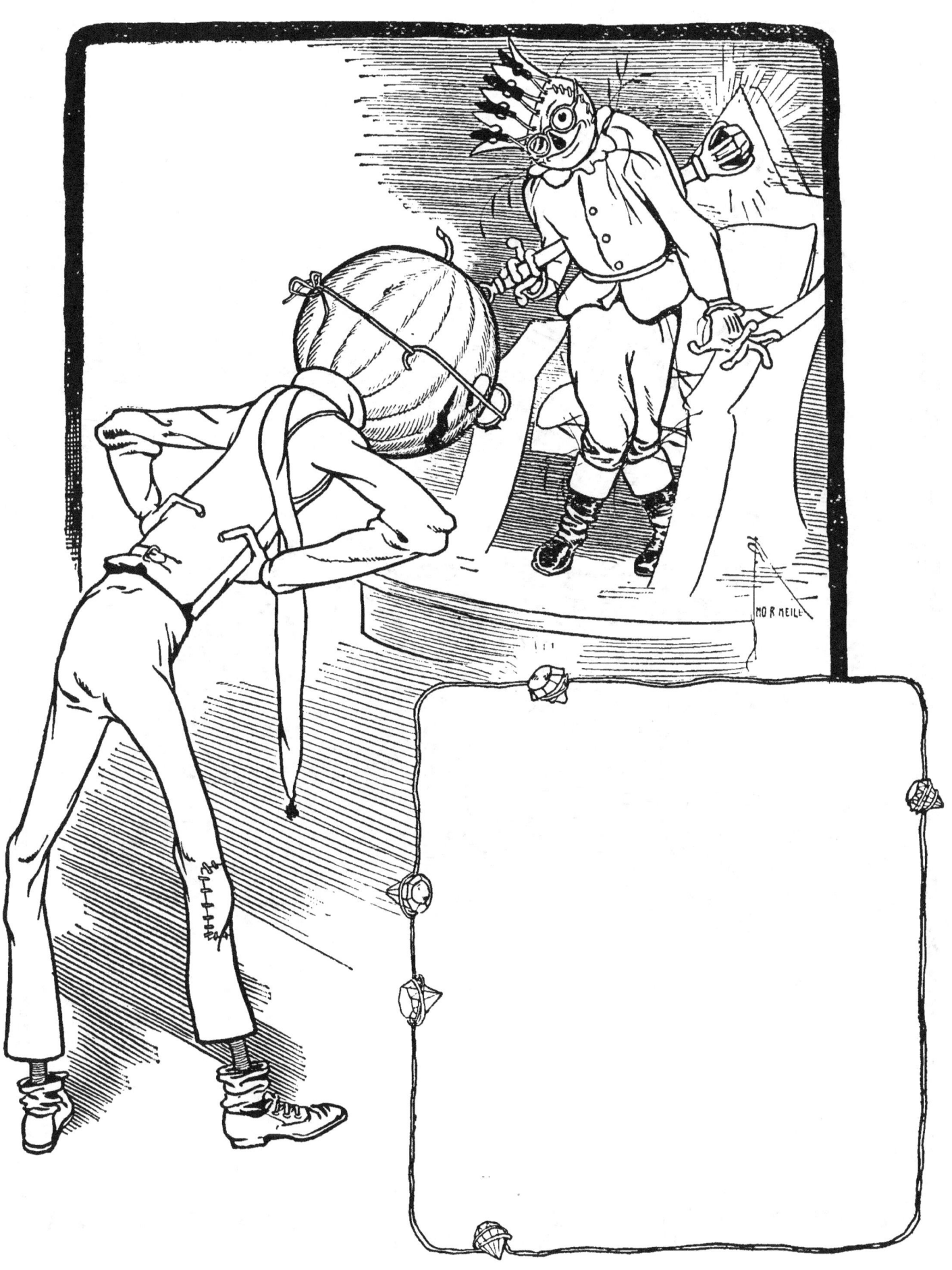

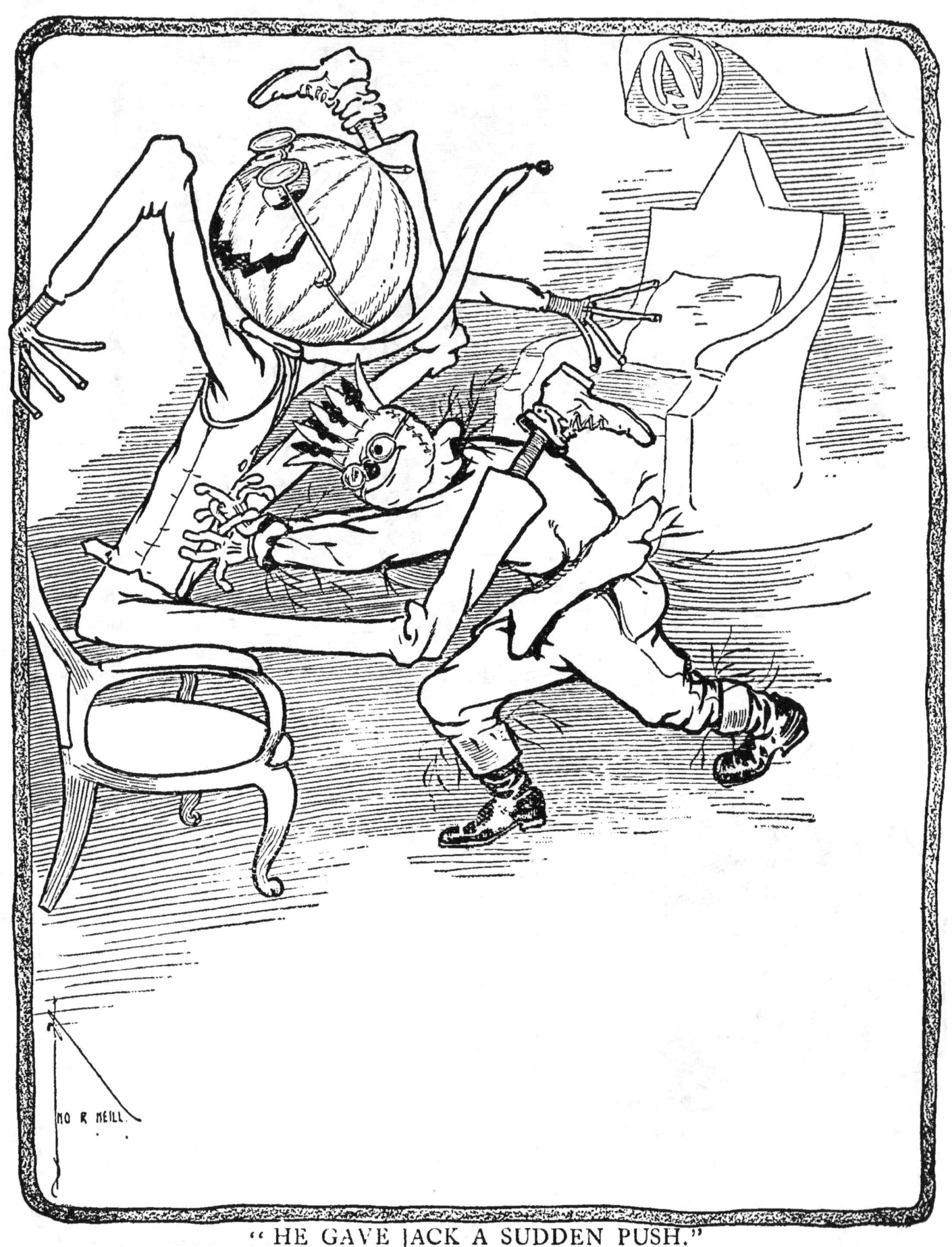

"HE GAVE JACK A SUDDEN PUSH."

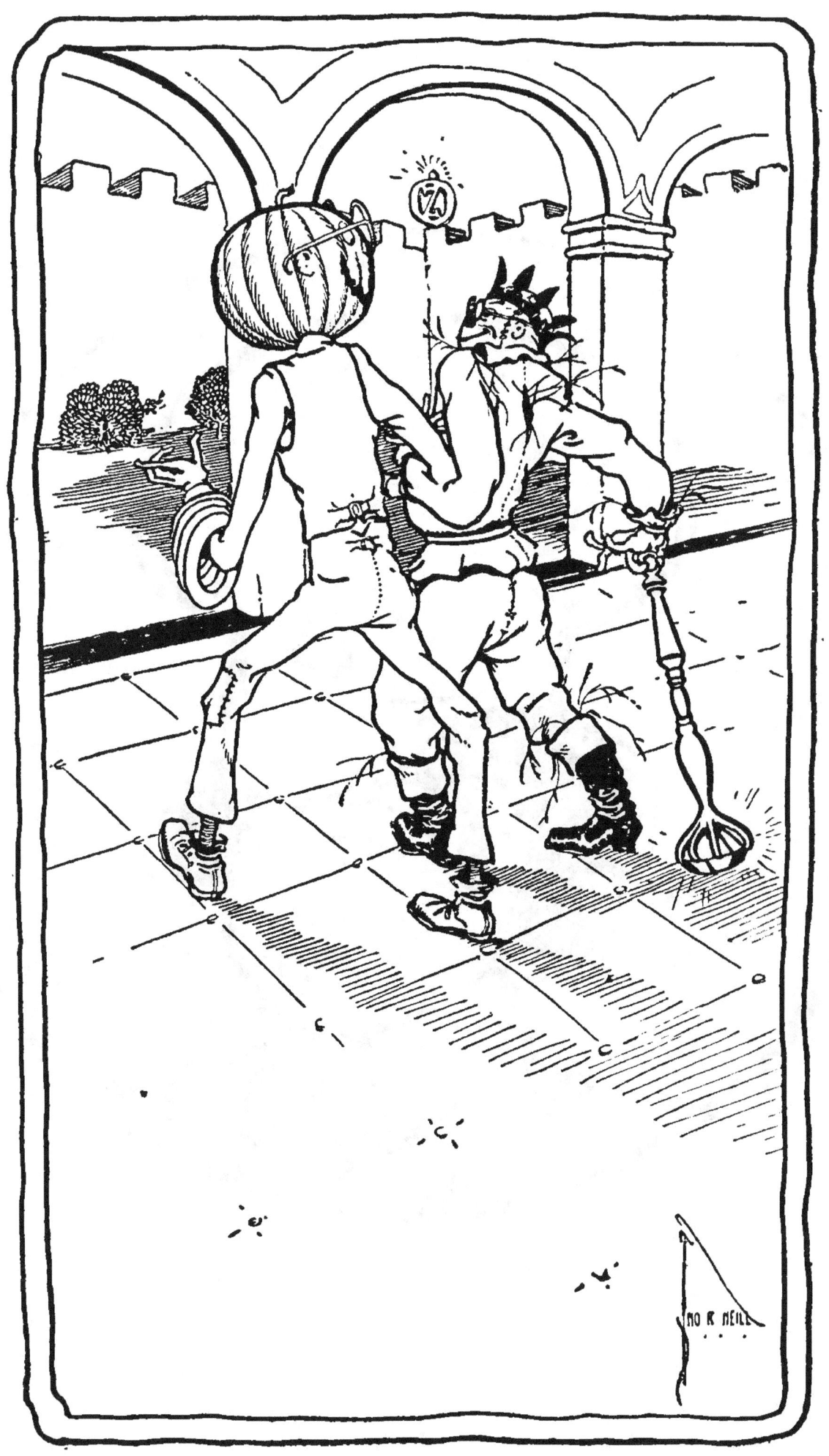

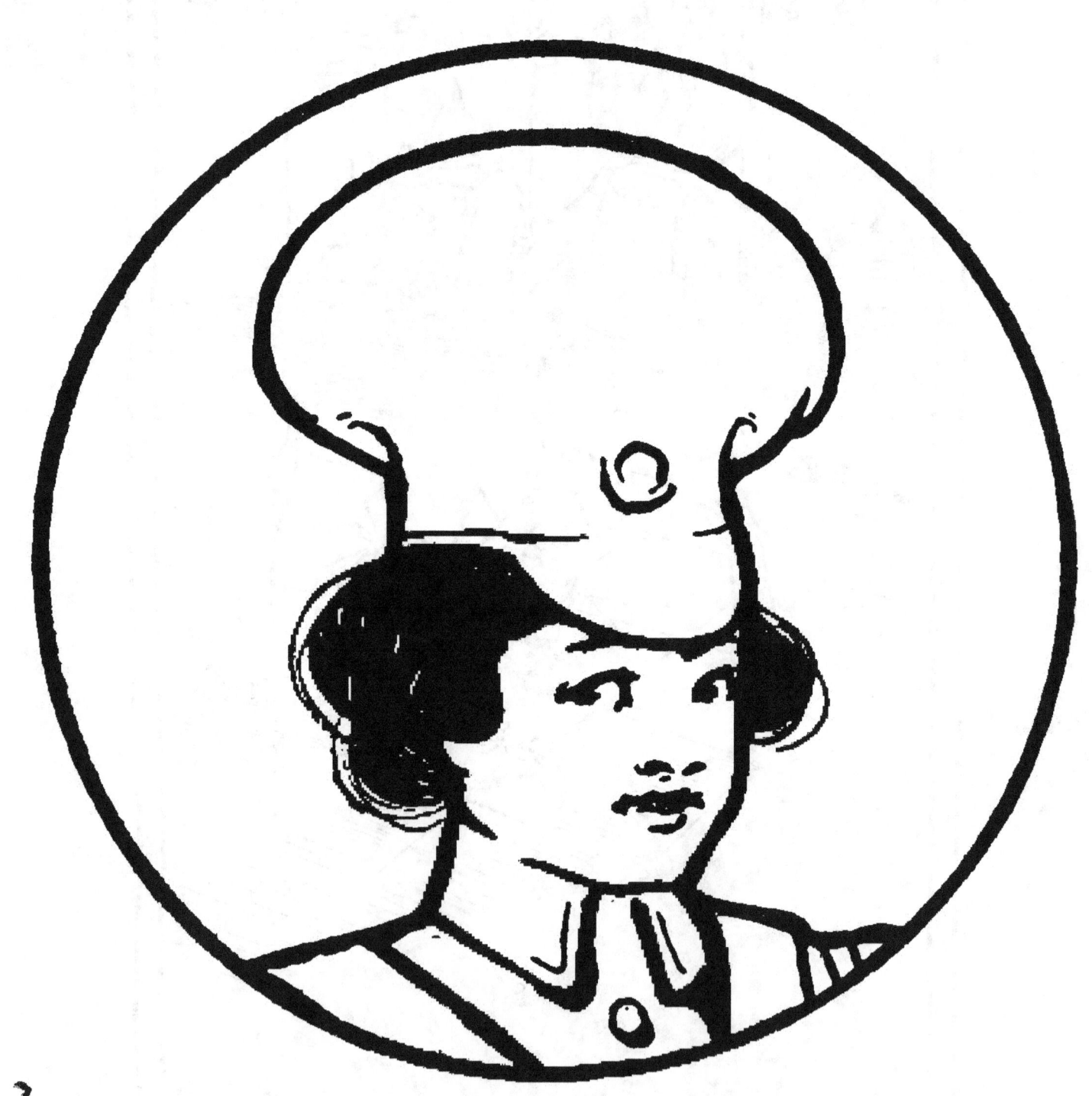

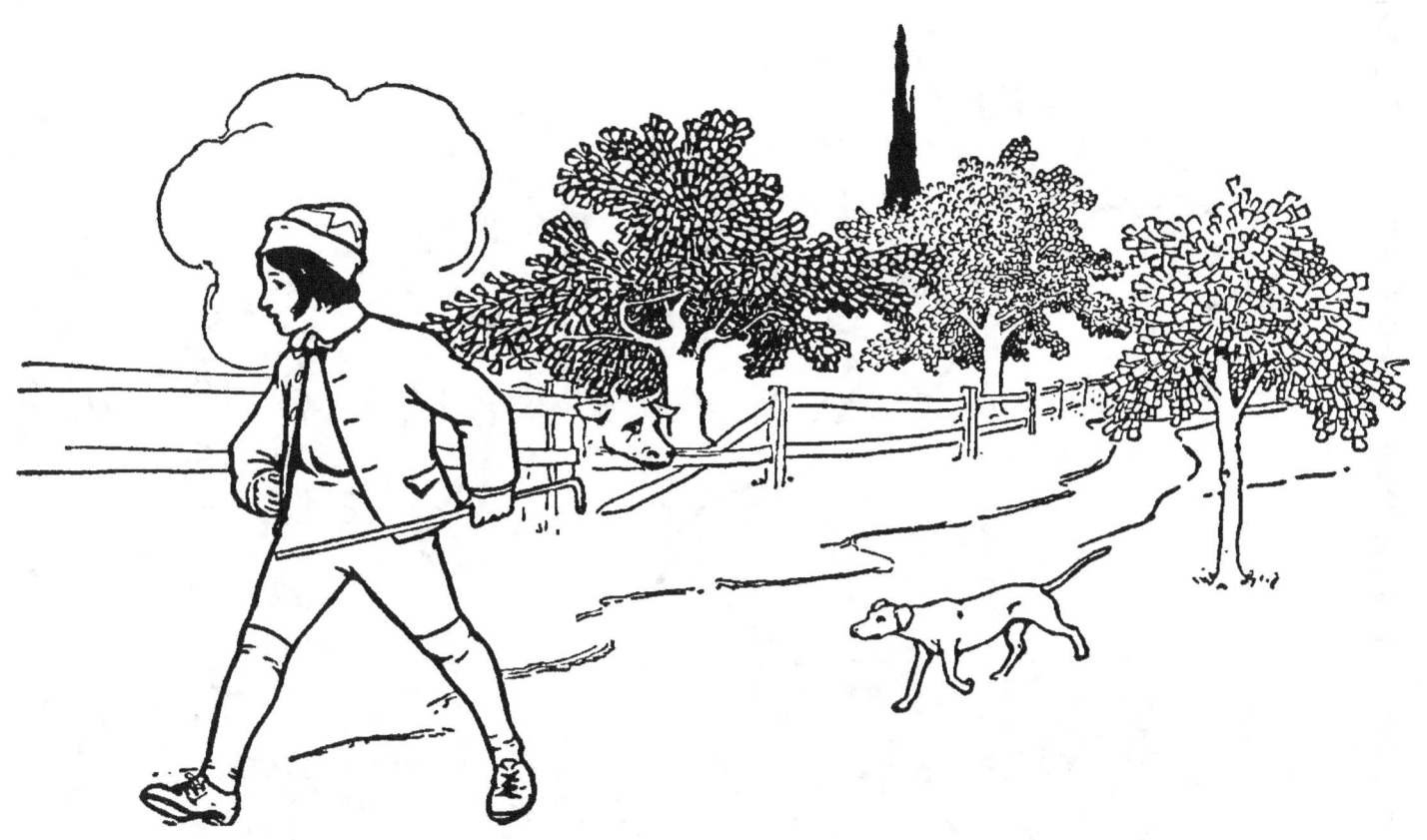

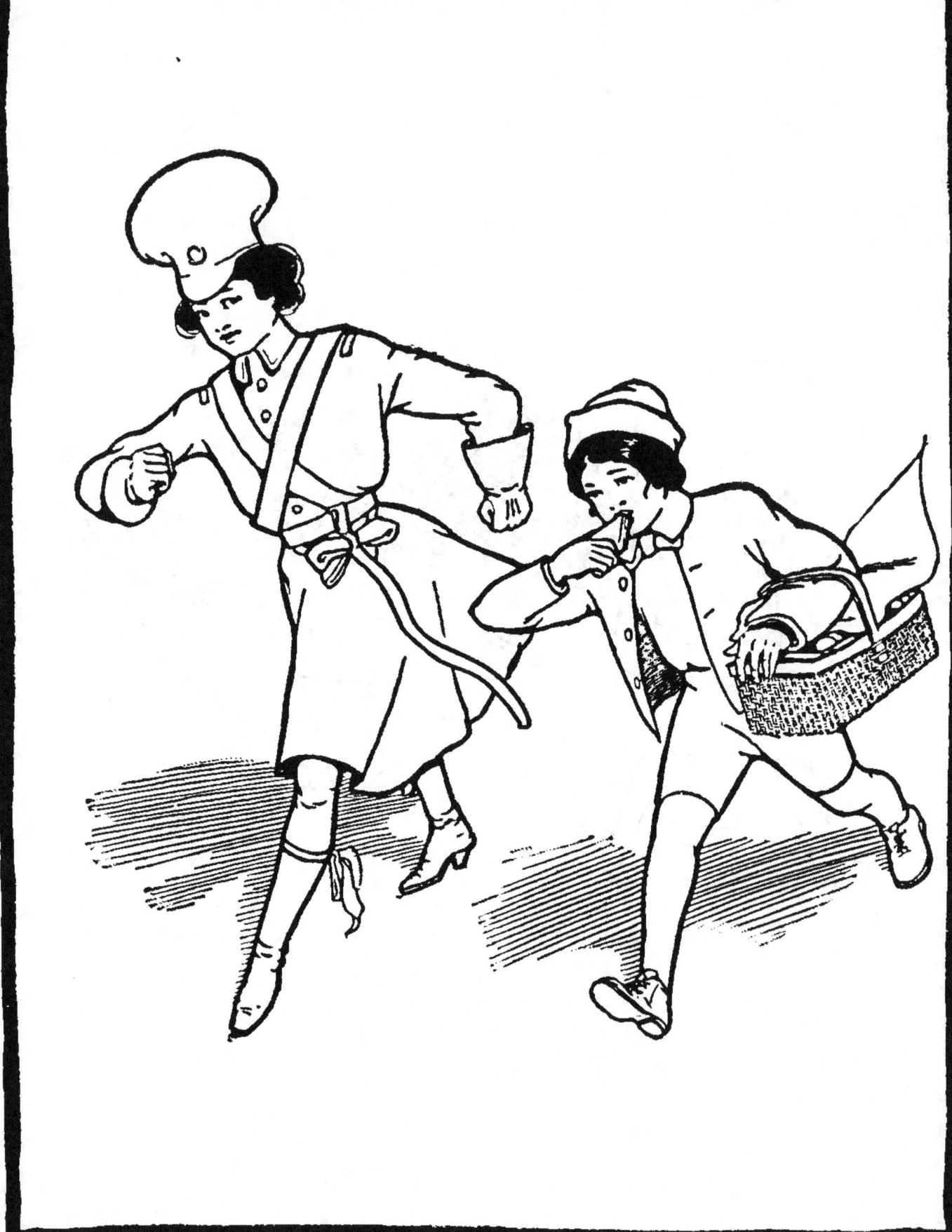

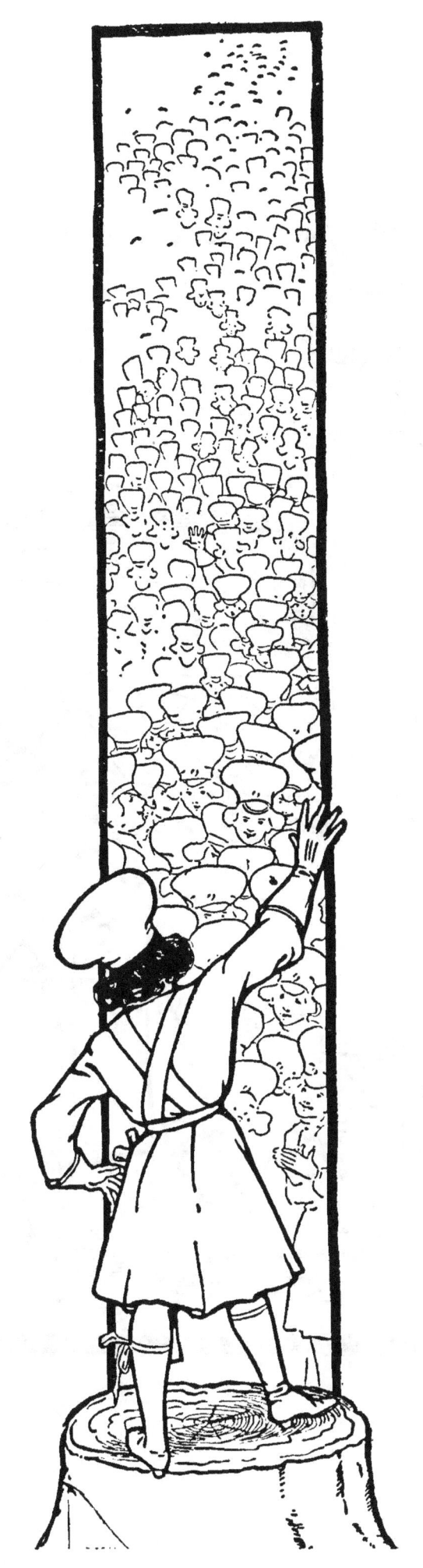

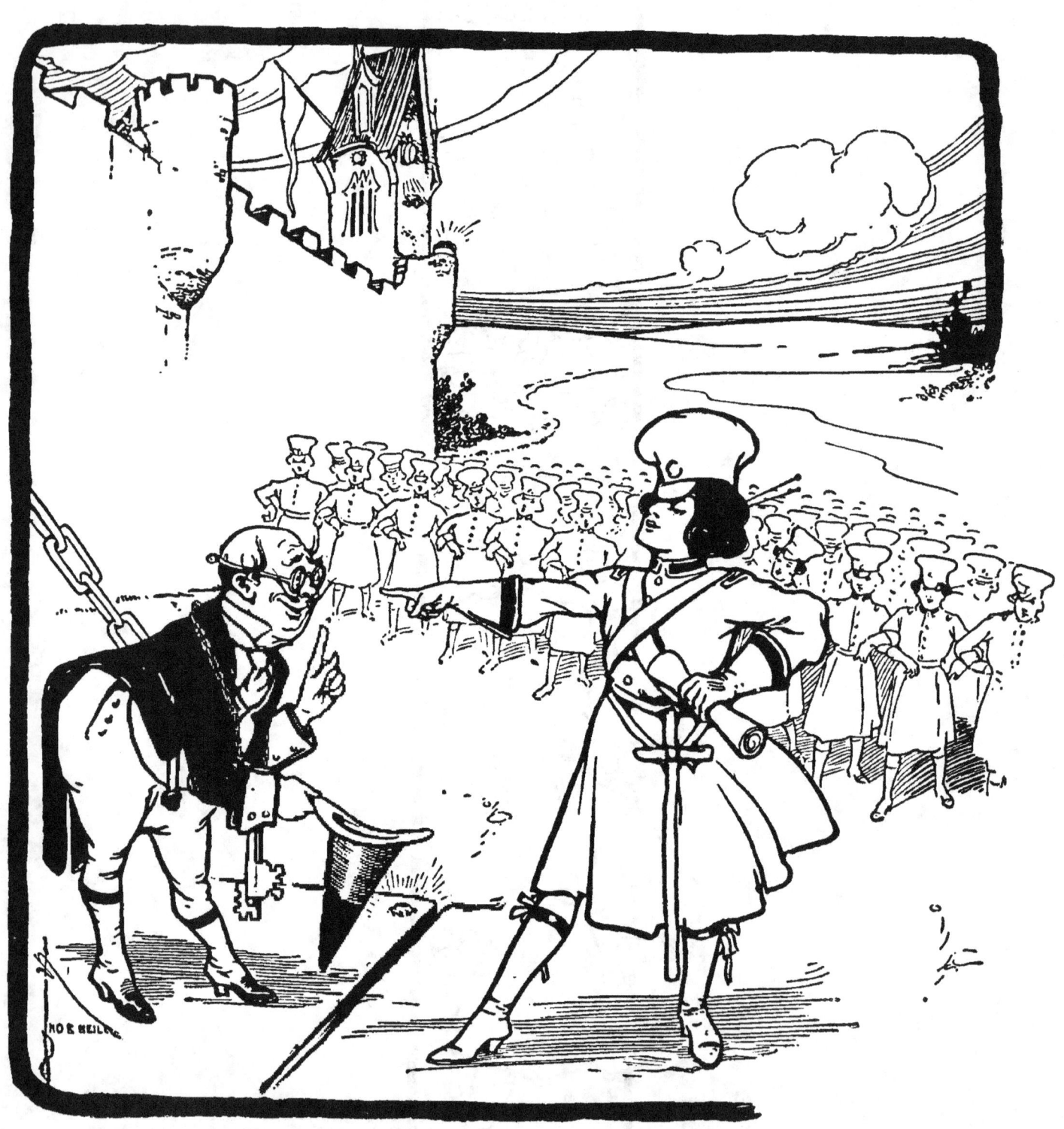

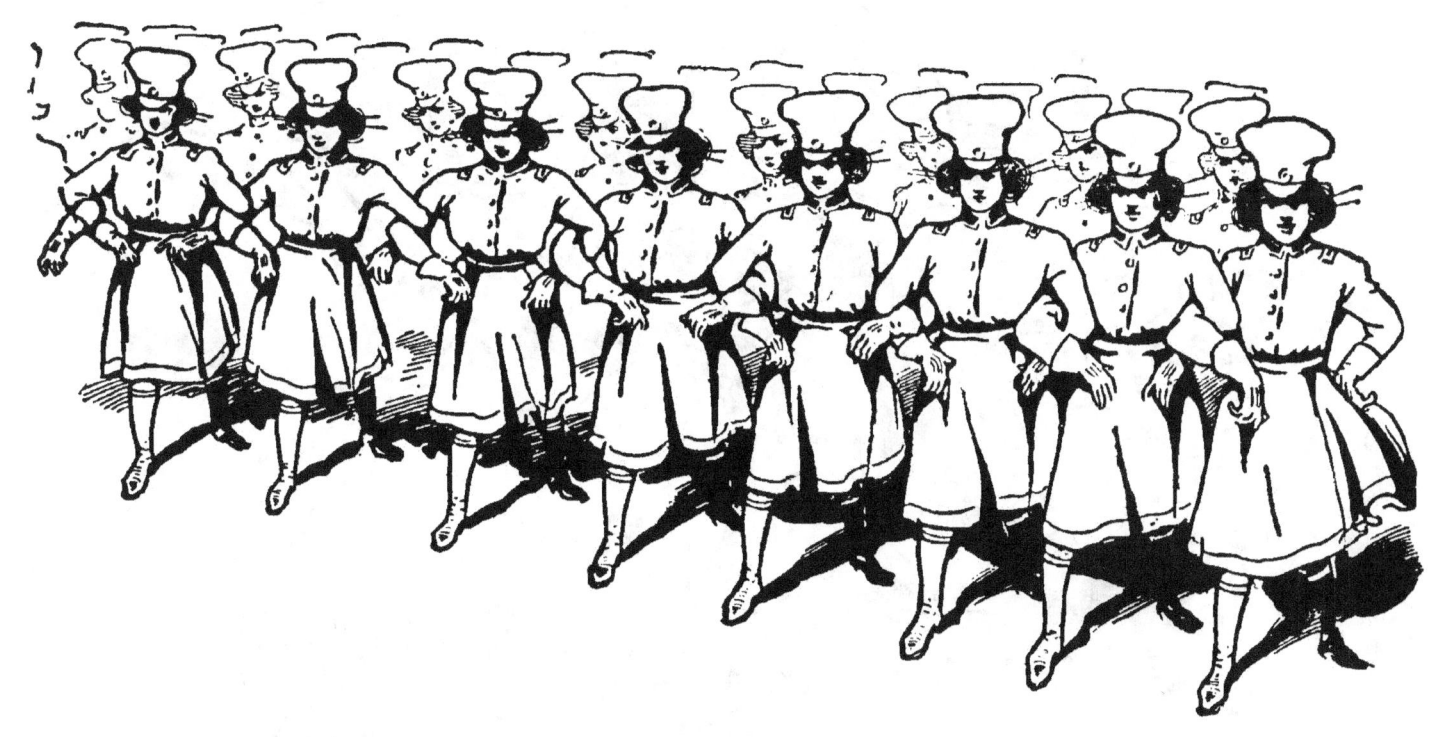

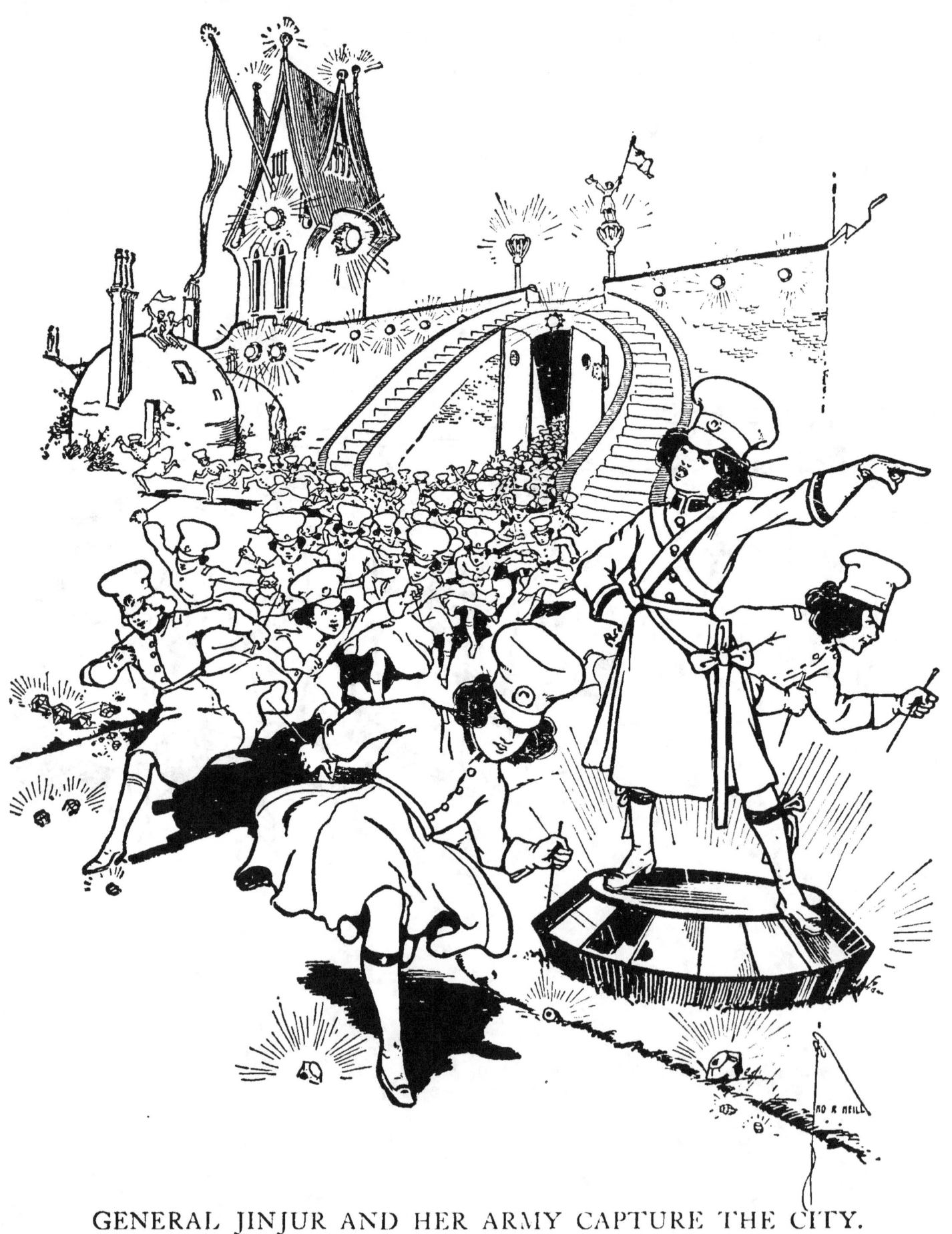

GENERAL JINJUR AND HER ARMY CAPTURE THE CITY.

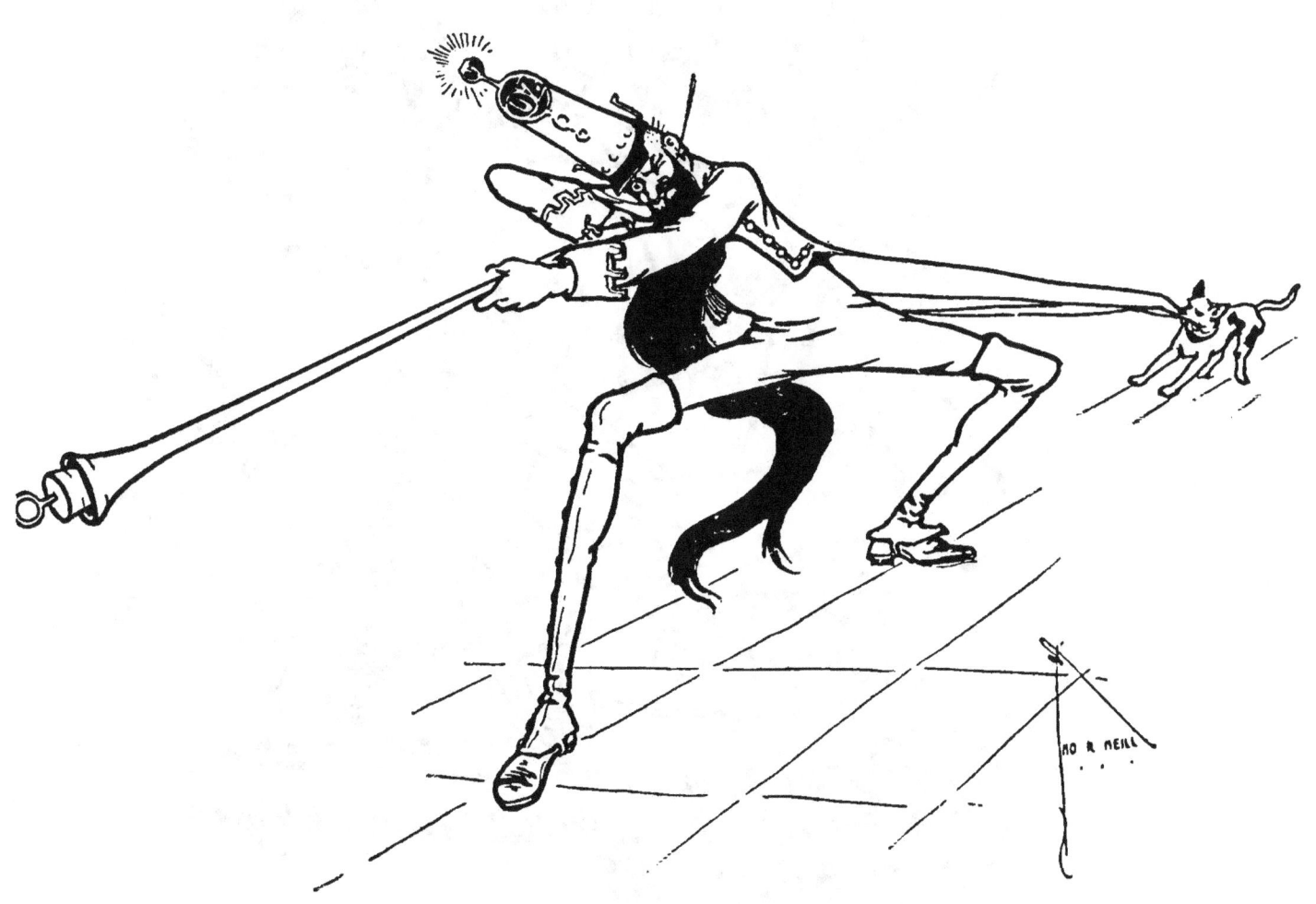

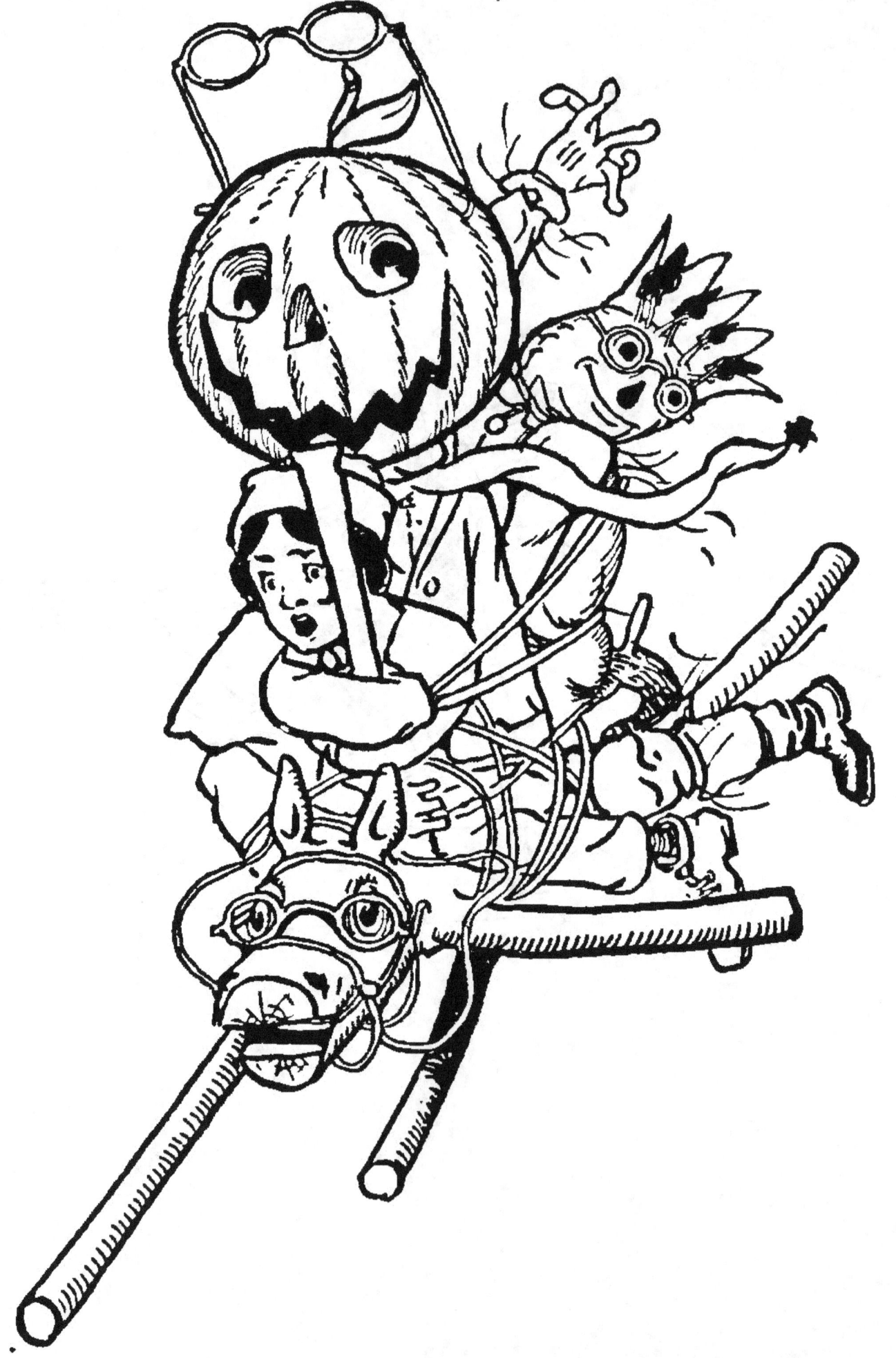

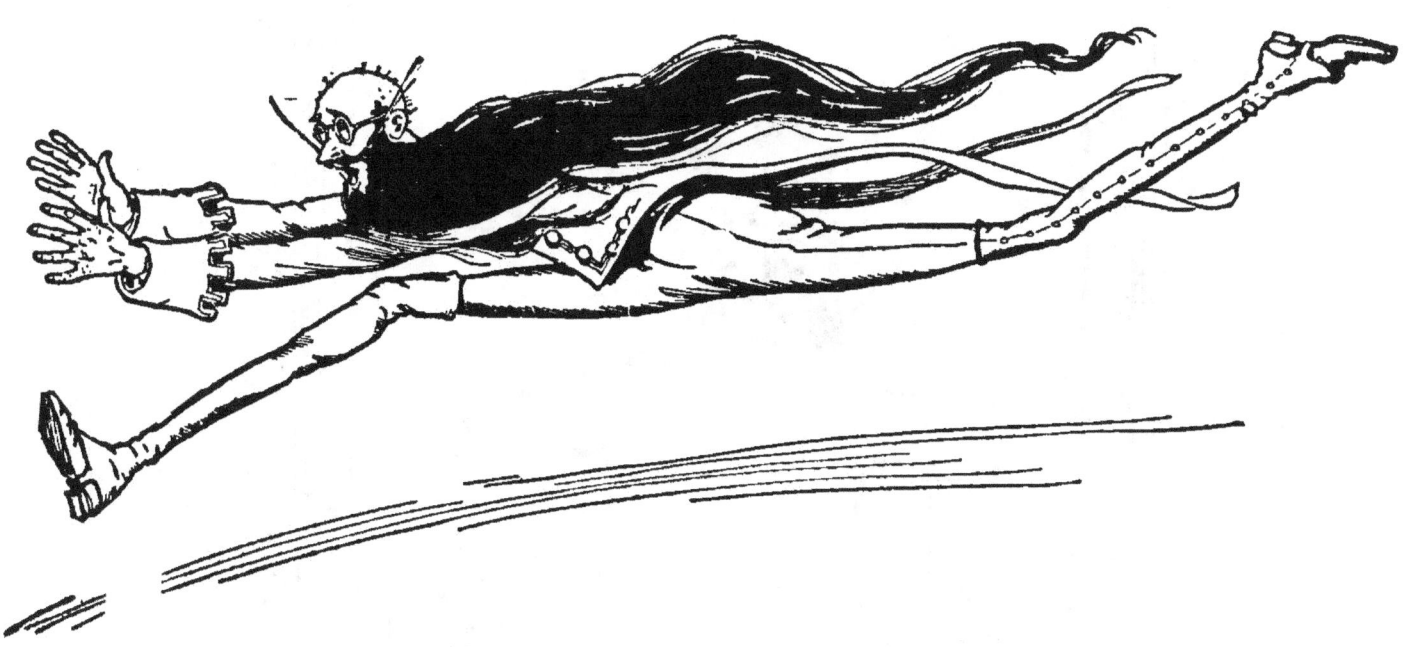

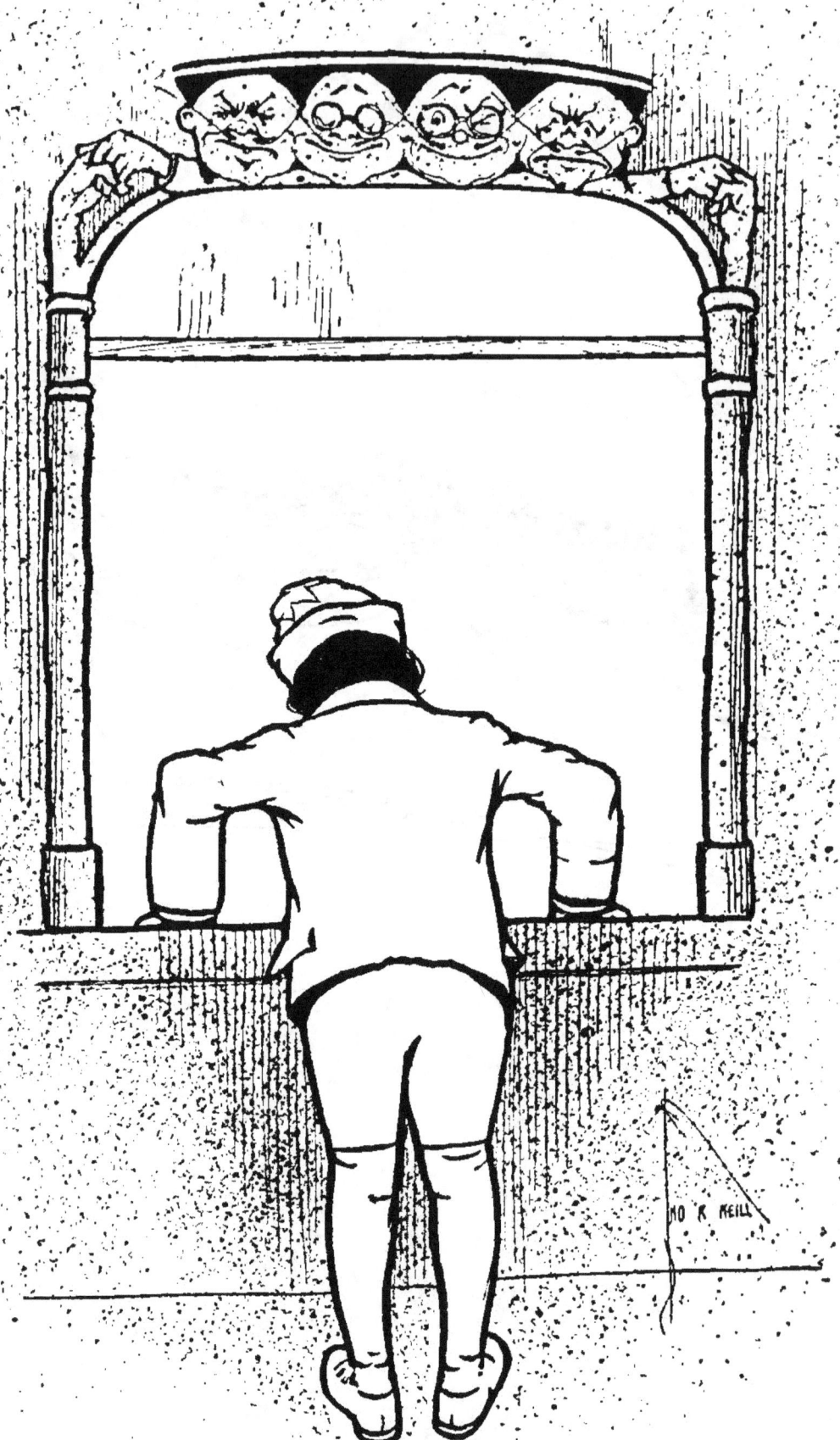

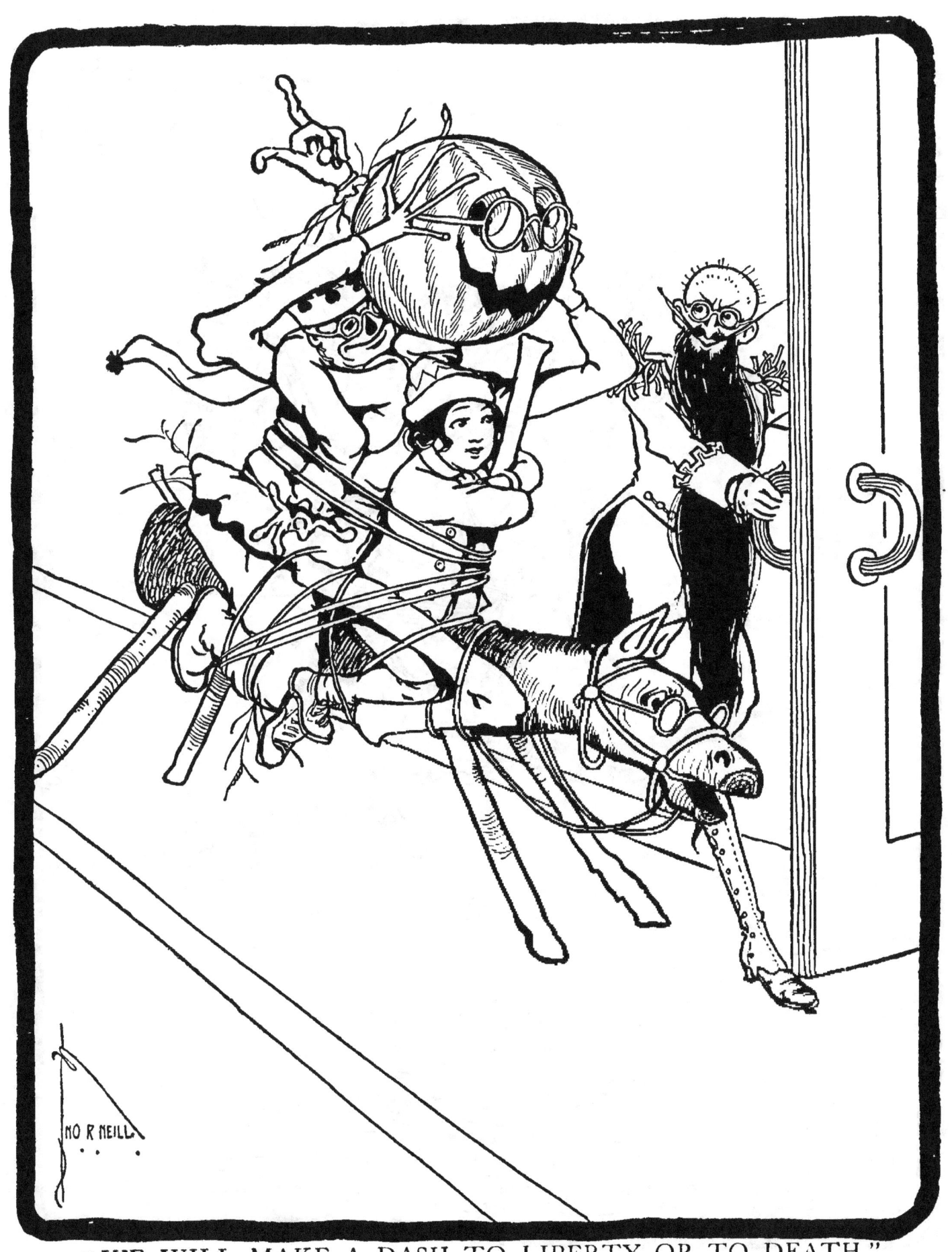

"WE WILL MAKE A DASH TO LIBERTY OR TO DEATH."

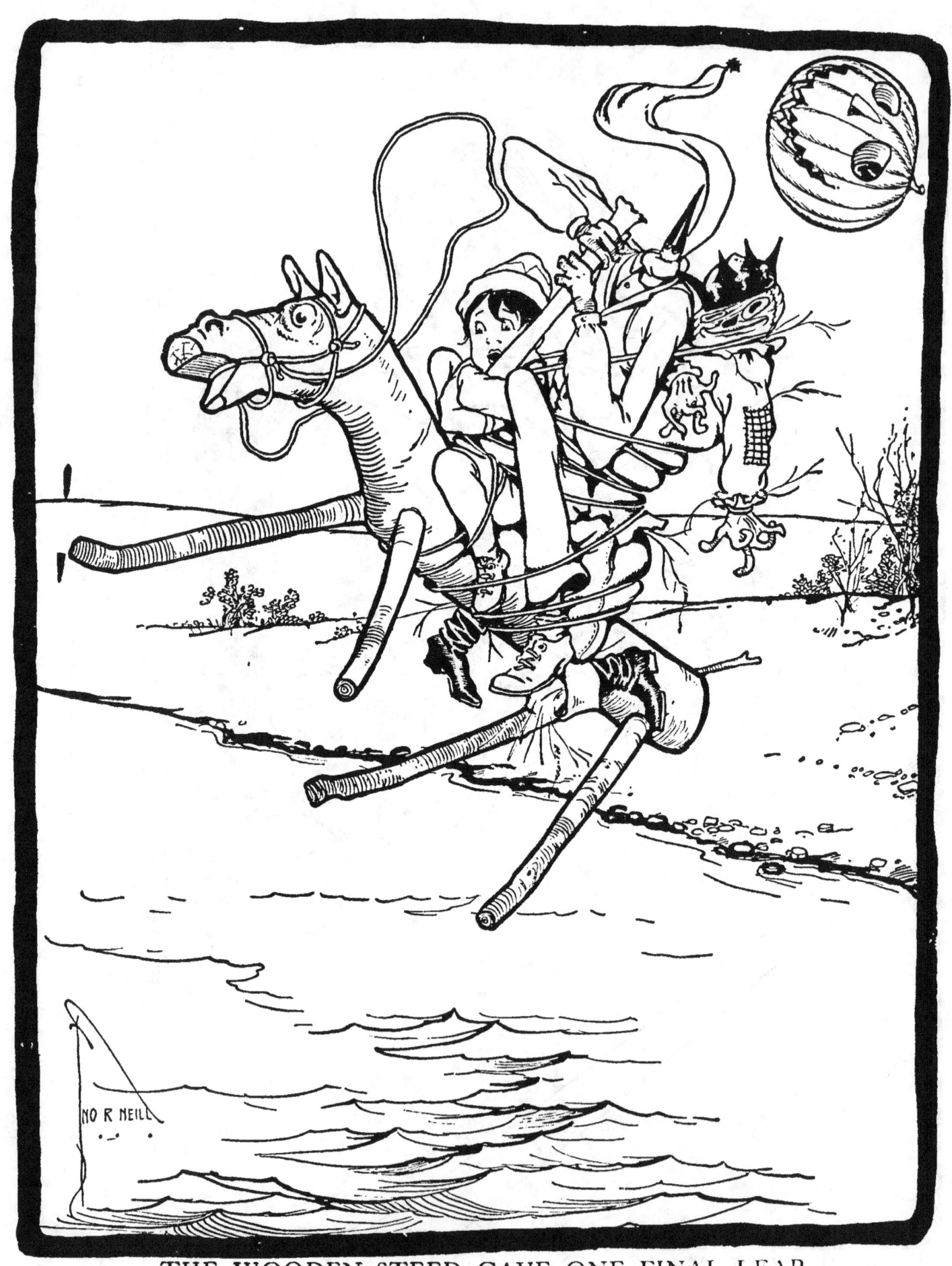

THE WOODEN STEED GAVE ONE FINAL LEAP.

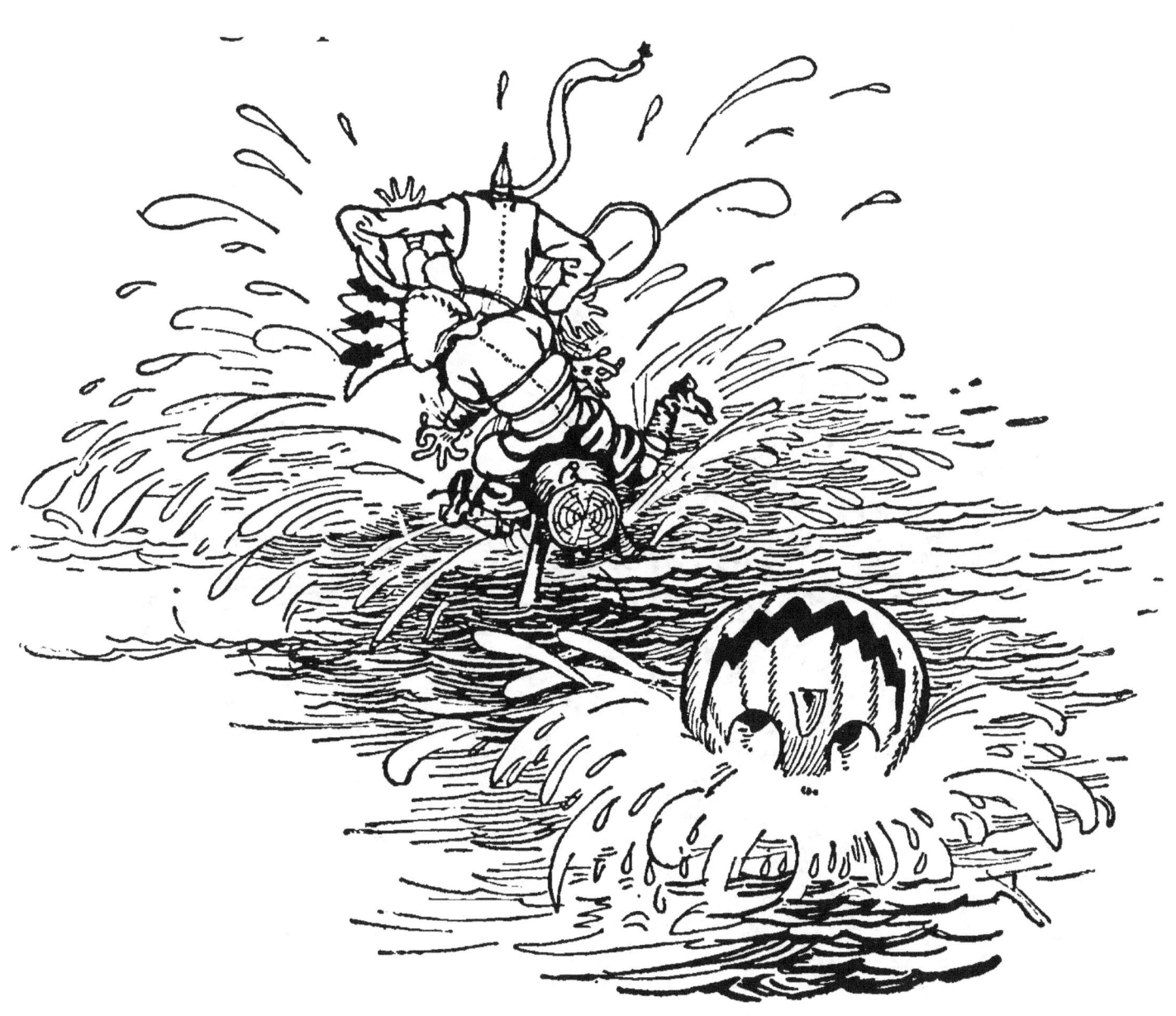

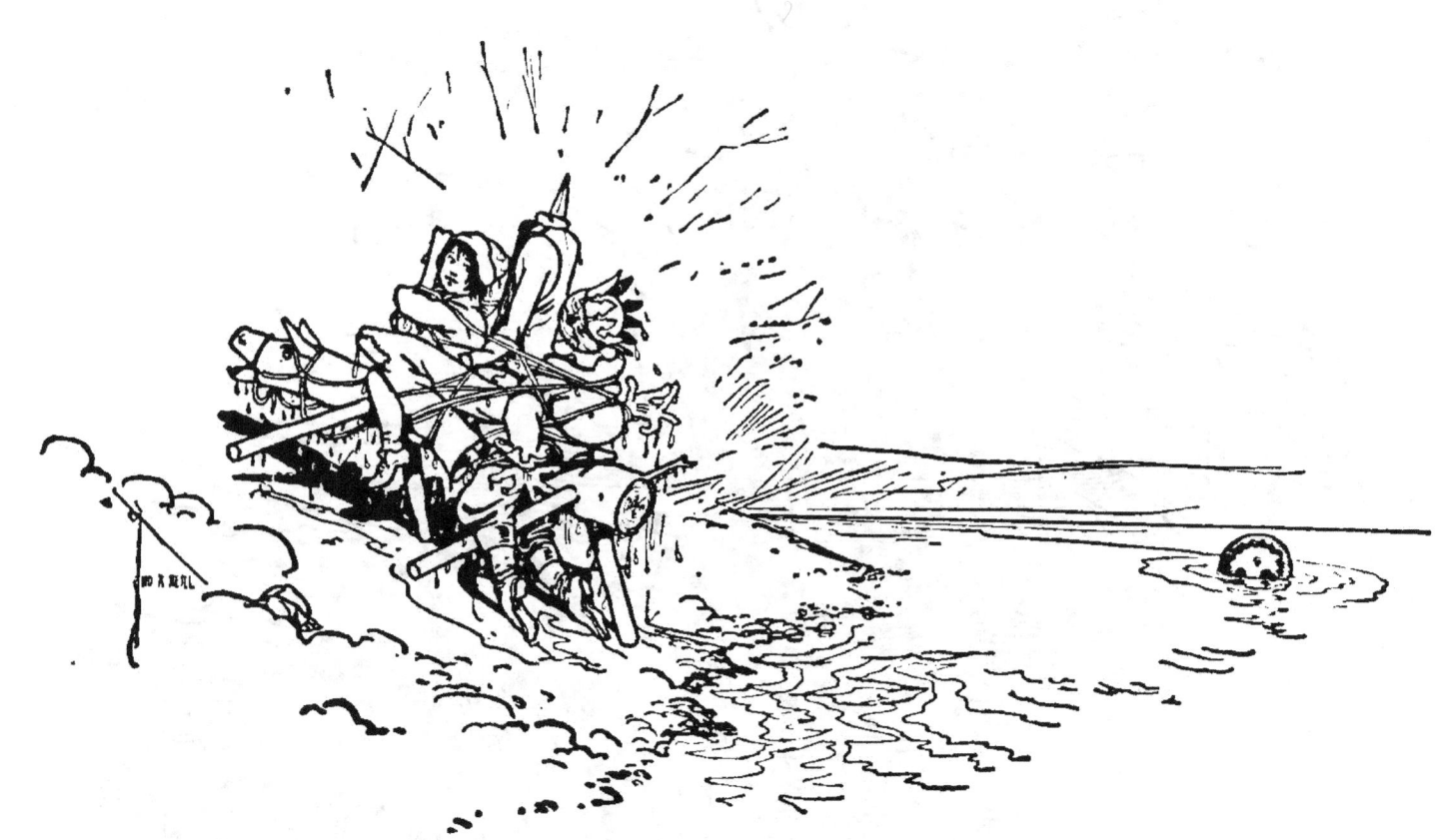

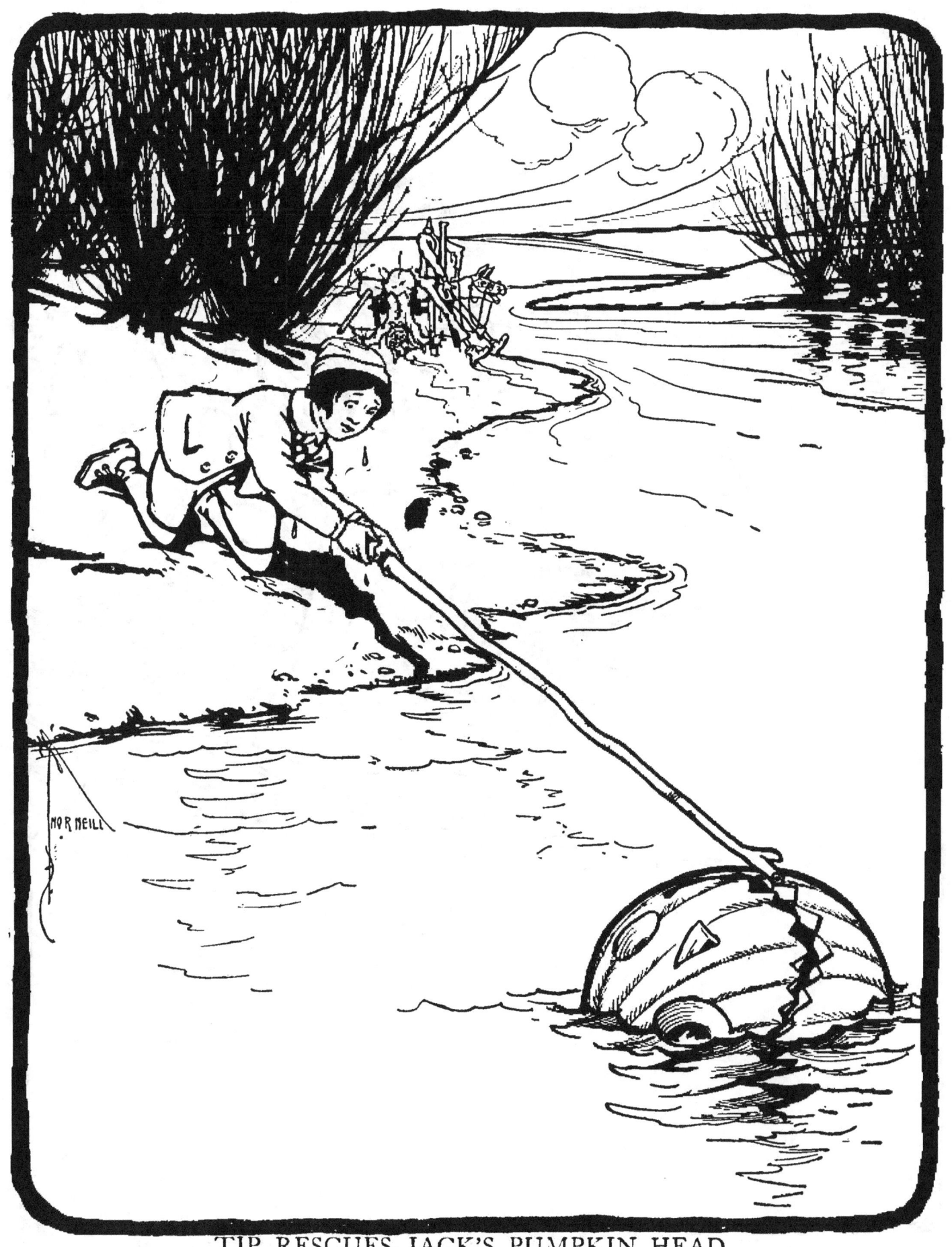

TIP RESCUES JACK'S PUMPKIN HEAD.

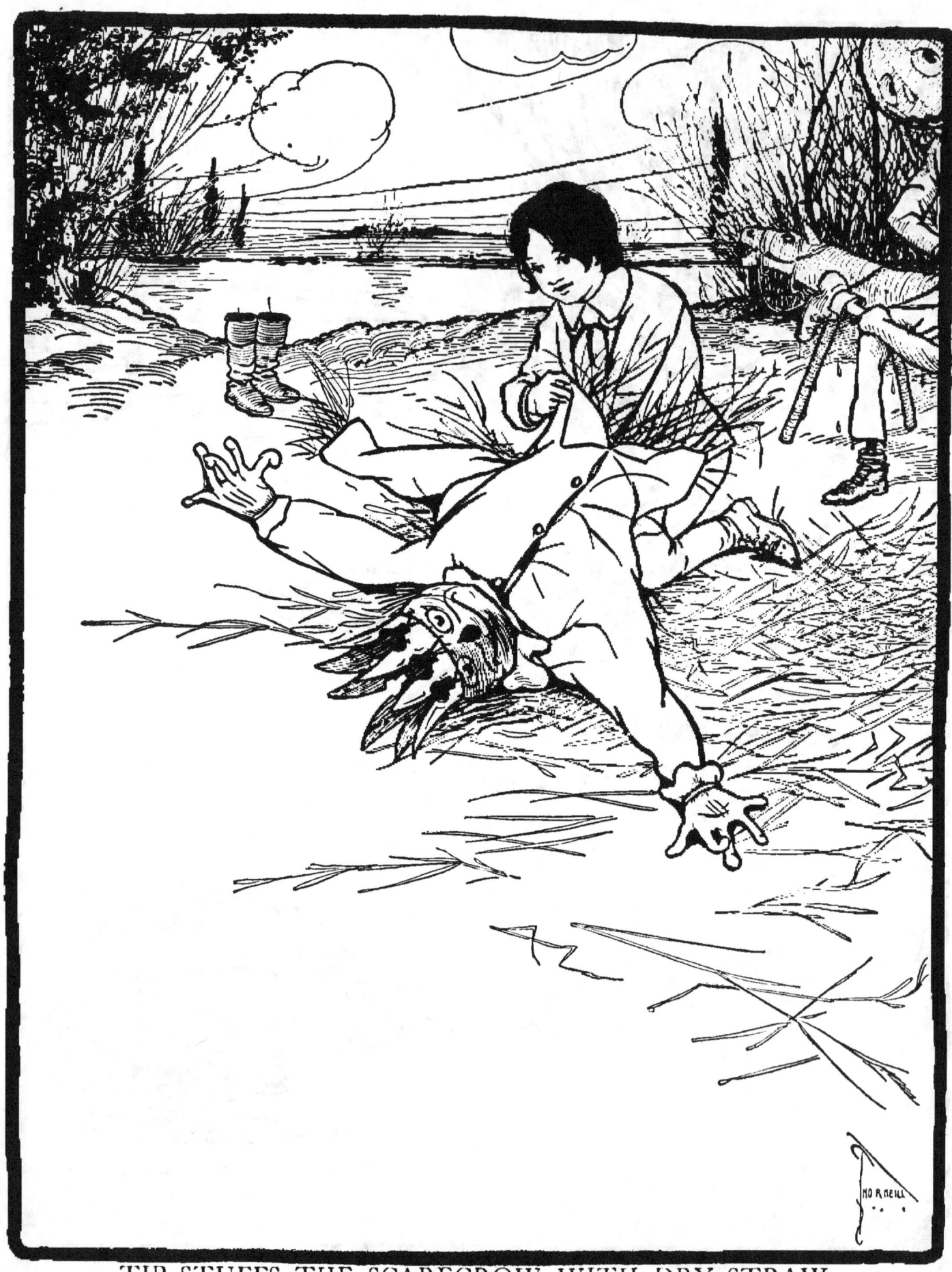

TIP STUFFS THE SCARECROW WITH DRY STRAW.

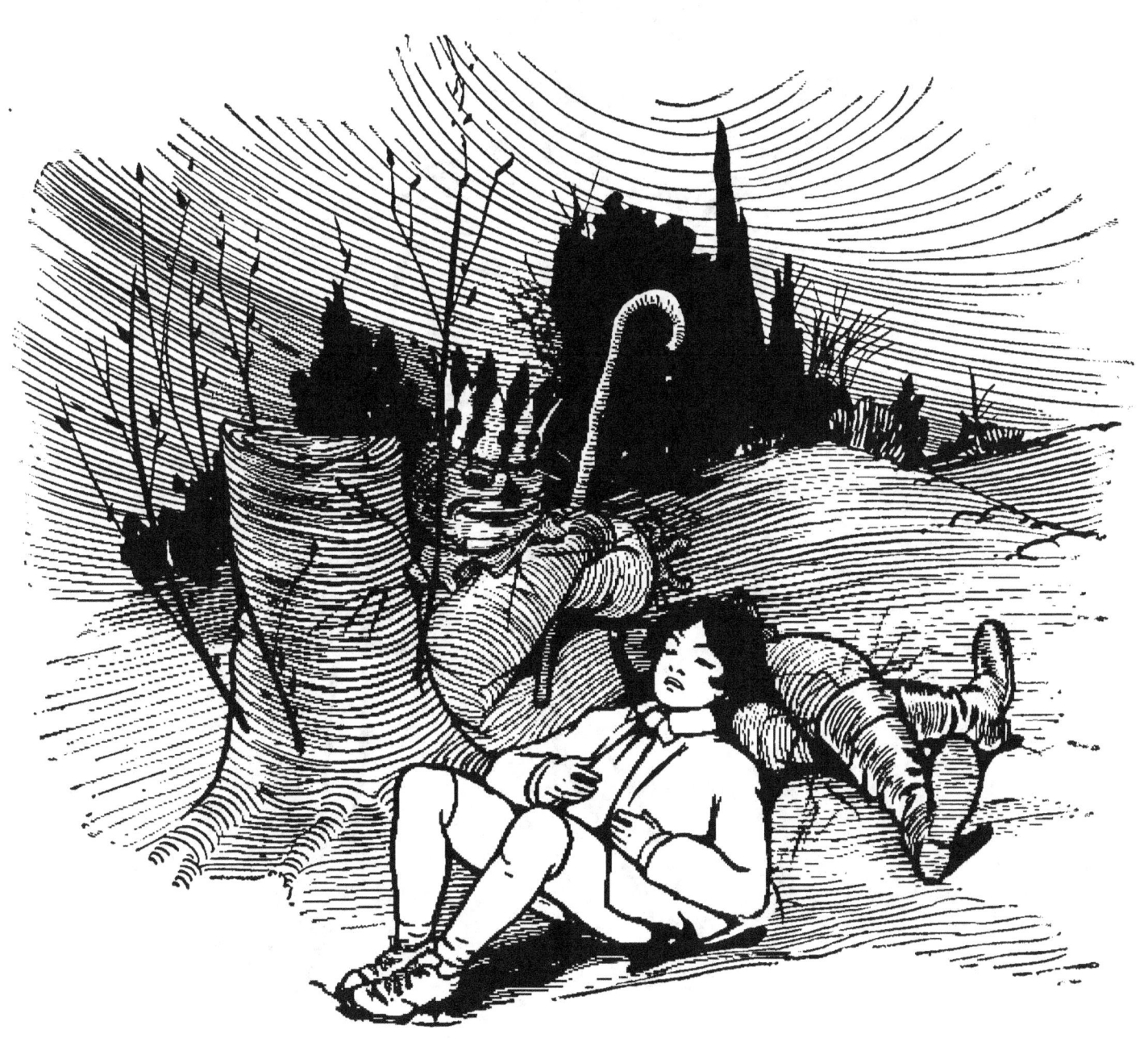

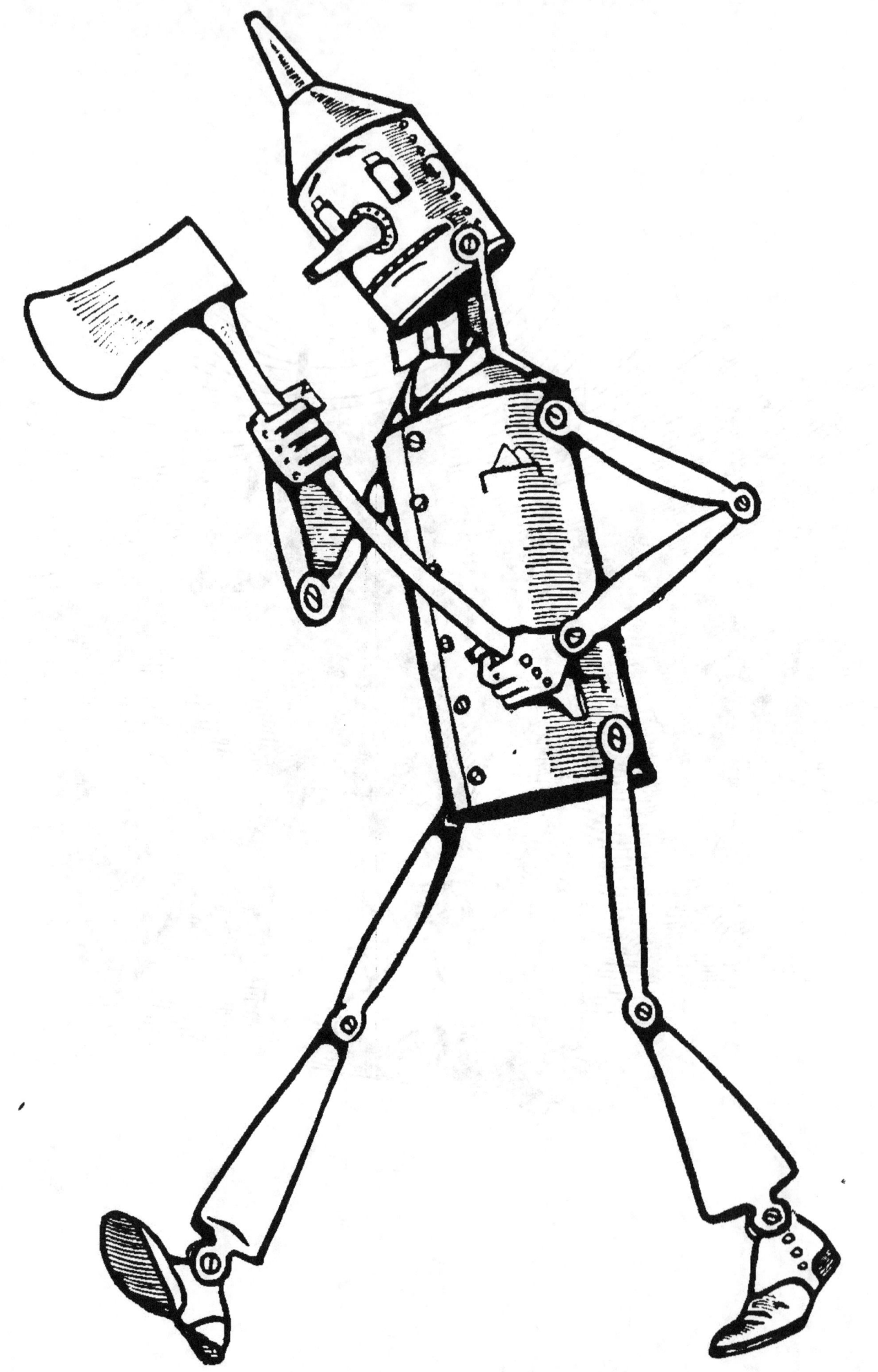

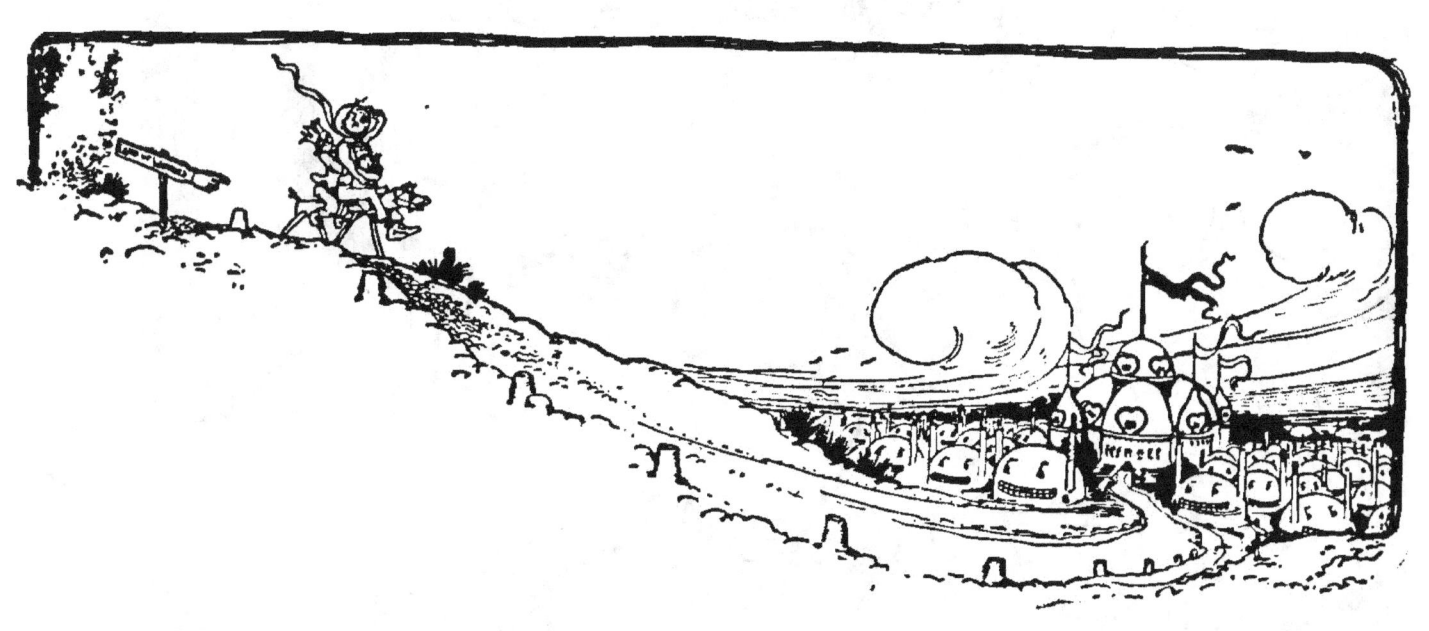

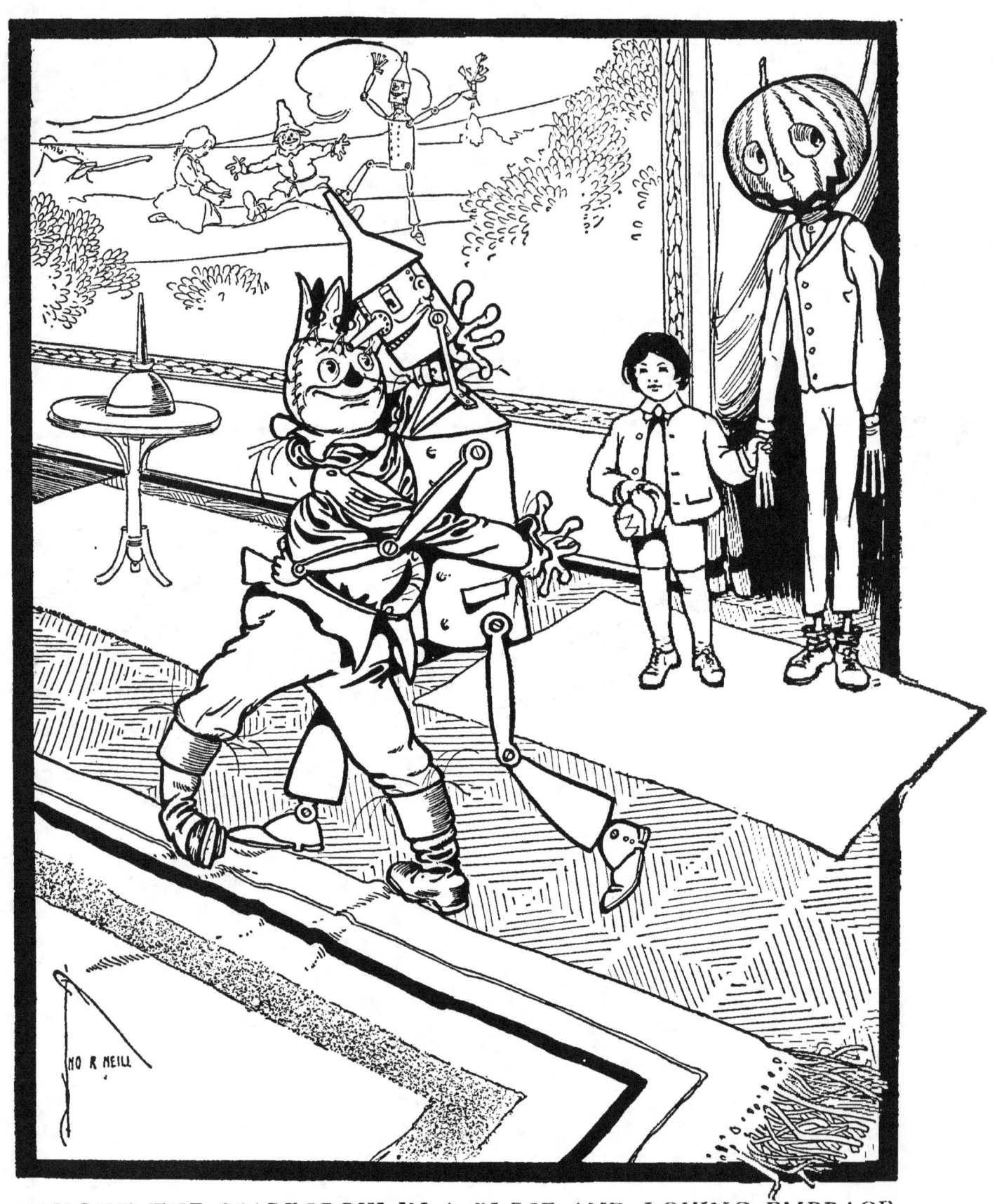

CAUGHT THE SCARECROW IN A CLOSE AND LOVING EMBRACE.

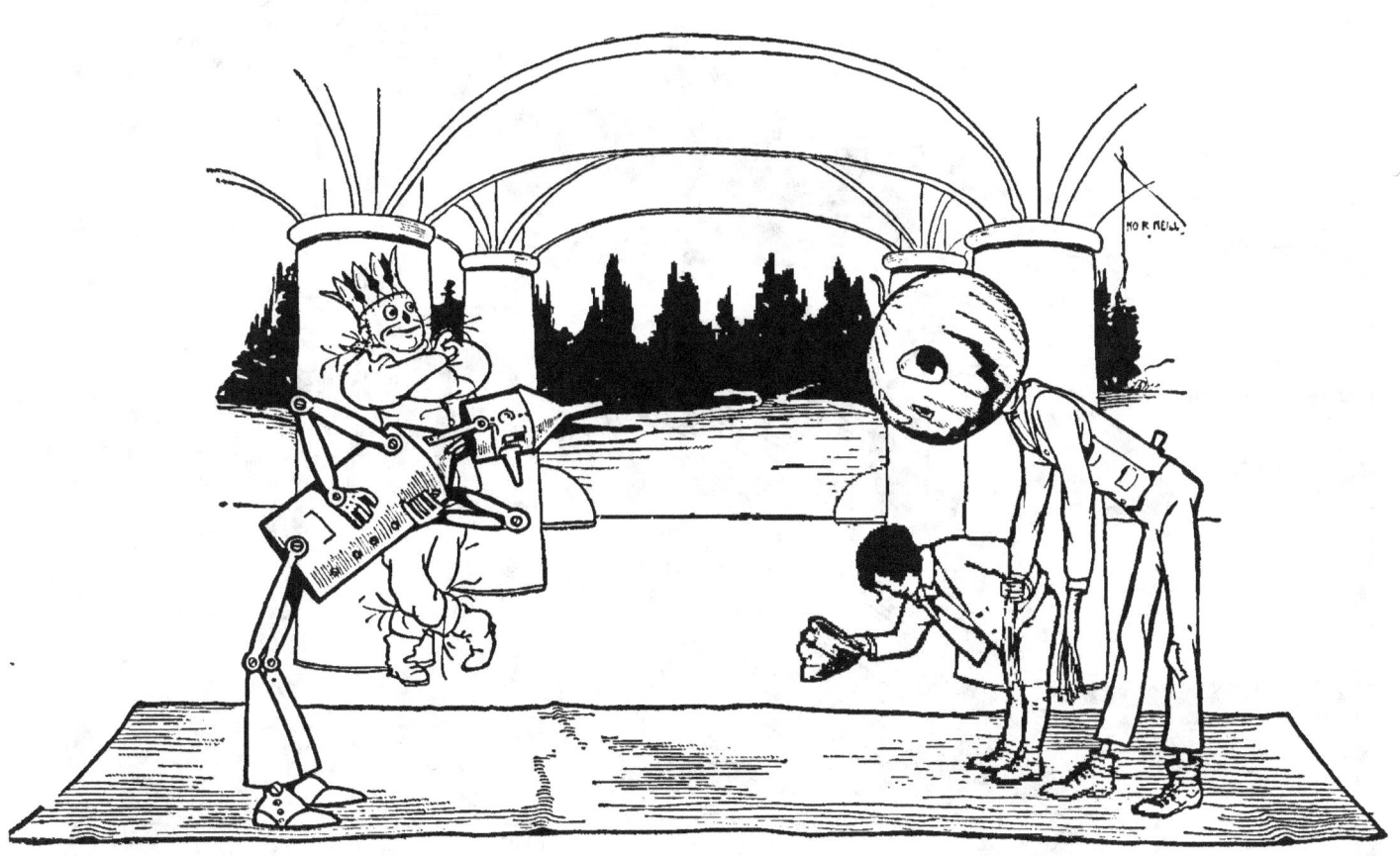

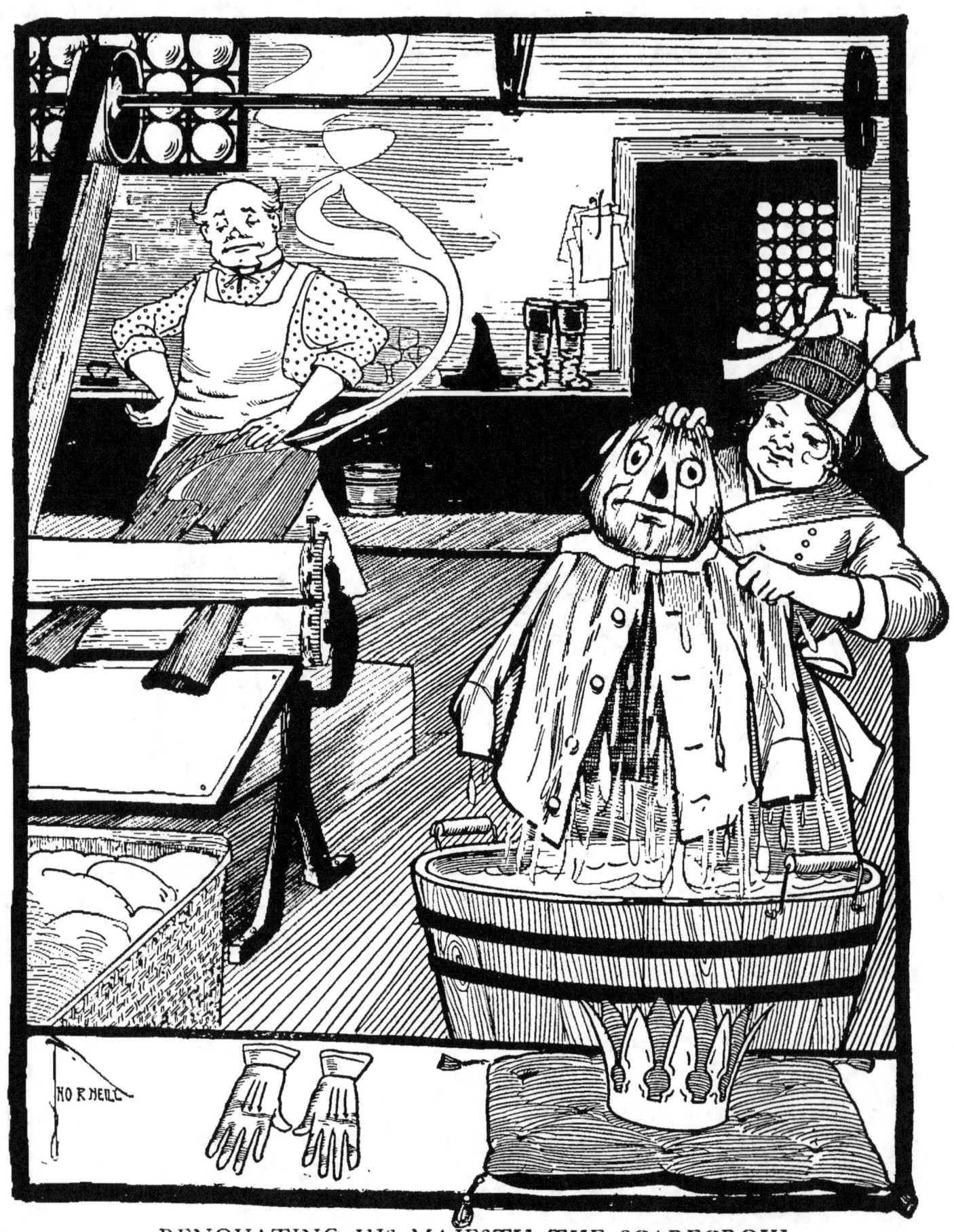

RENOVATING HIS MAJESTY, THE SCARECROW.

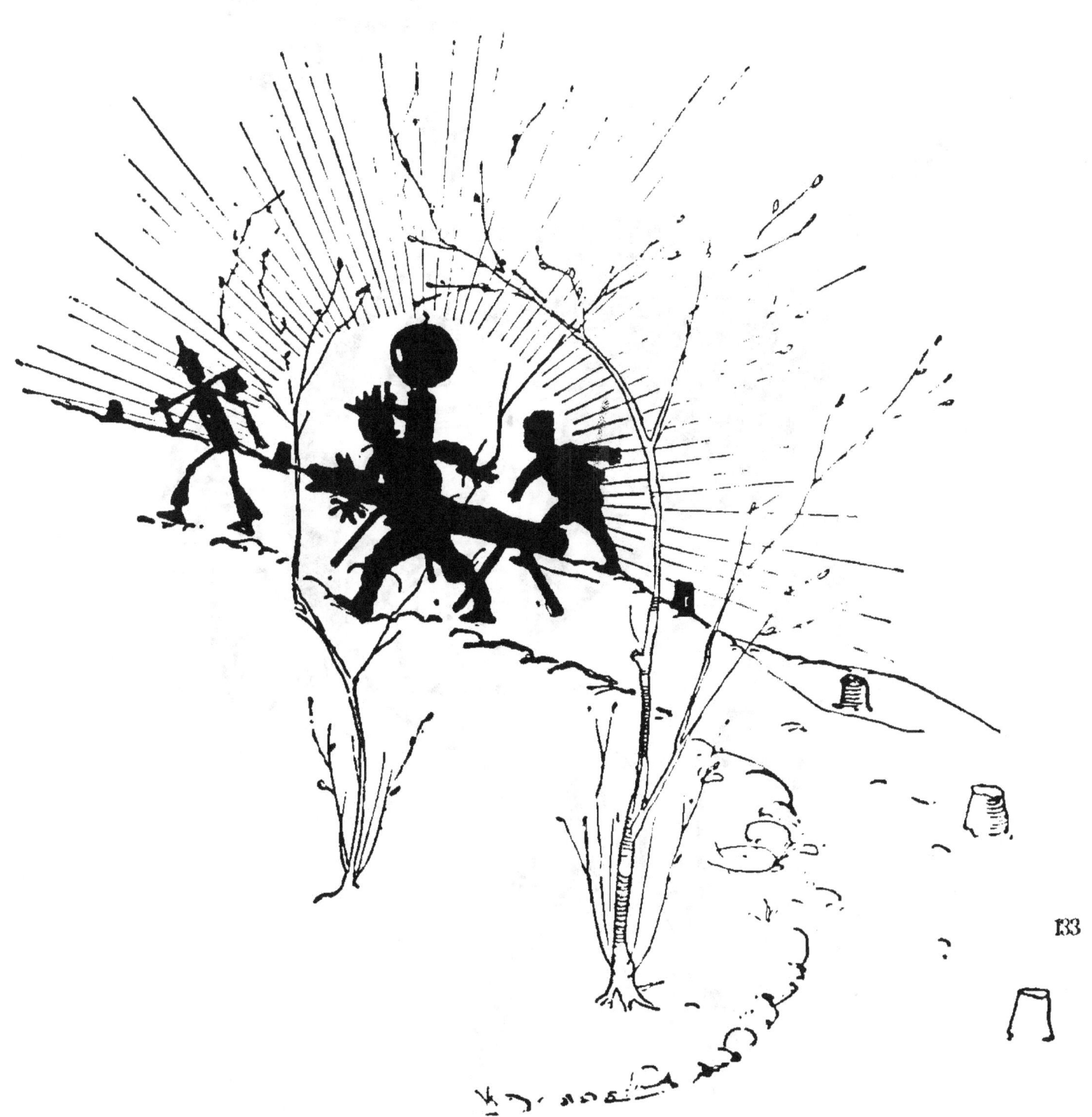

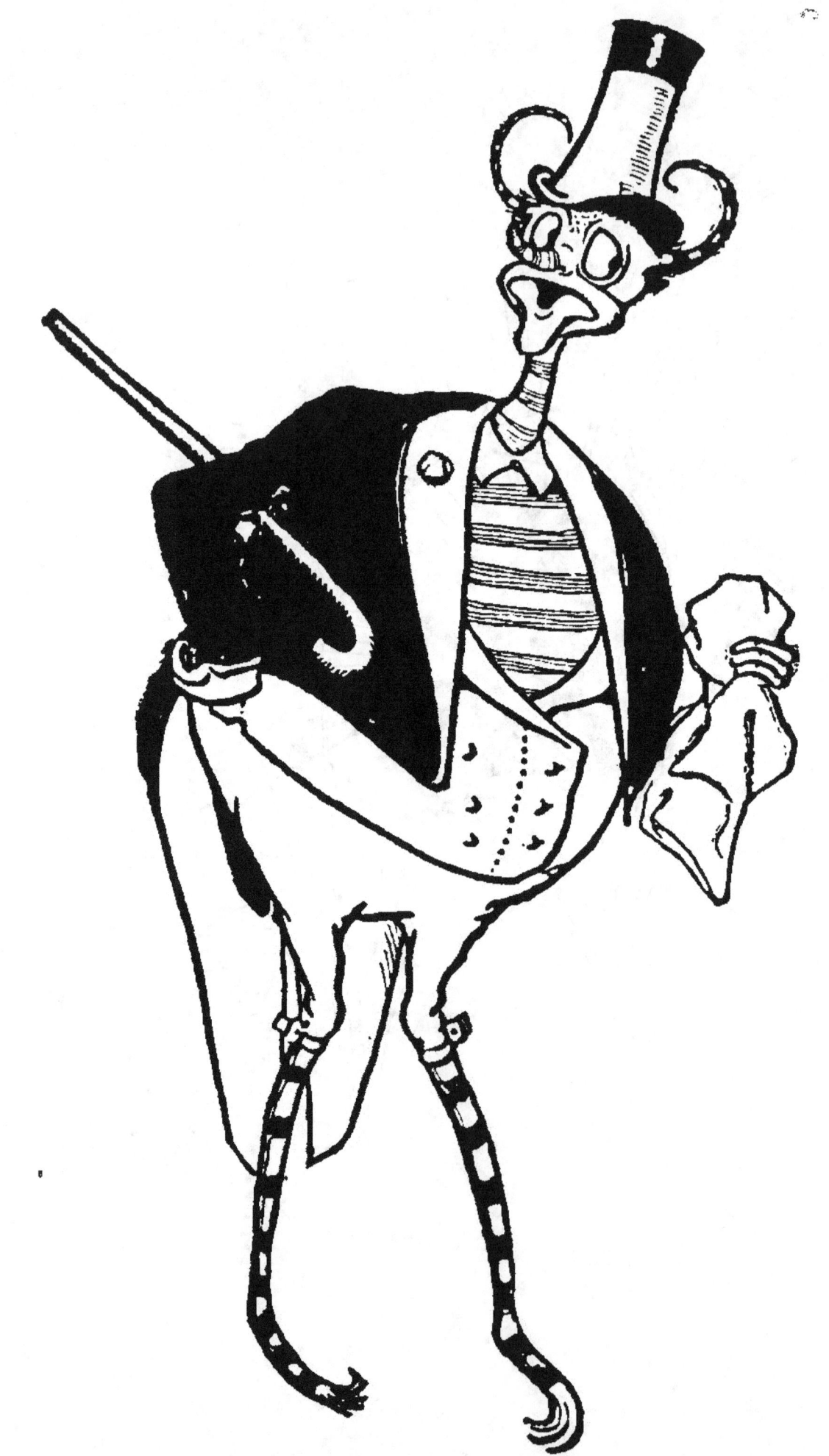

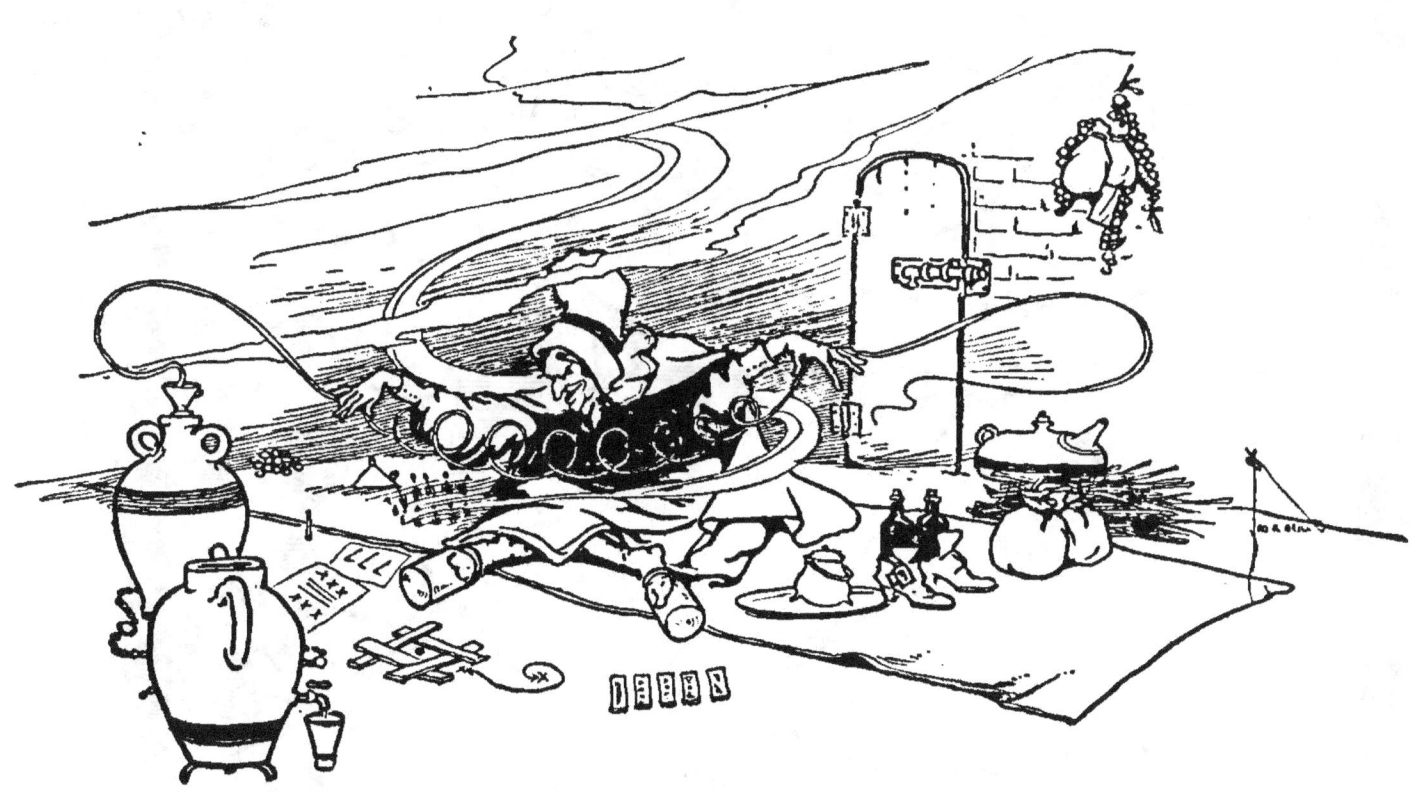

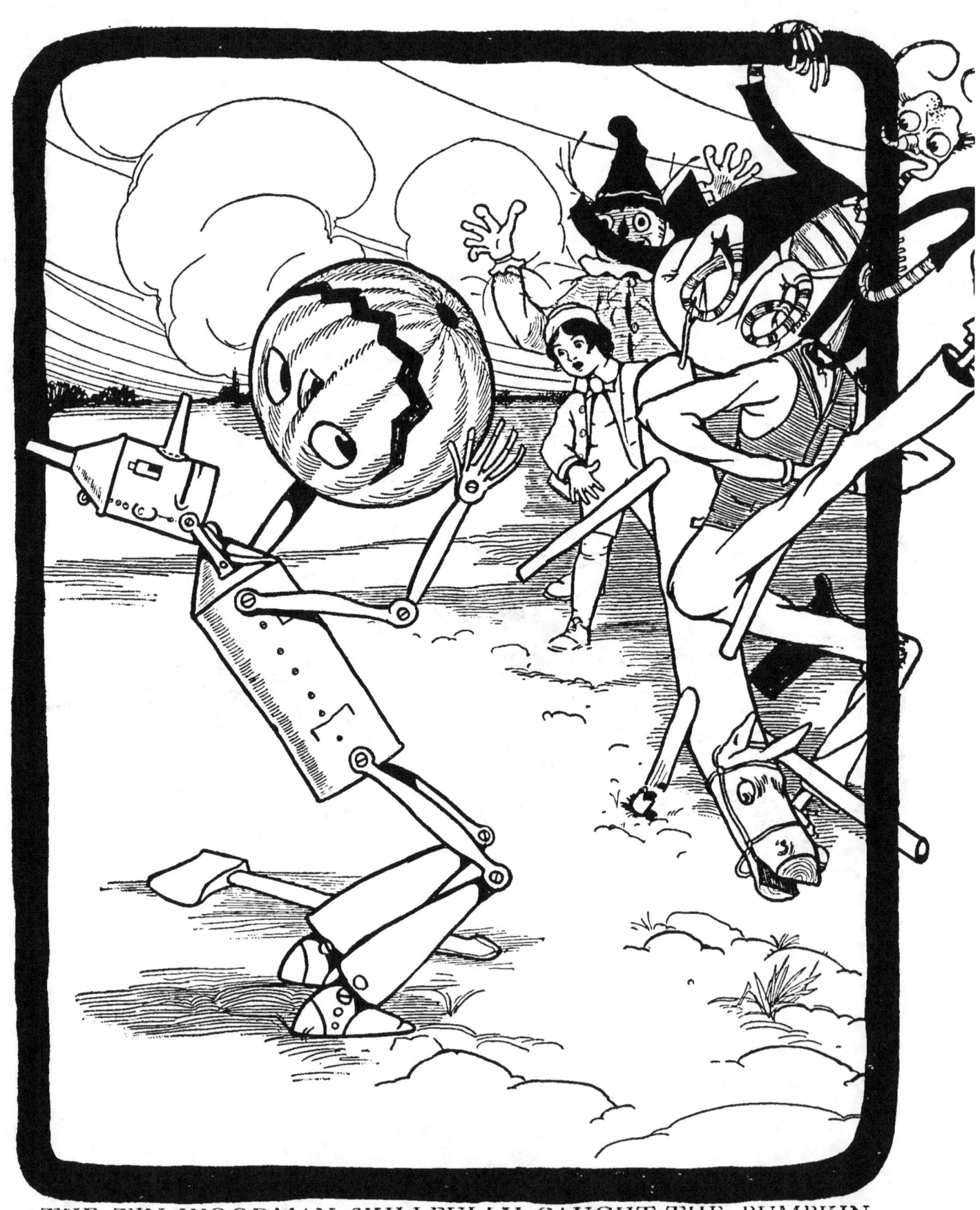

THE TIN WOODMAN SKILLFULLY CAUGHT THE PUMPKIN

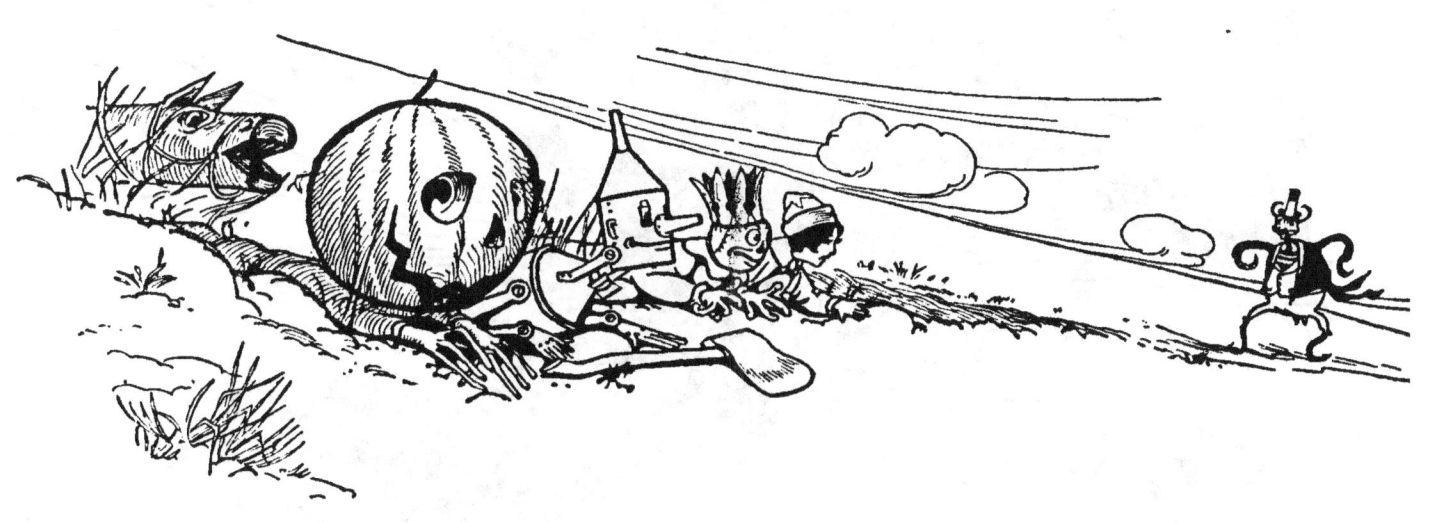

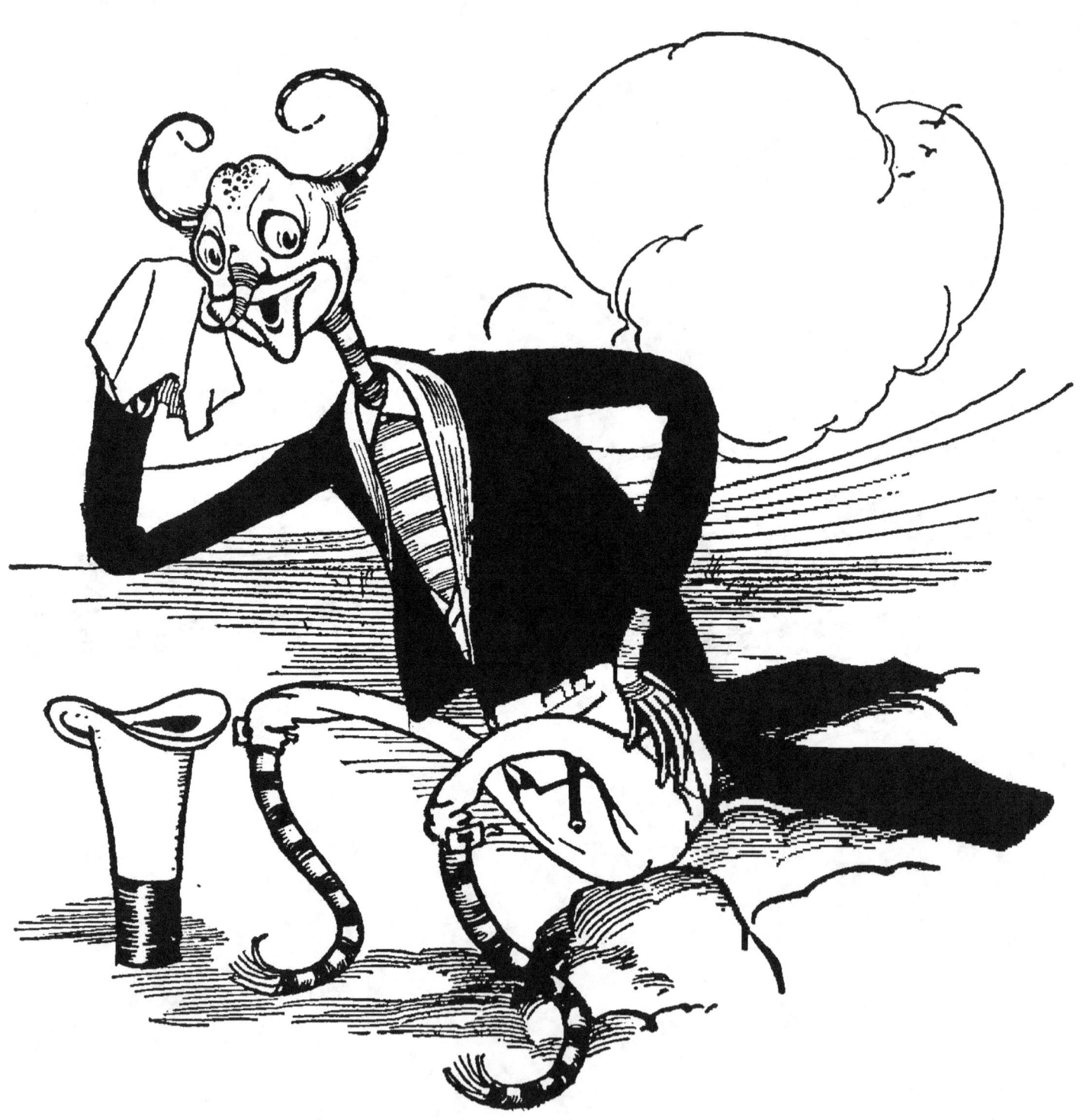

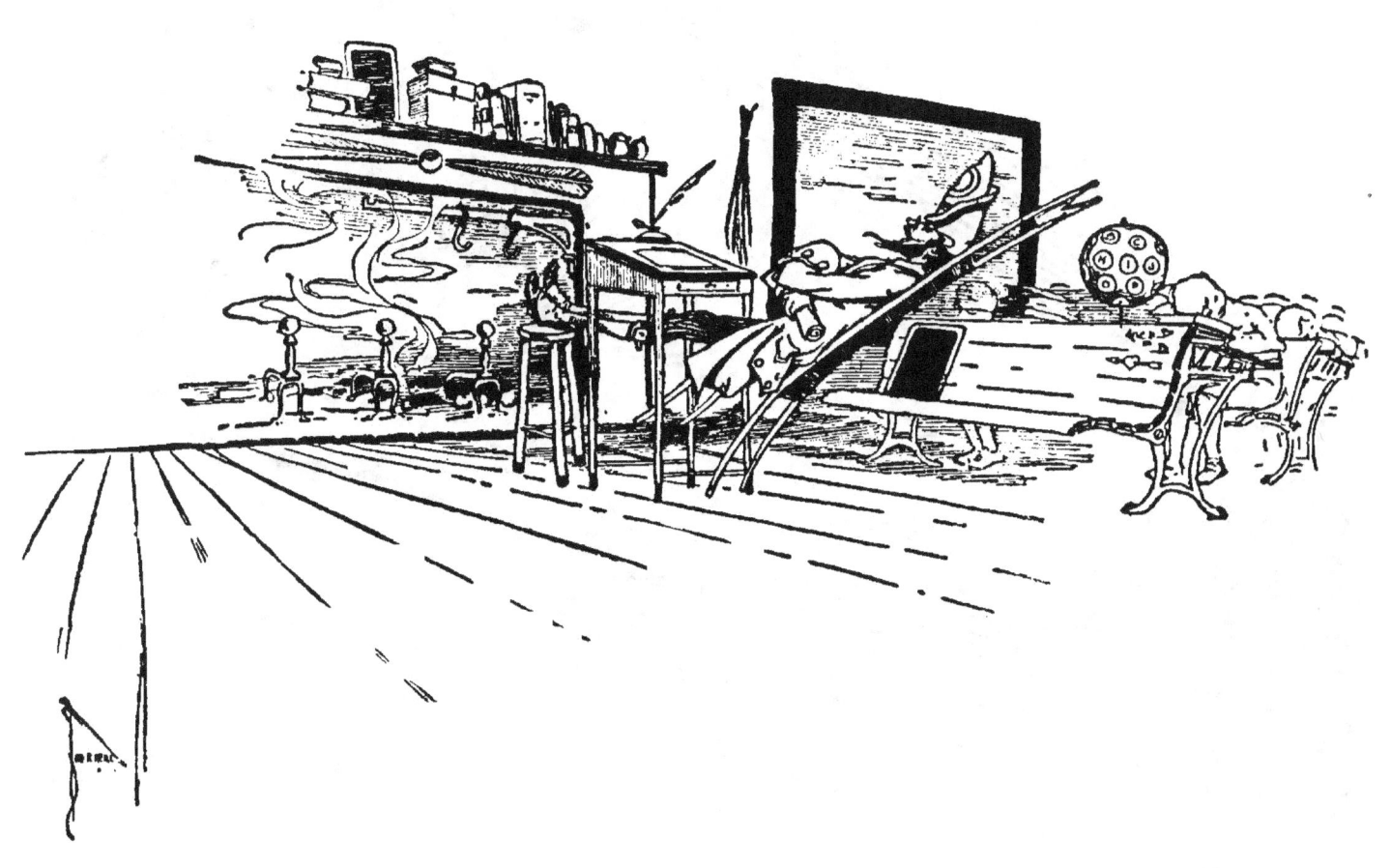

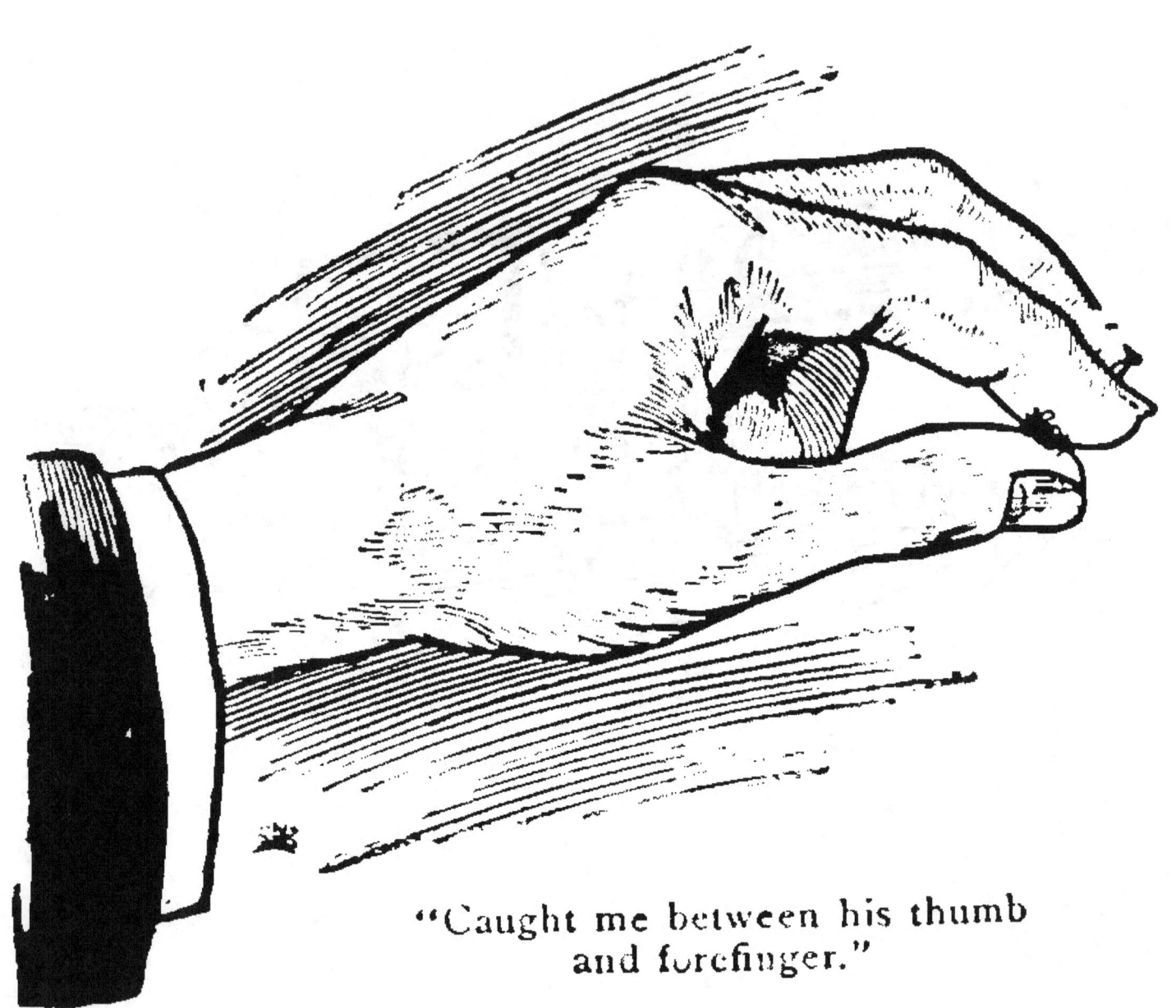

"Caught me between his thumb
and forefinger."

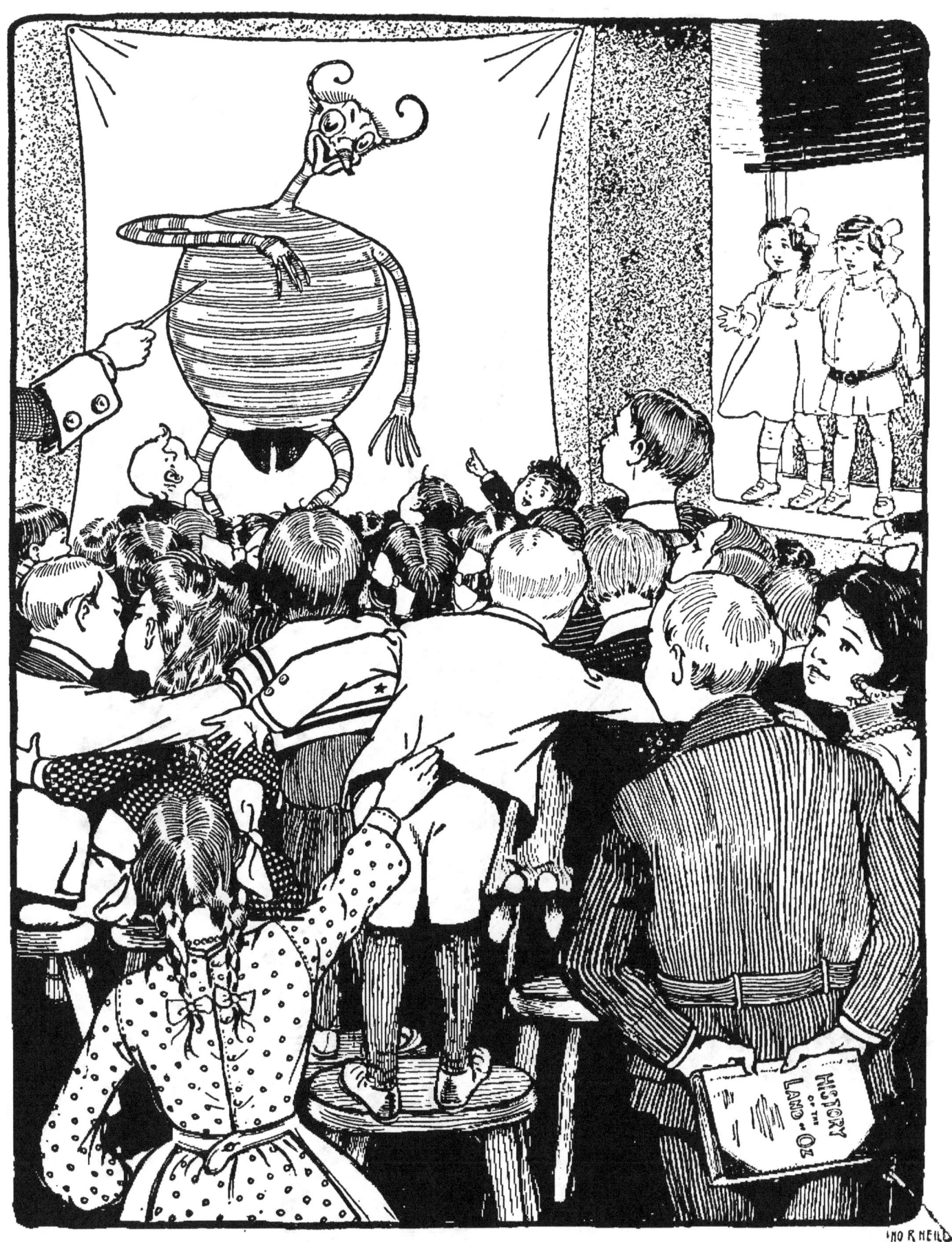

"THE STUDENTS STOOD UP ON THEIR STOOLS."

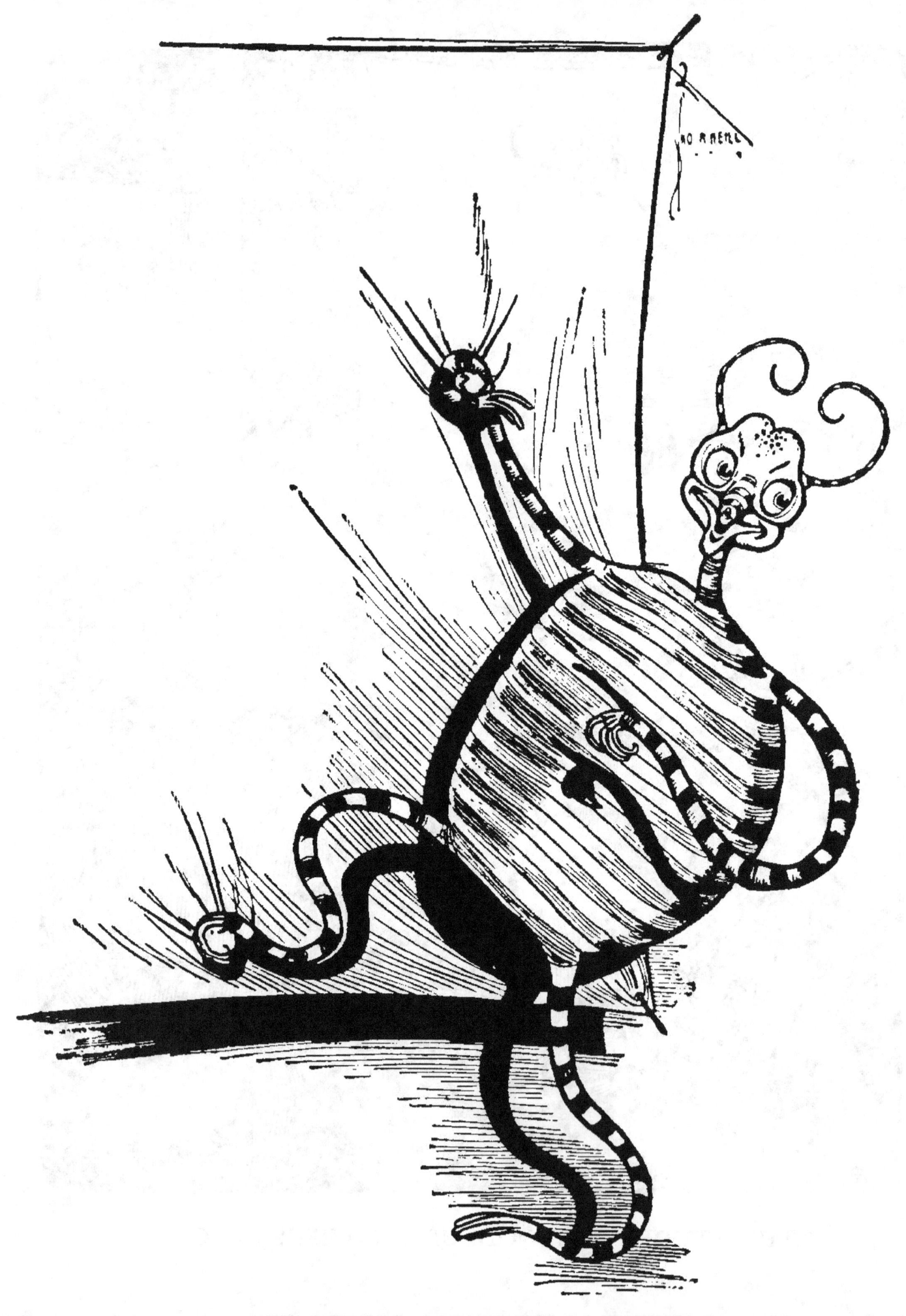

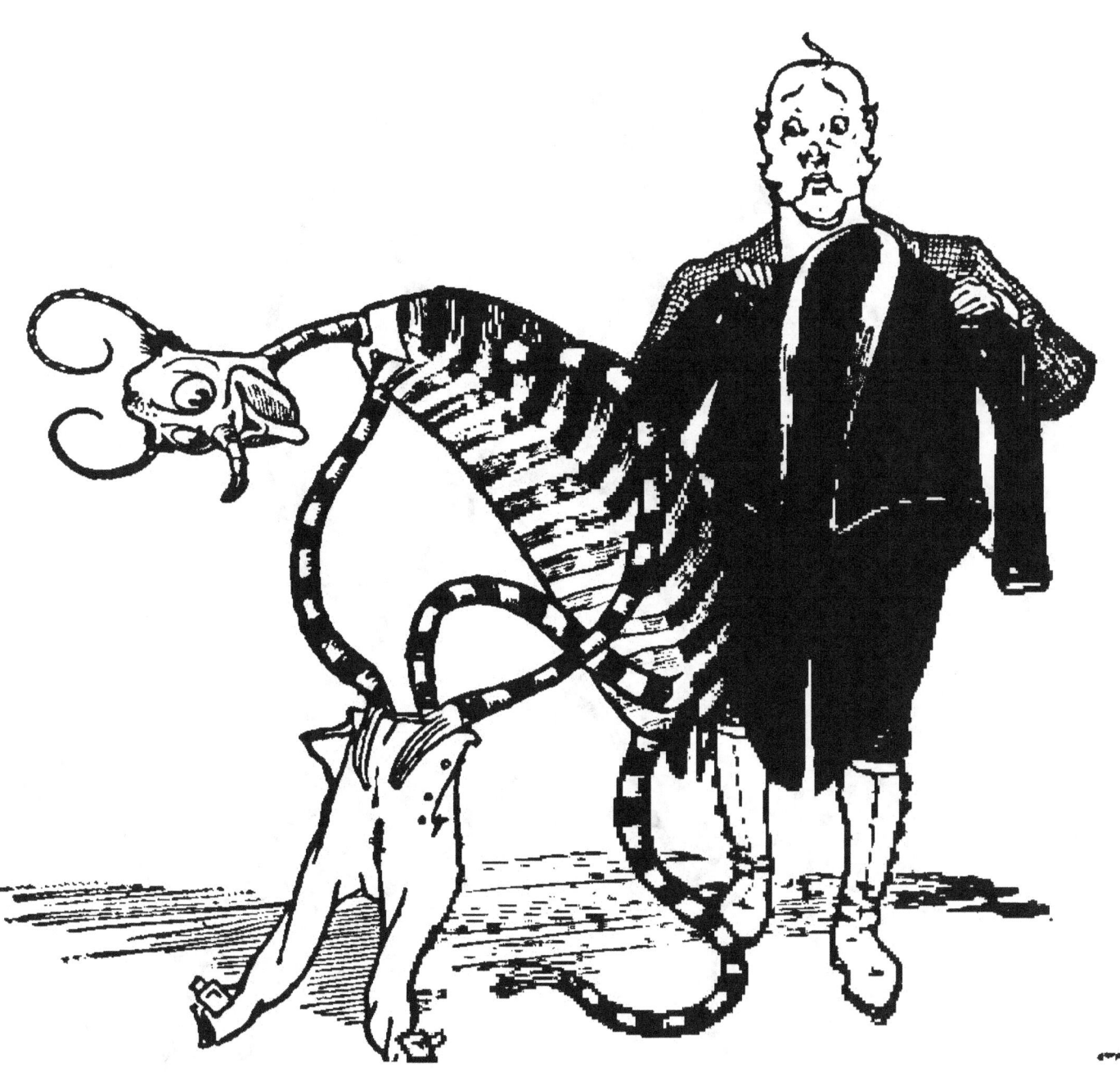

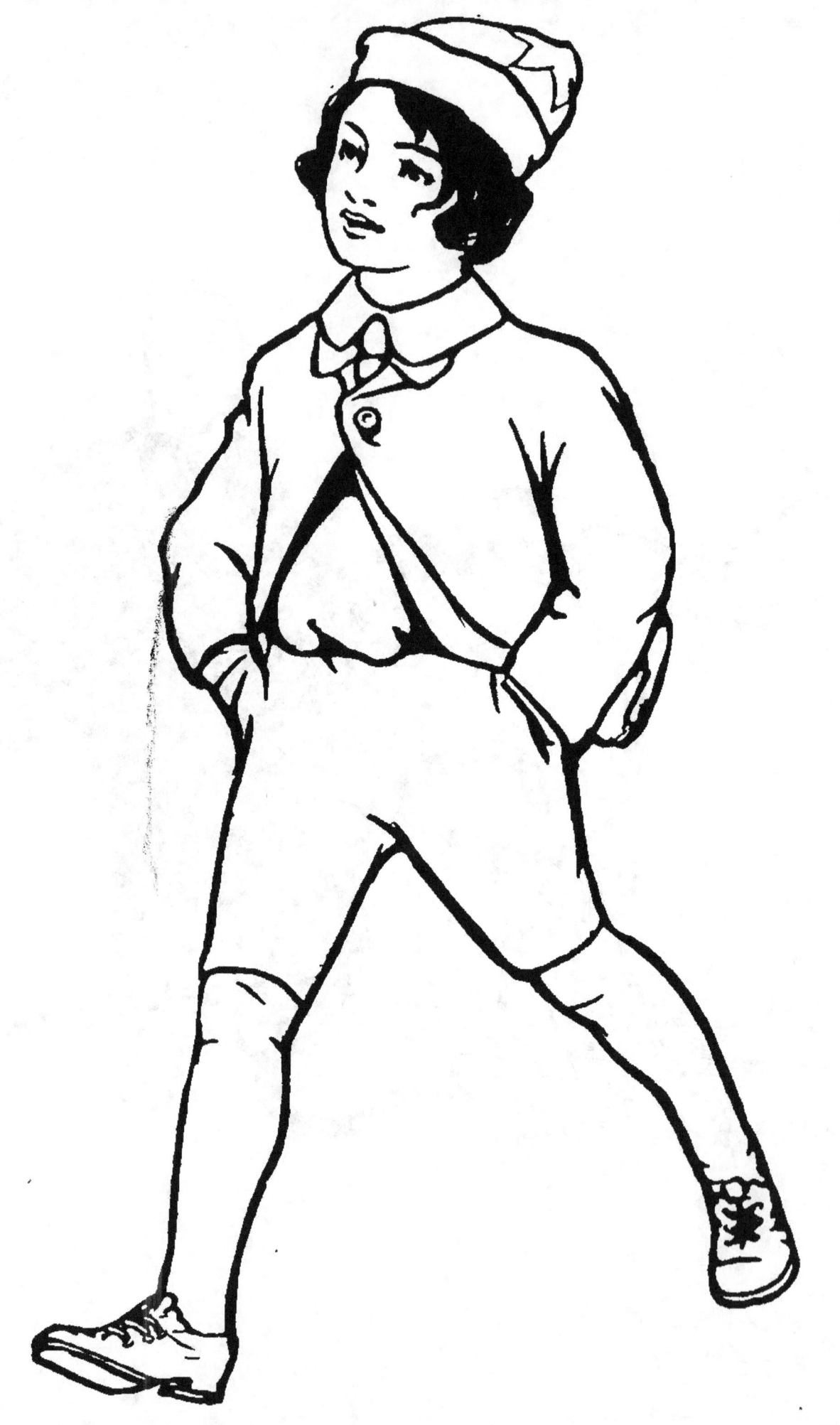

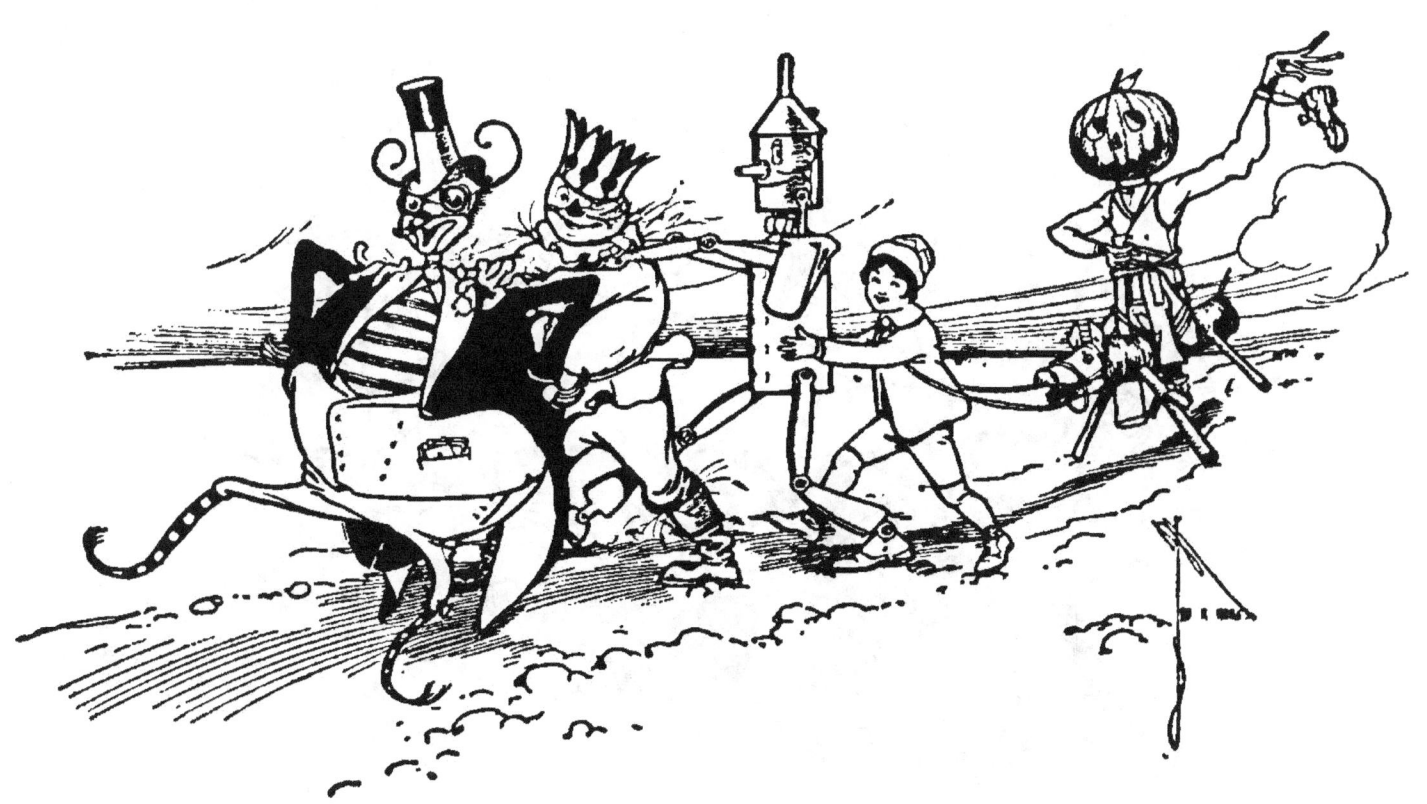

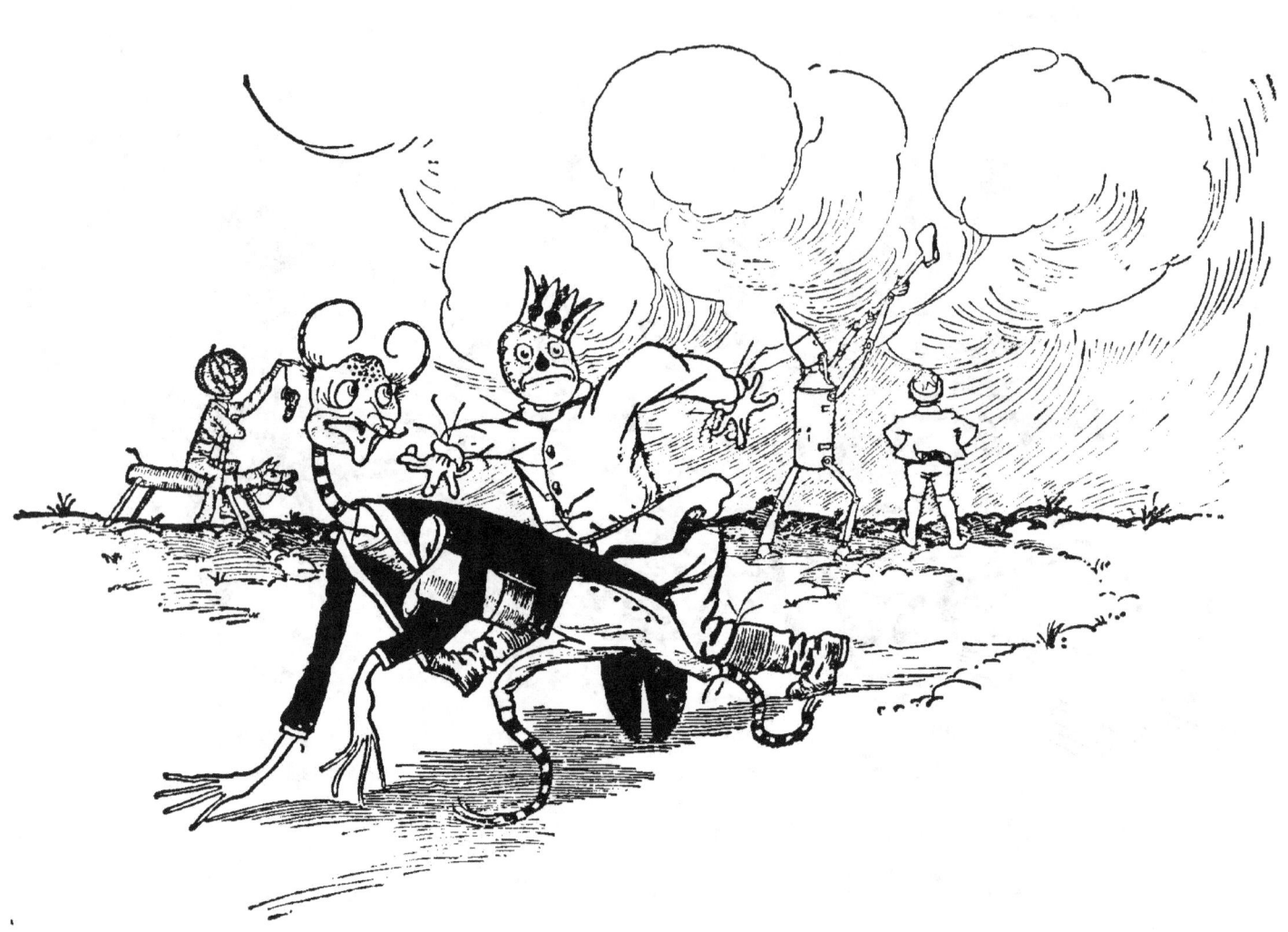

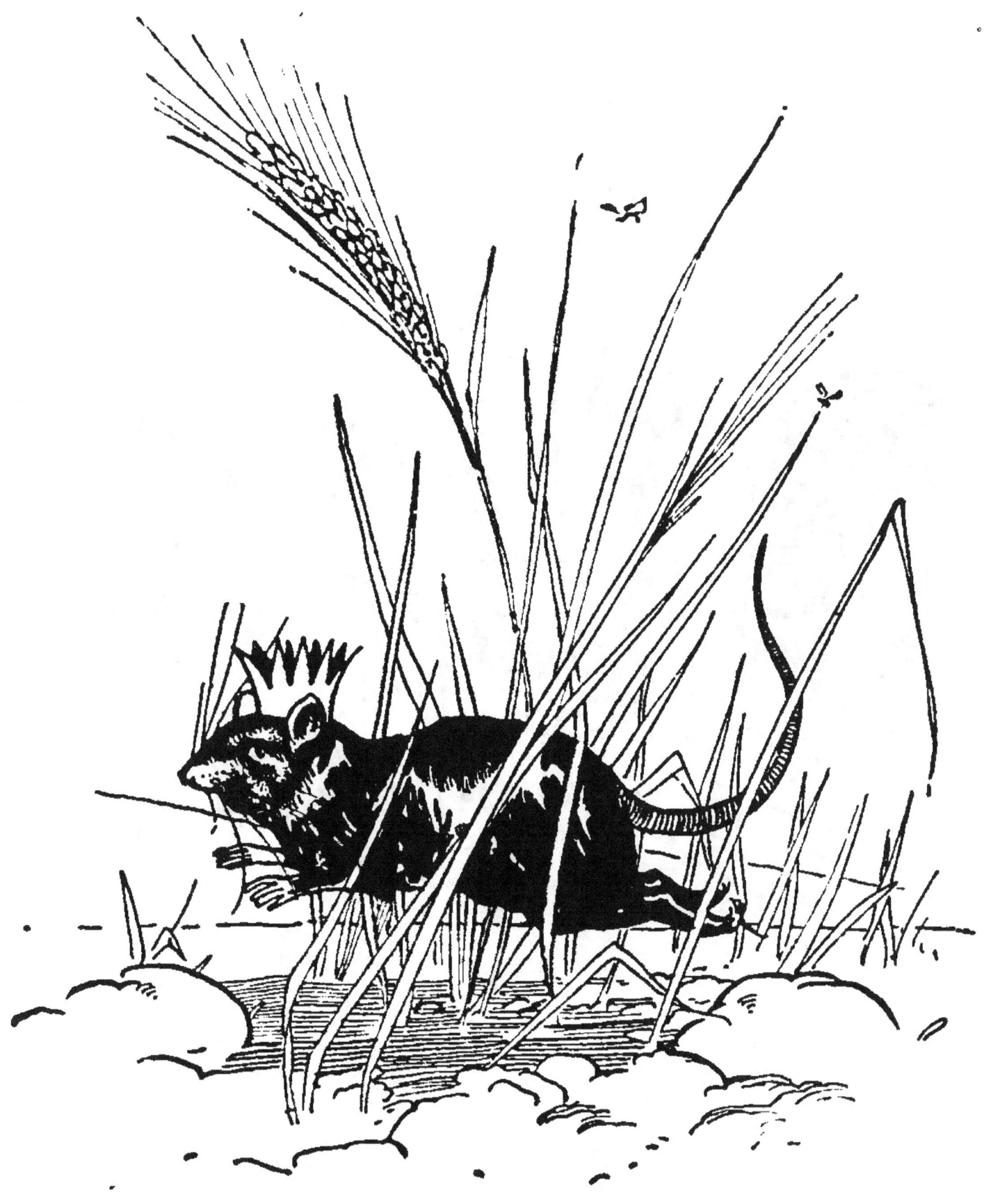

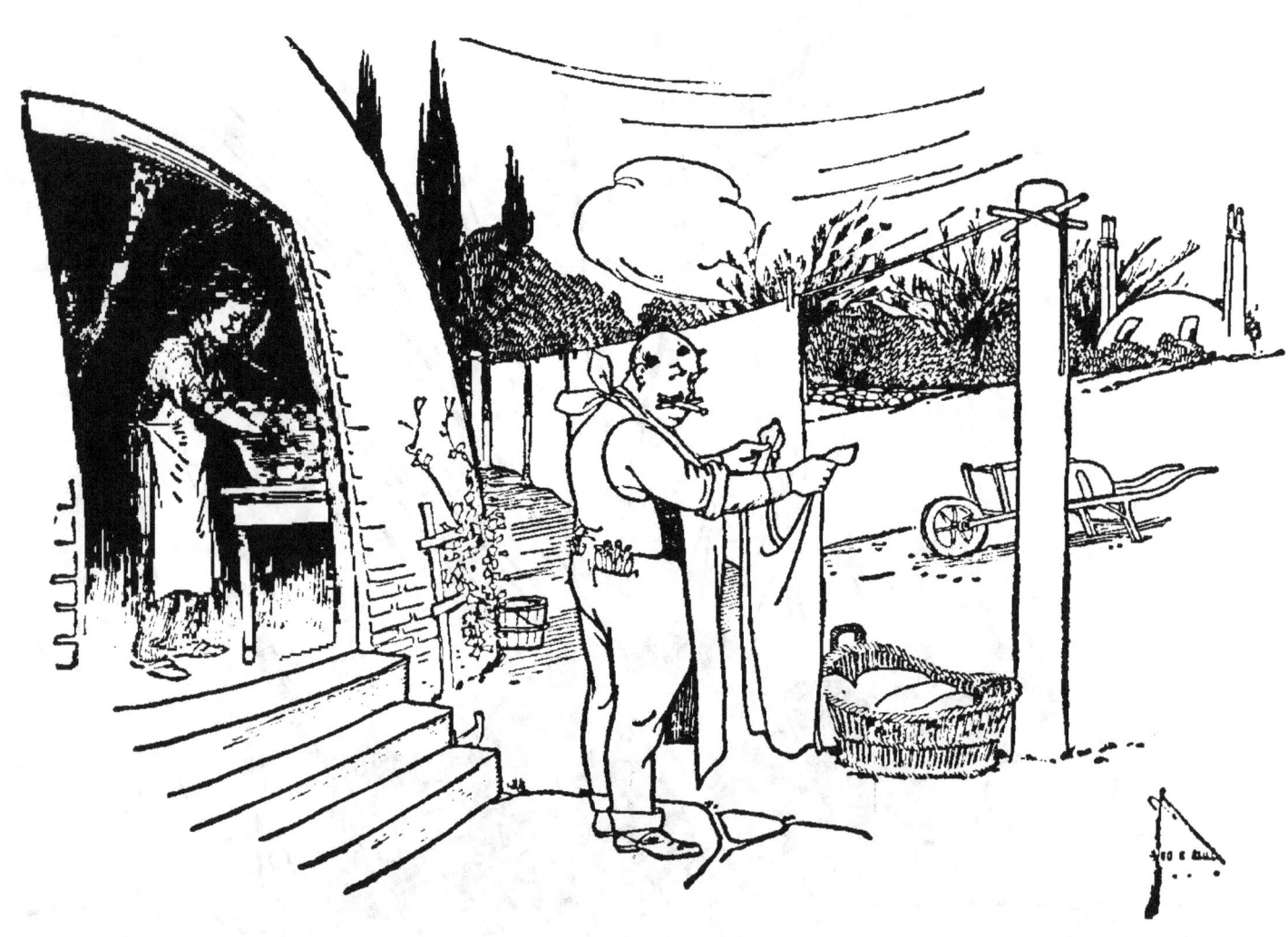

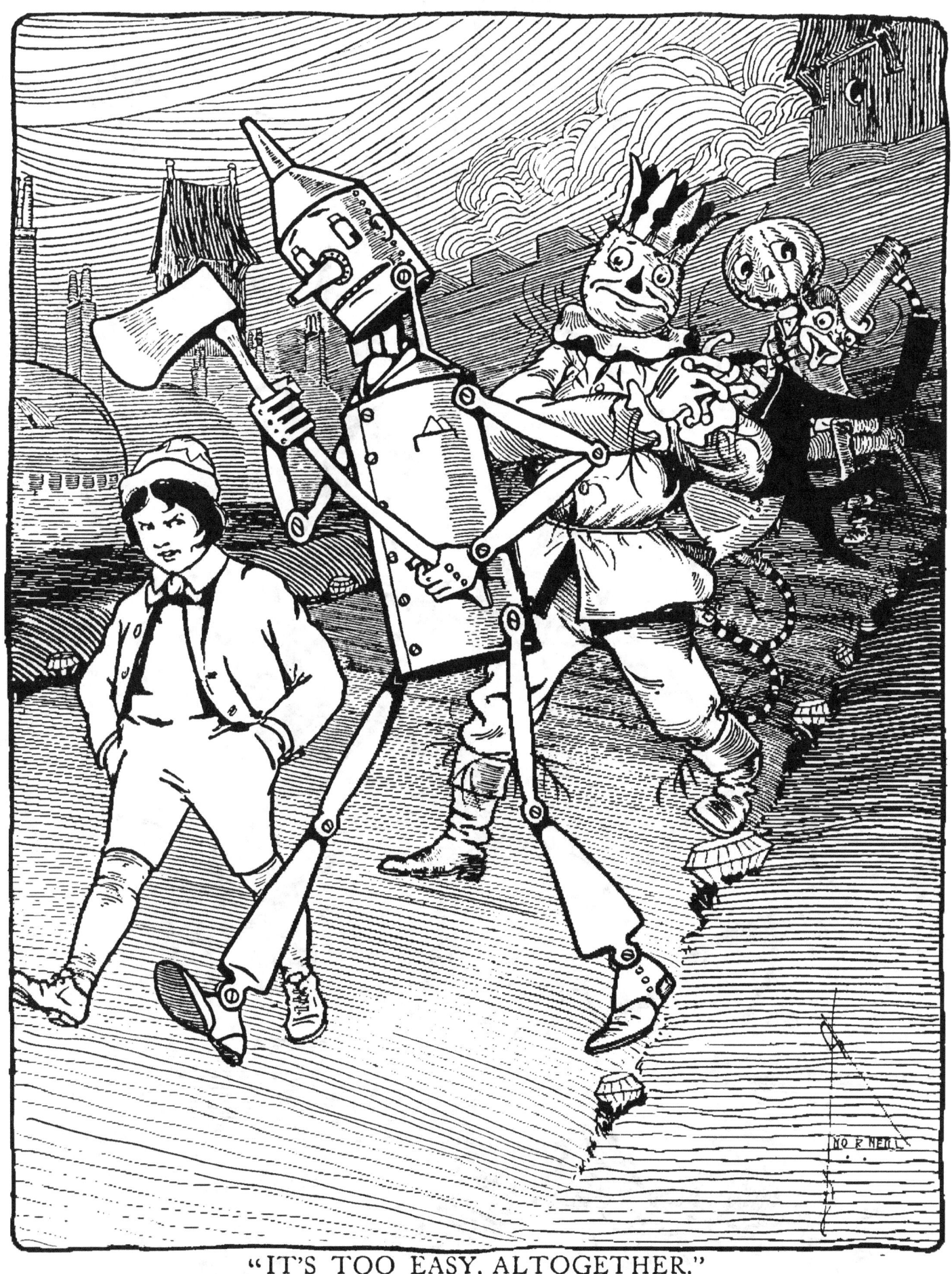

"IT'S TOO EASY, ALTOGETHER."

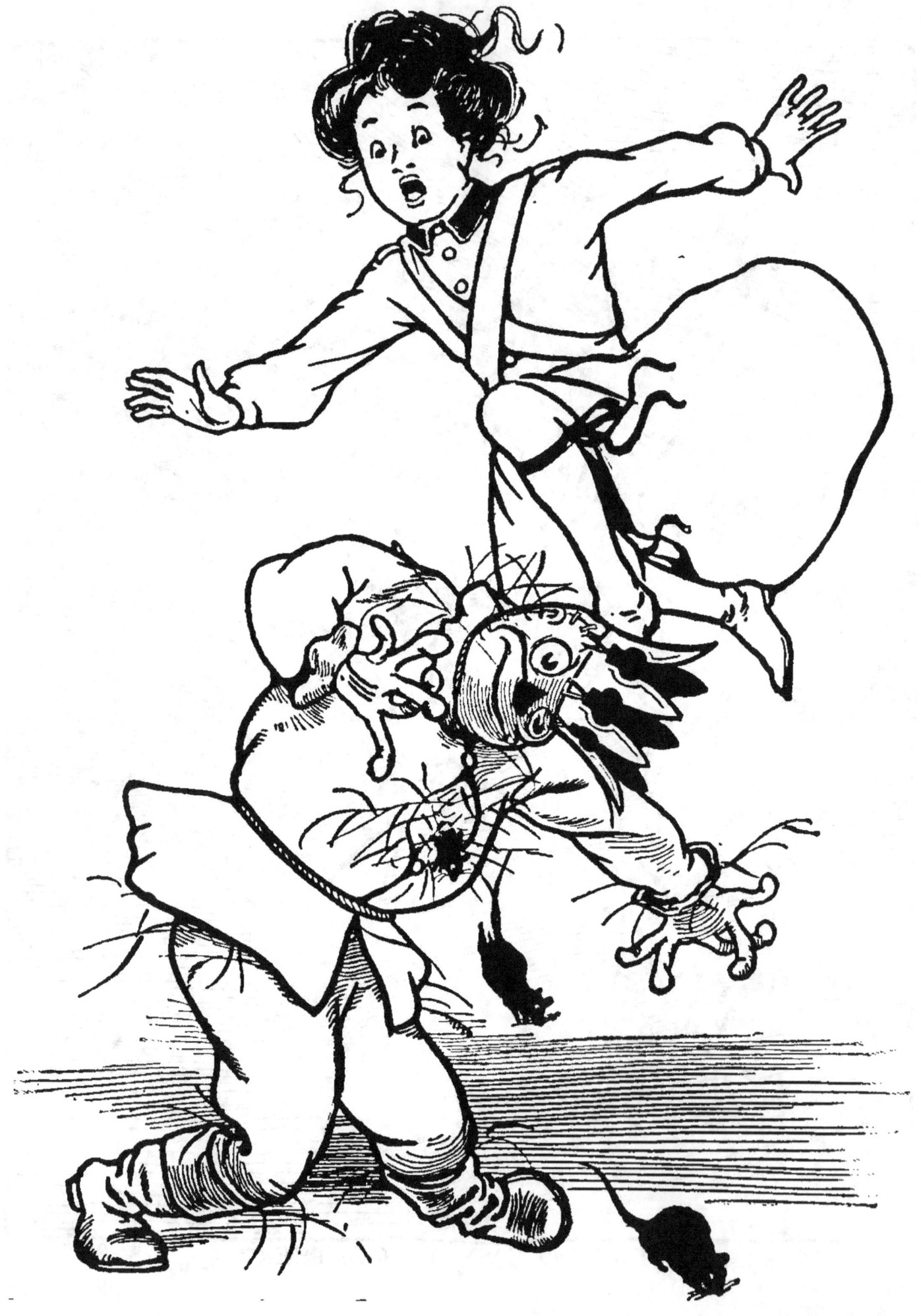

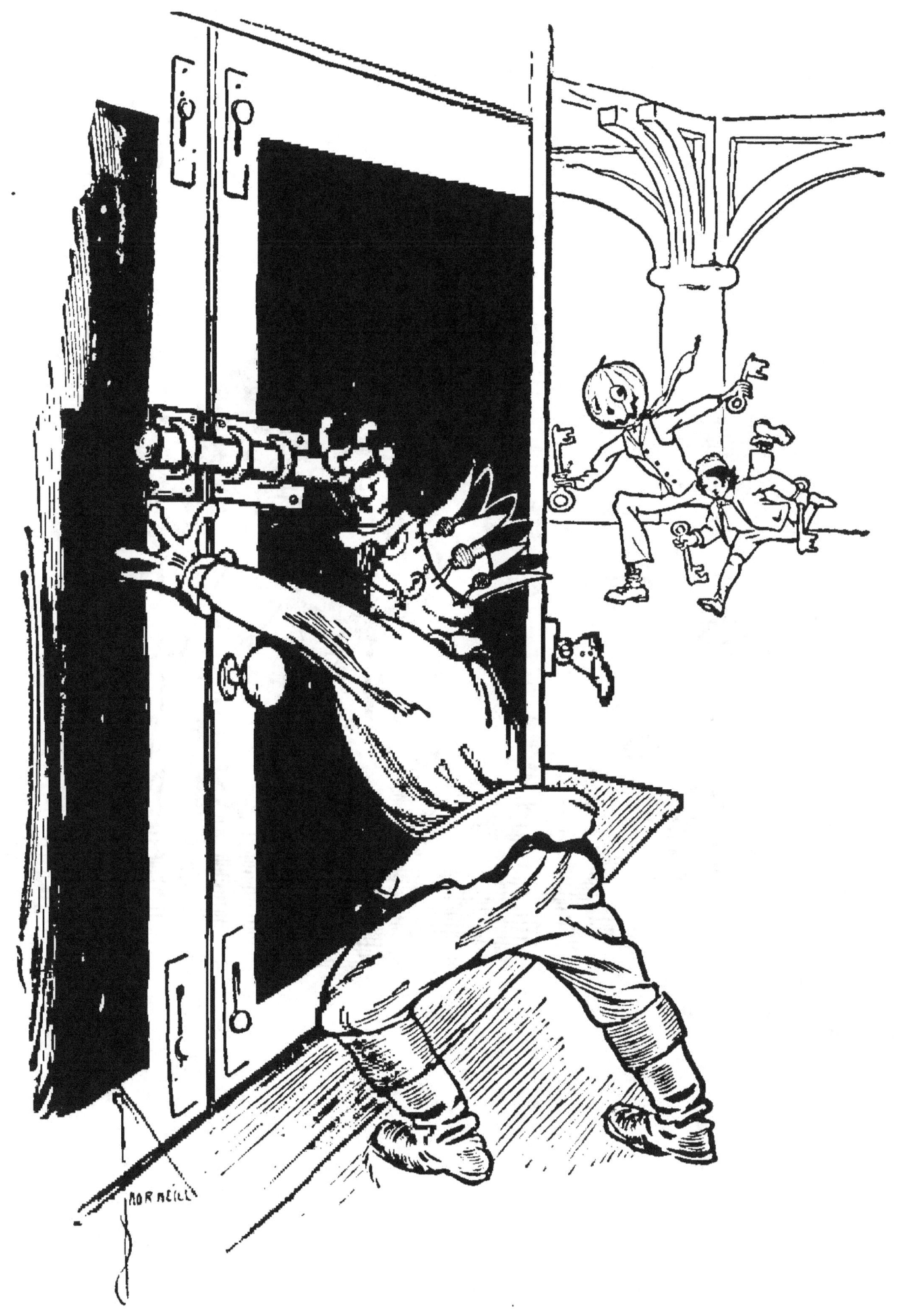

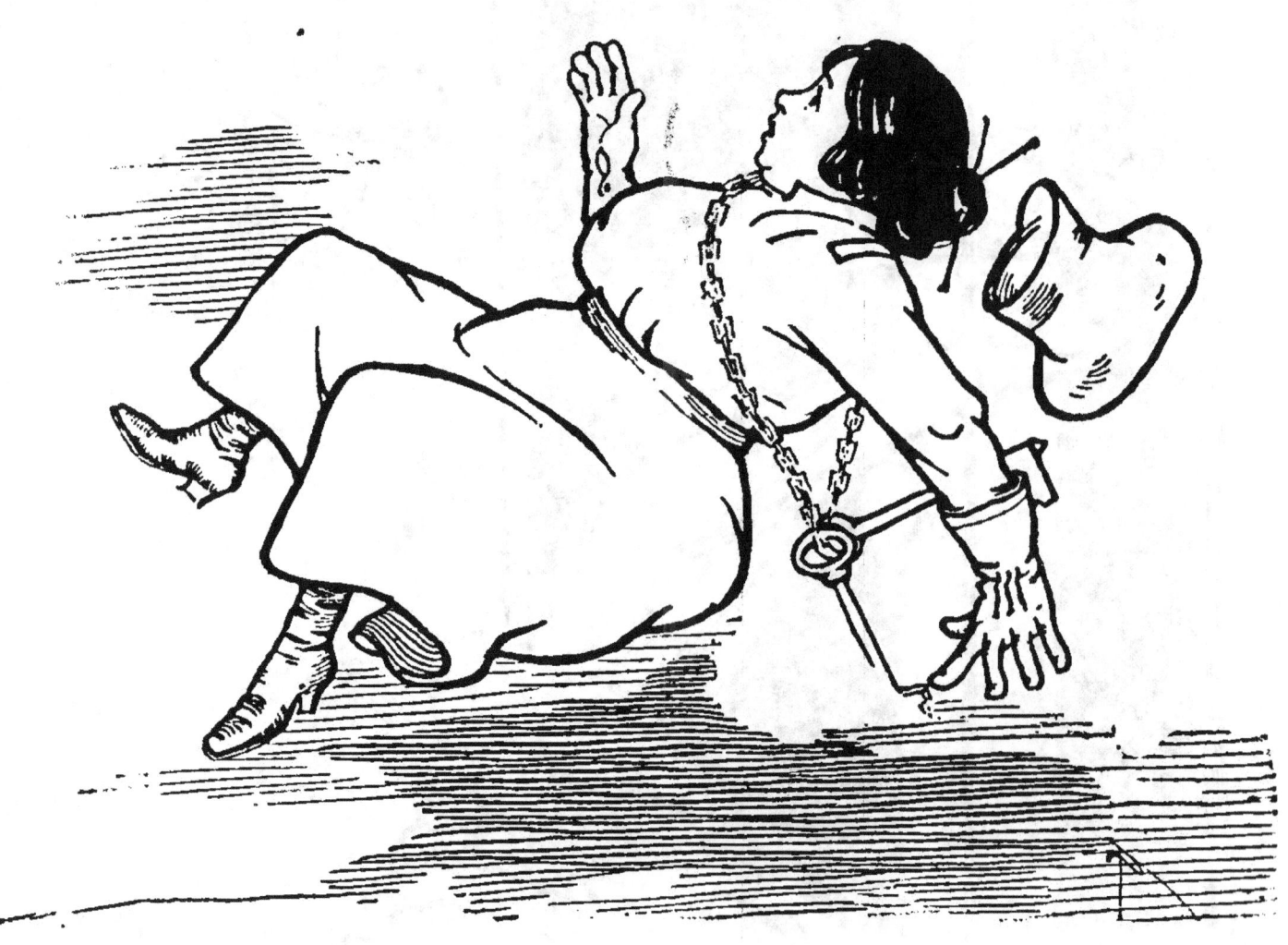

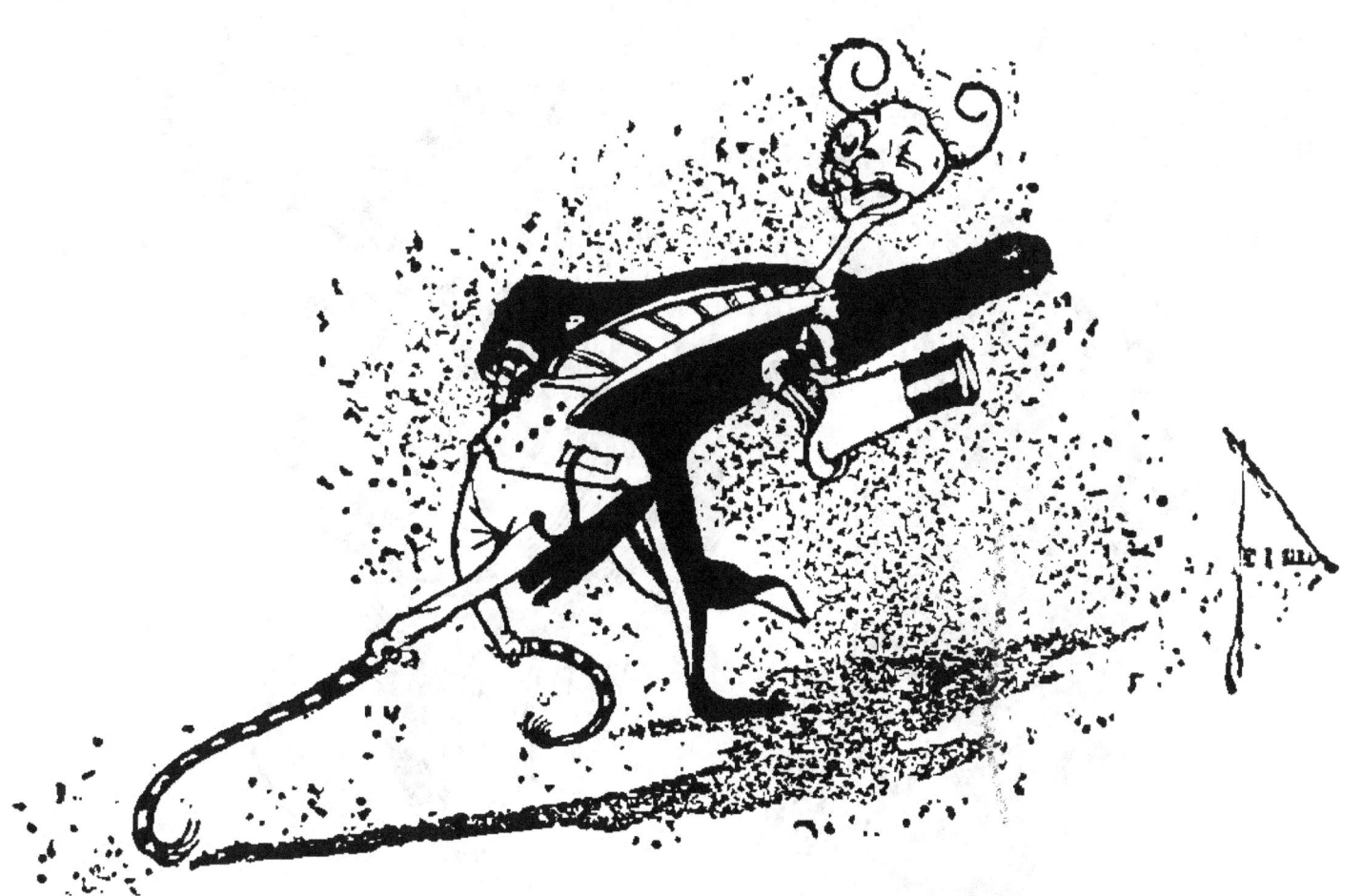

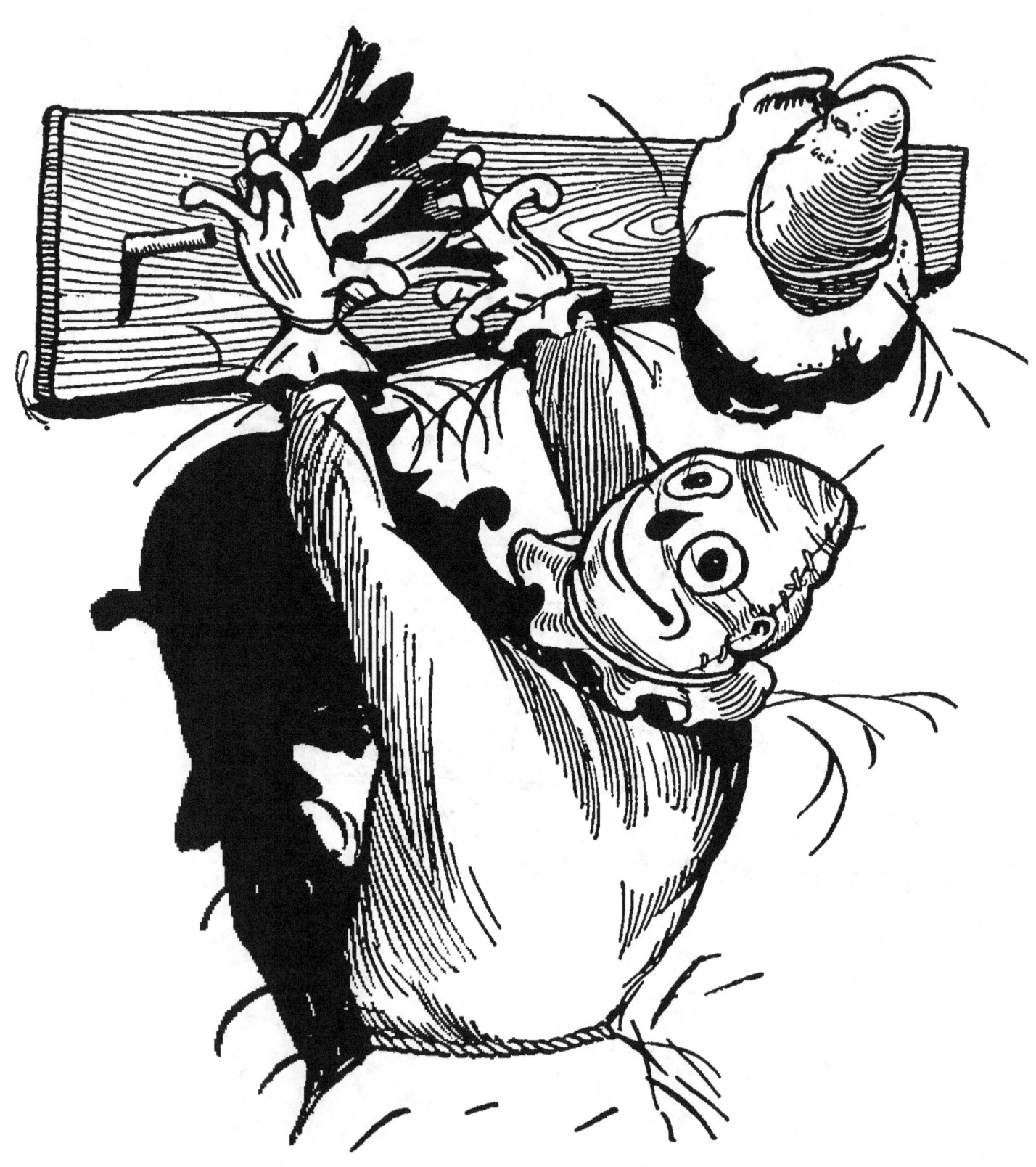

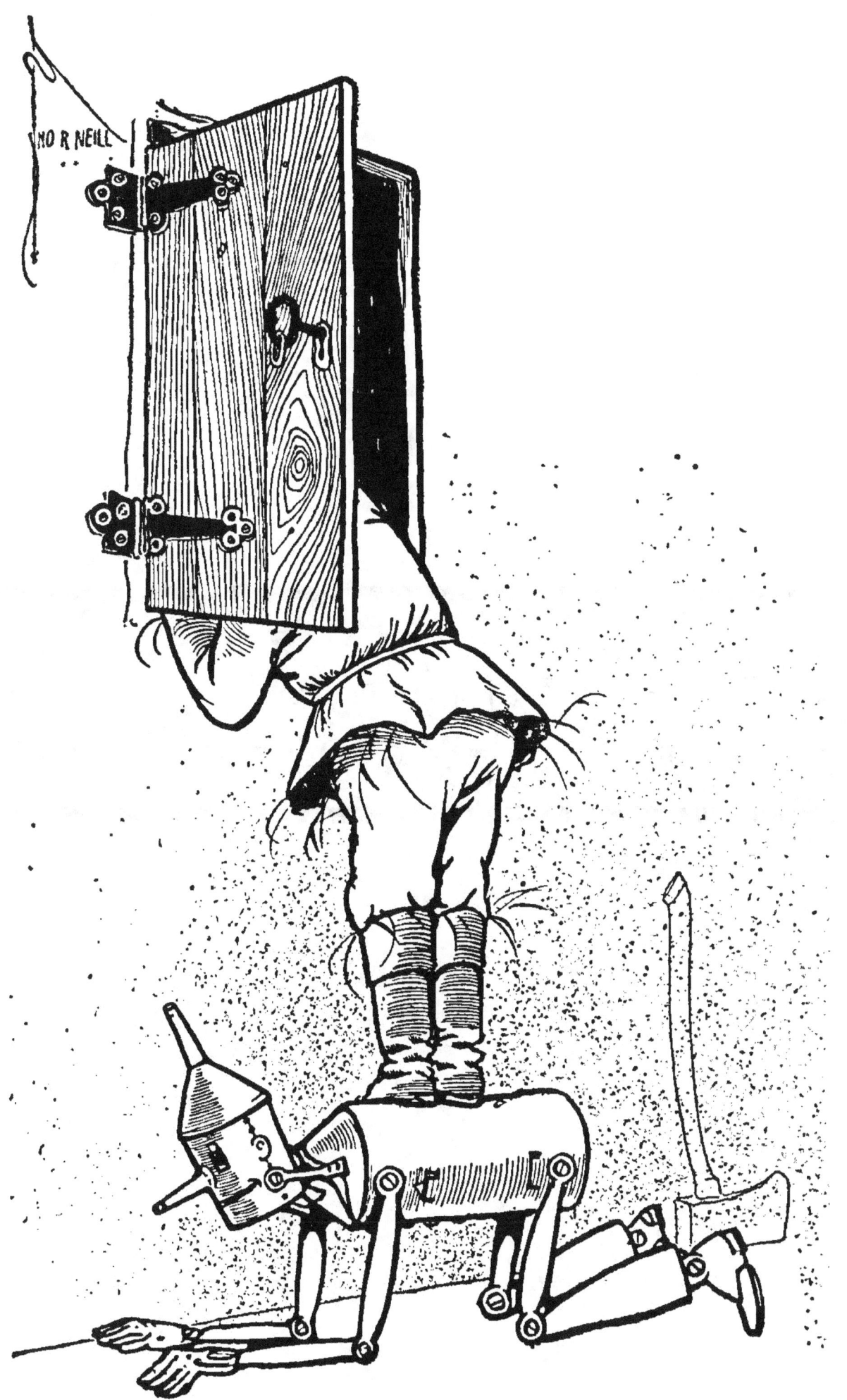

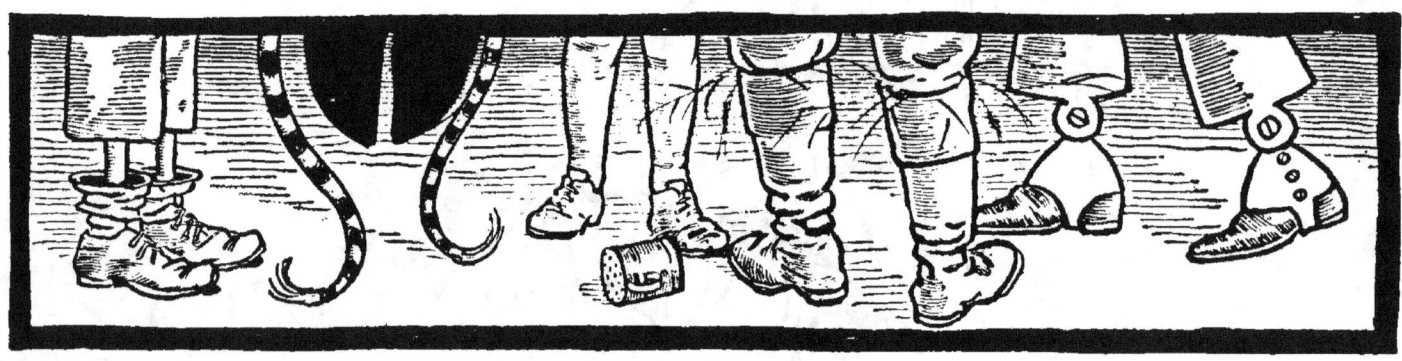

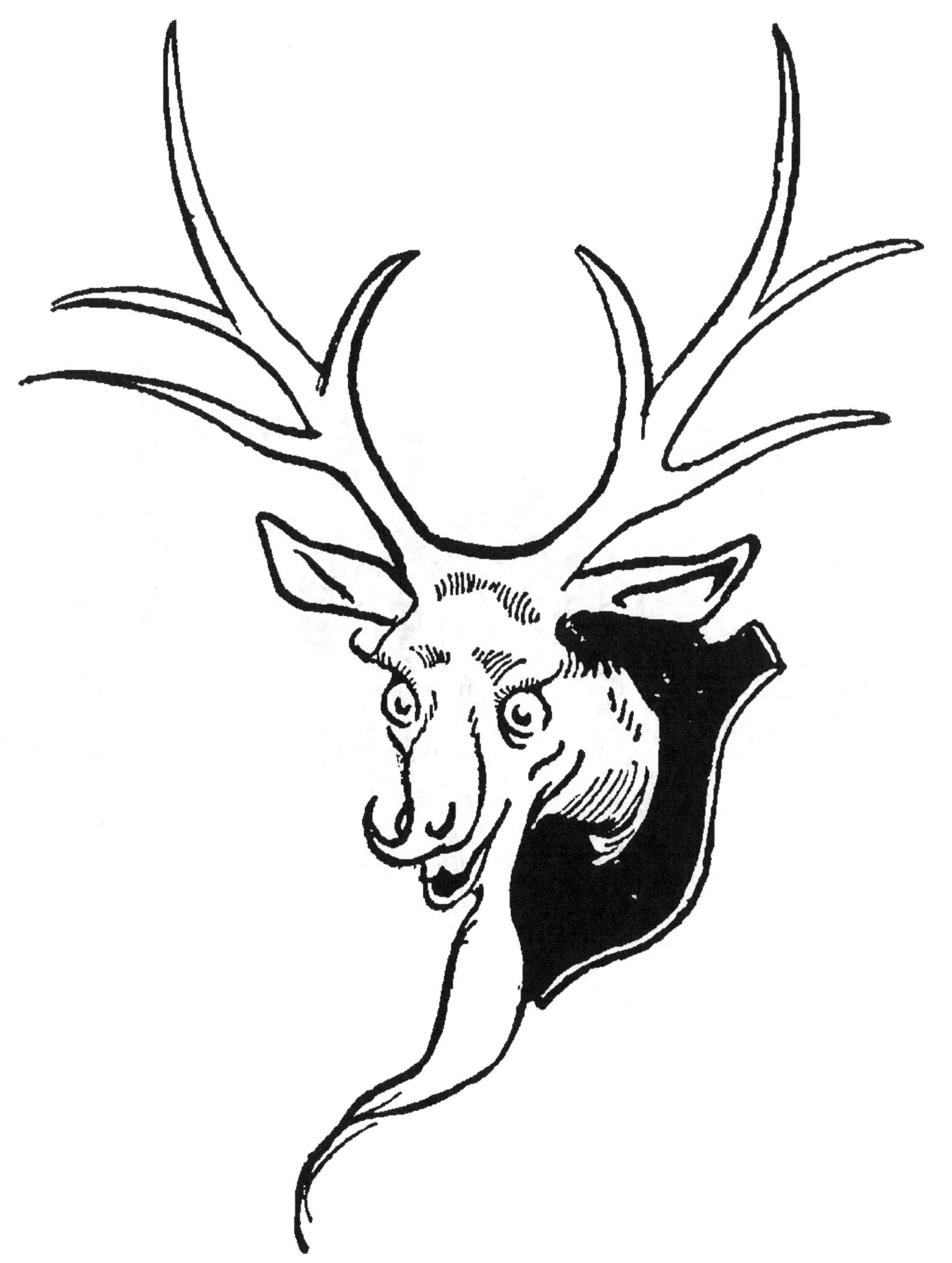

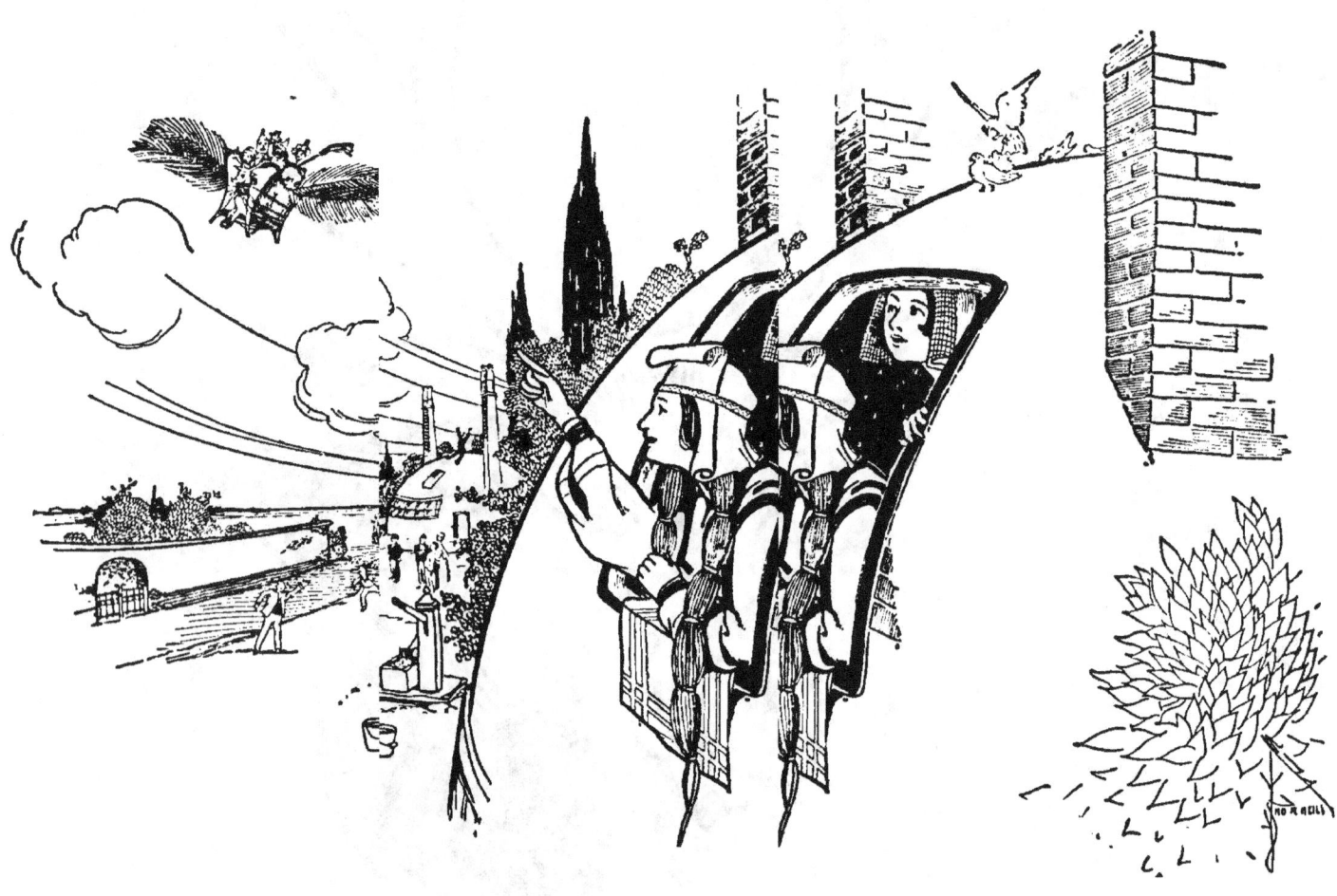

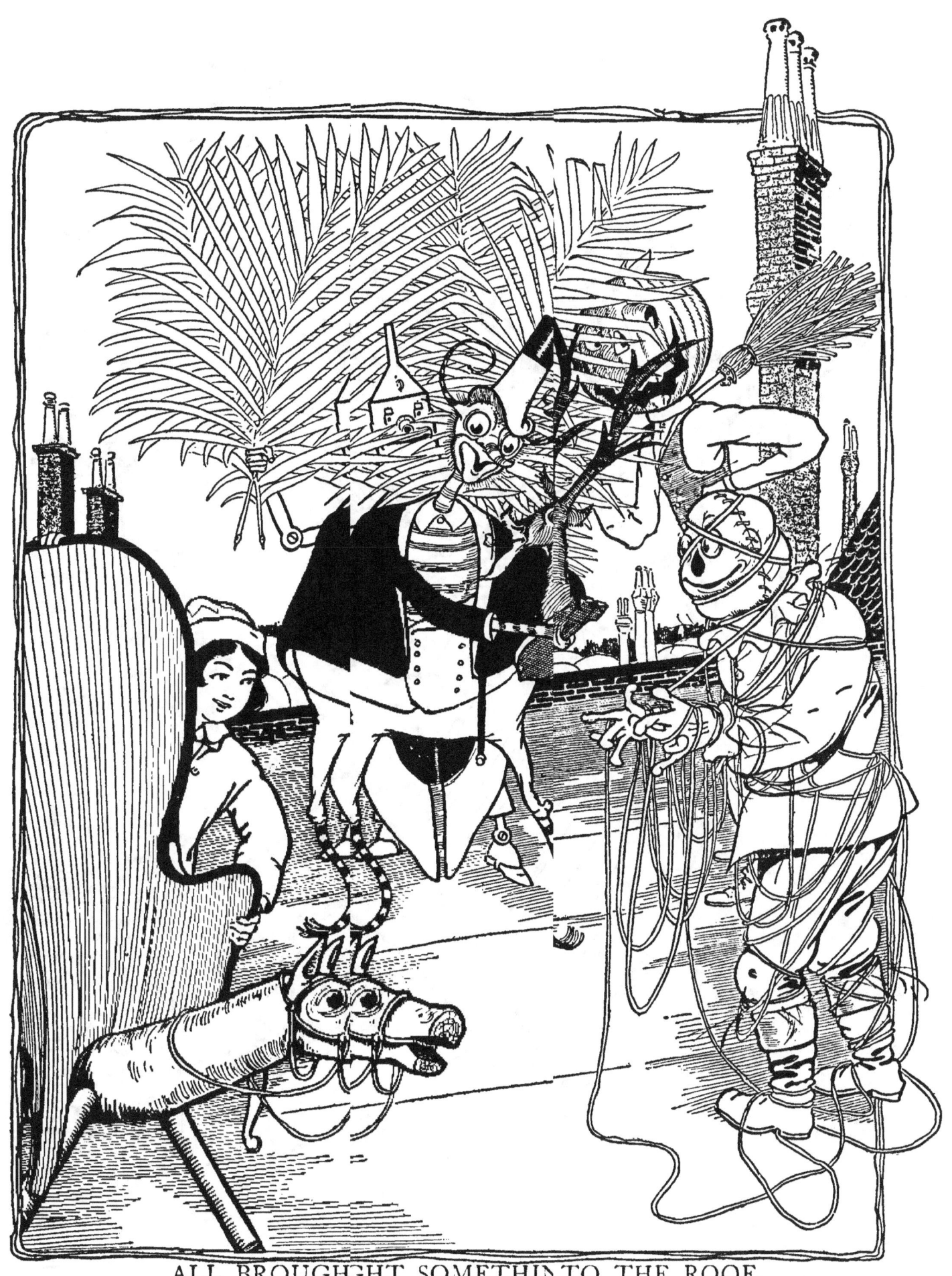

ALL BROUGHGHT SOMETHIN TO THE ROOF.

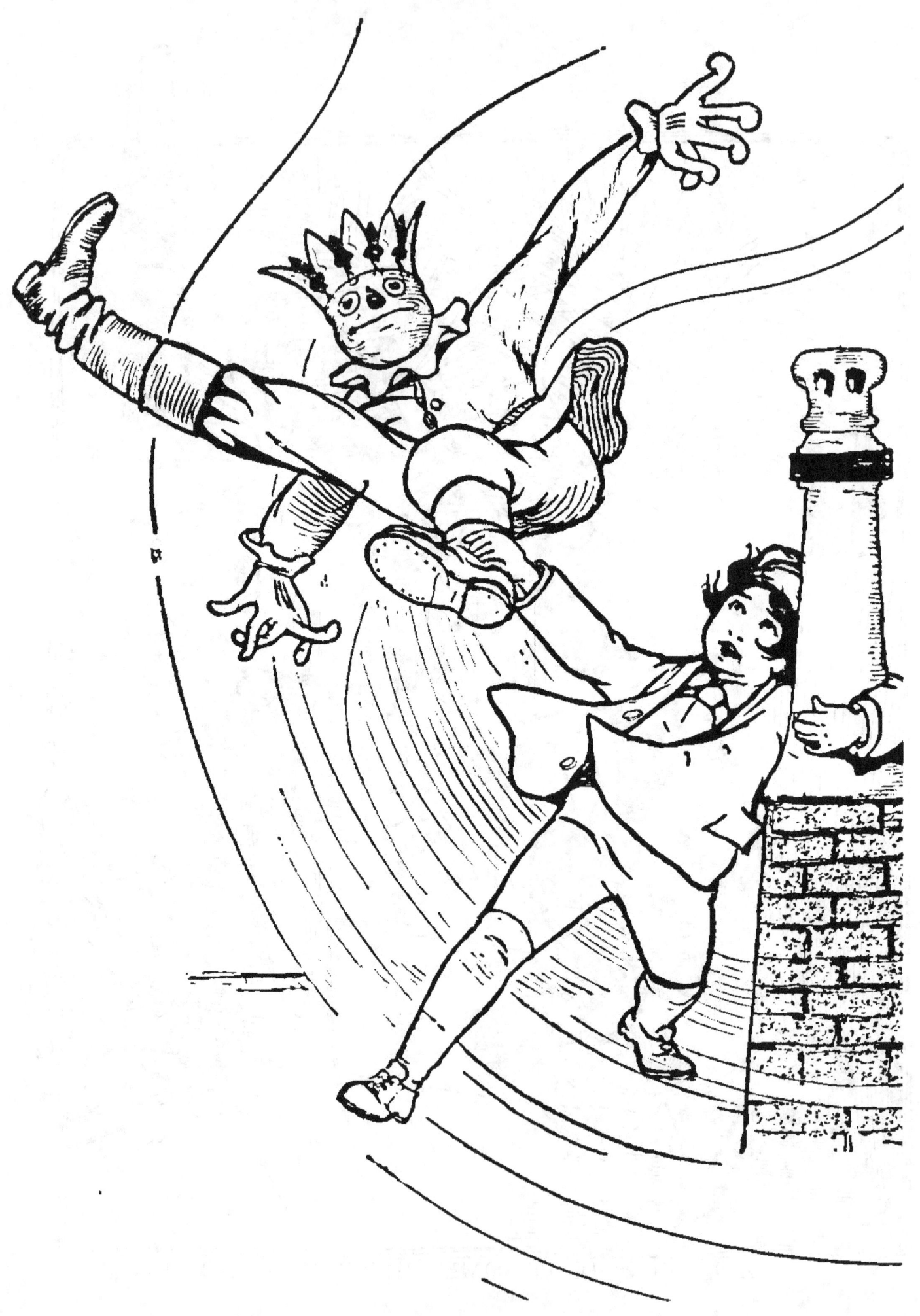

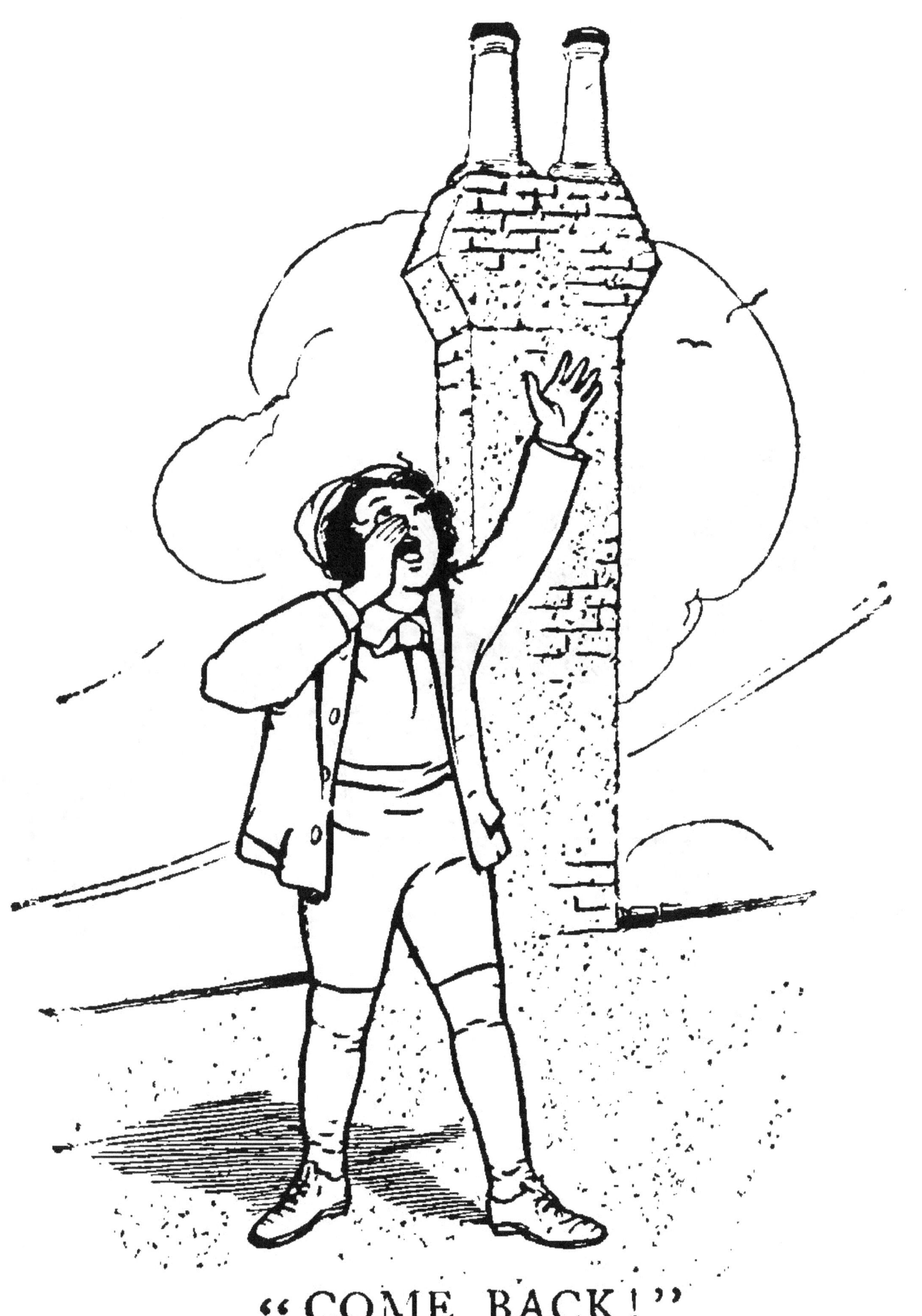

"COME BACK!"

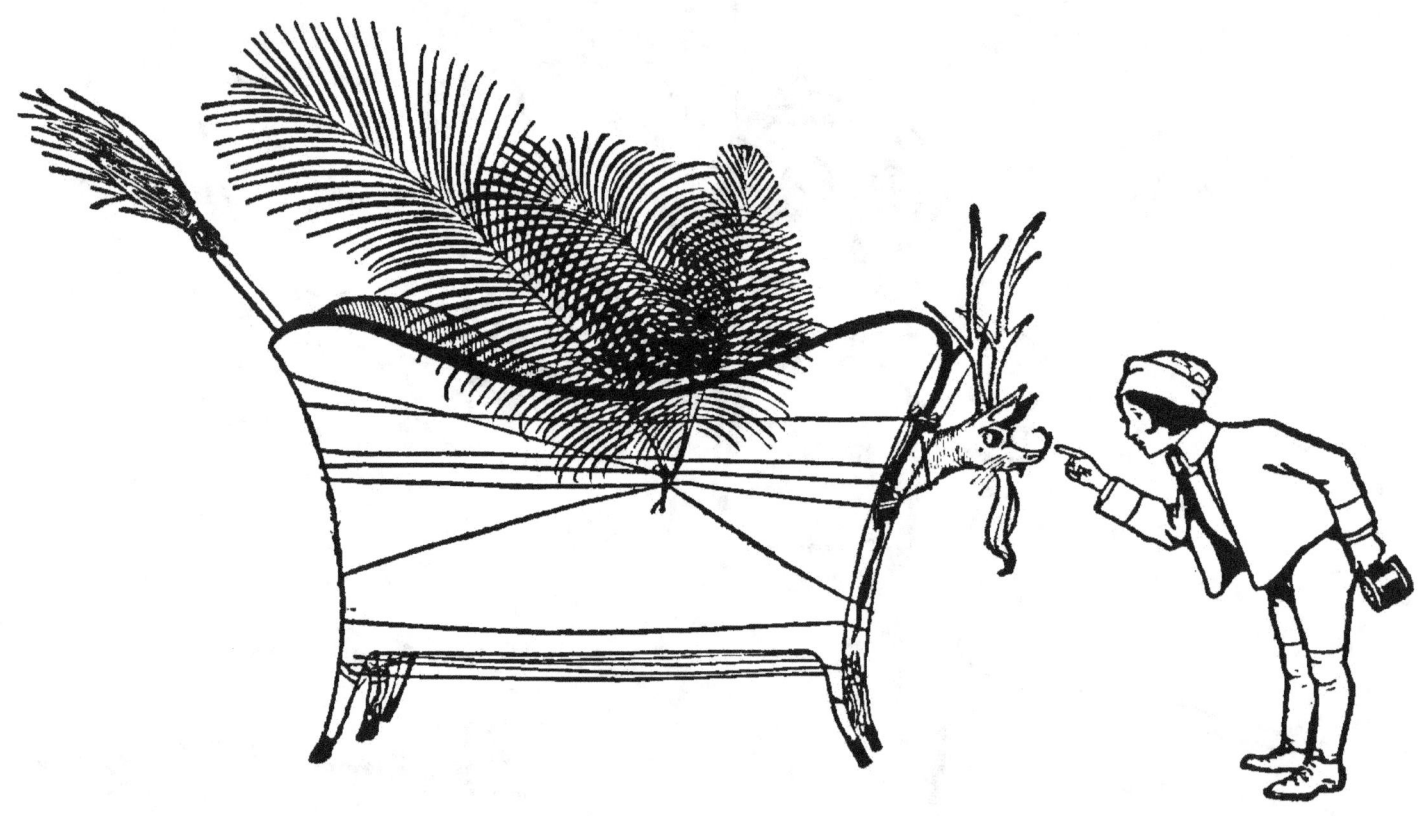

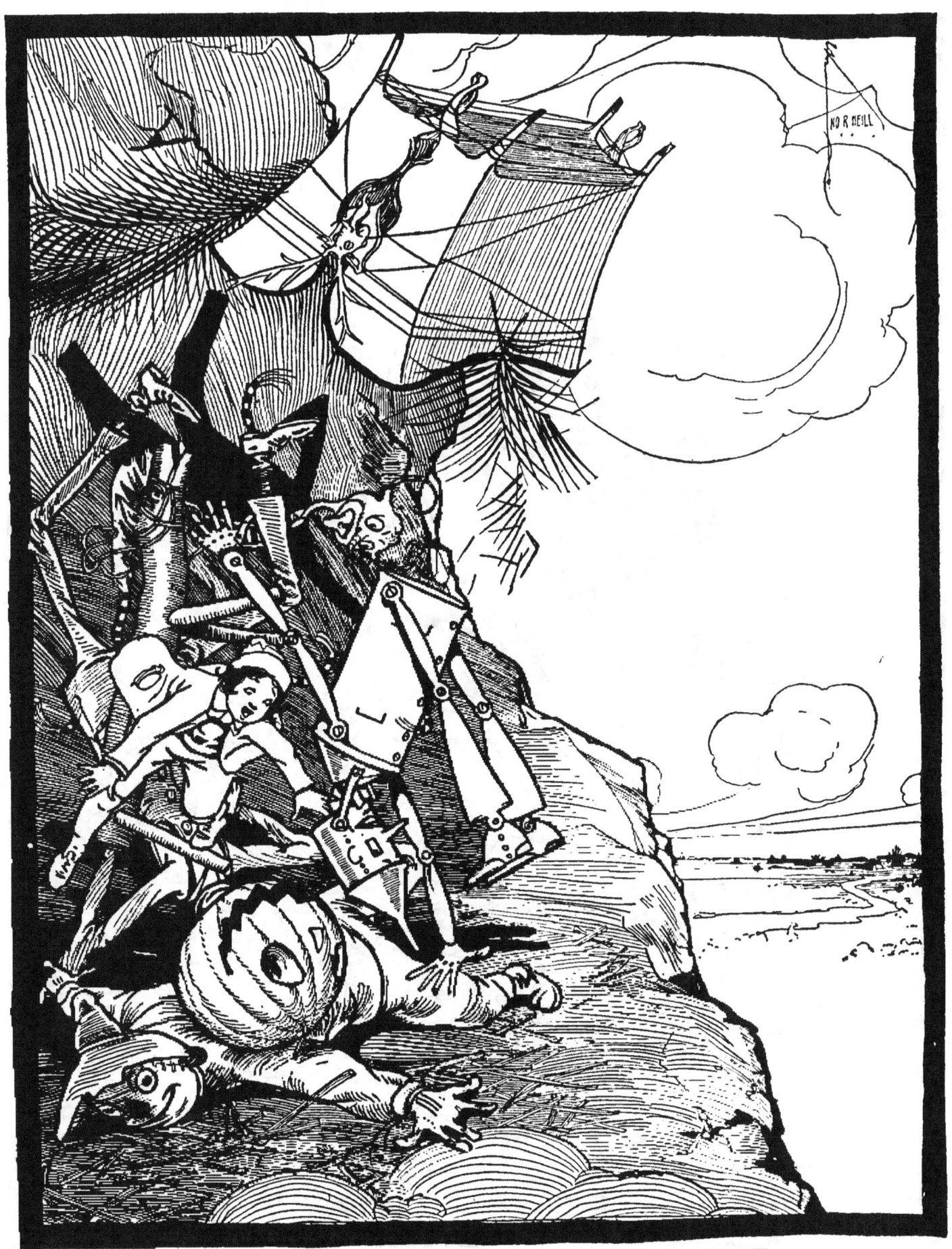

ALL WERE IMMEDIATELY DUMPED OUT.

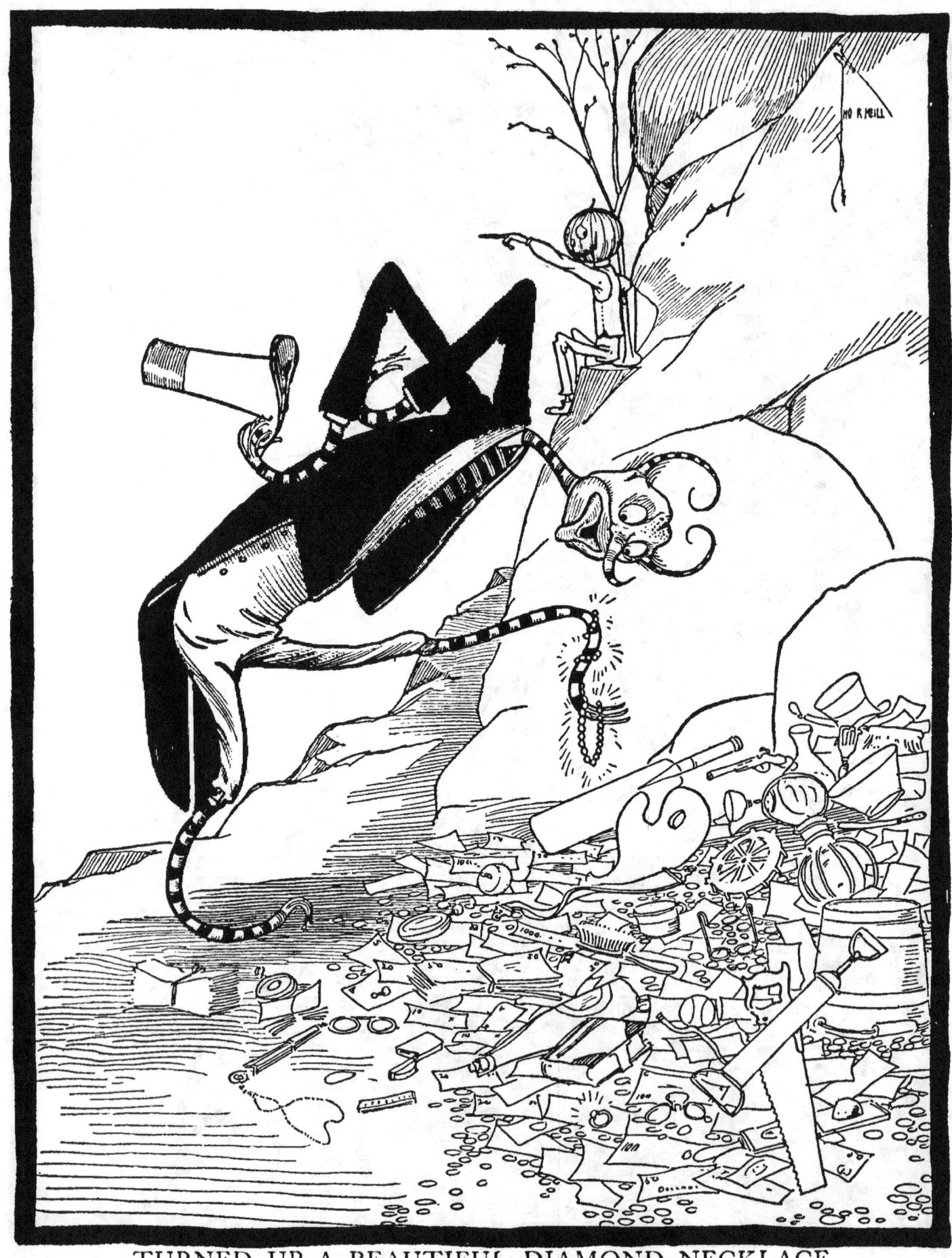

TURNED UP A BEAUTIFUL DIAMOND NECKLACE.

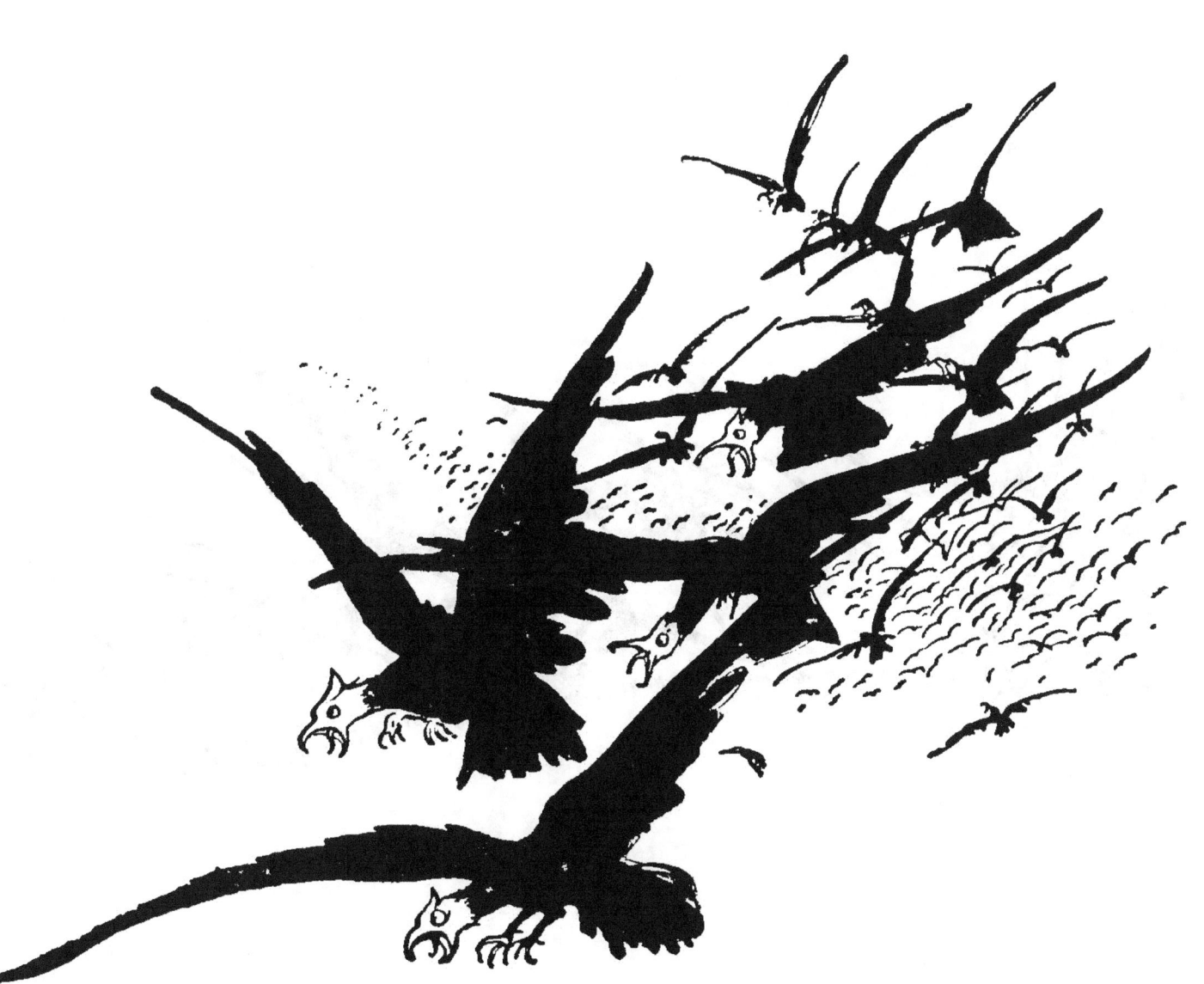

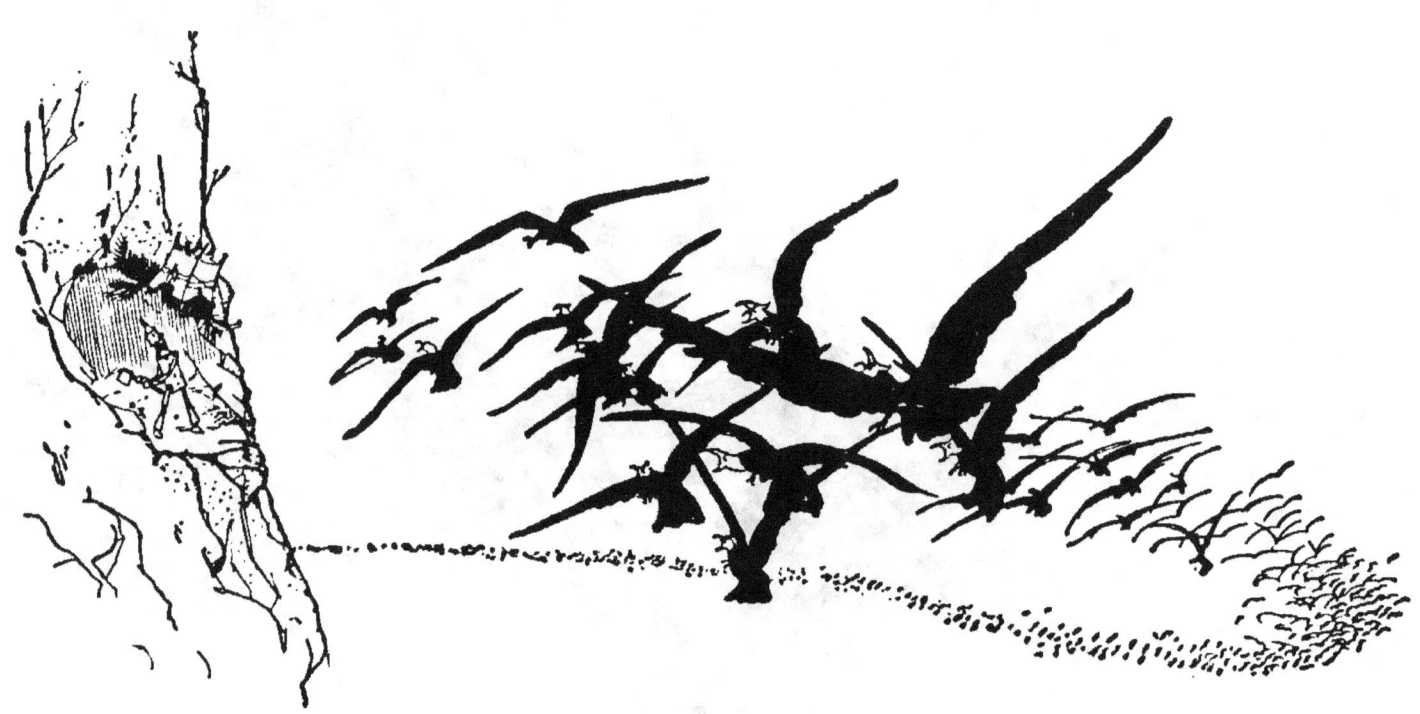

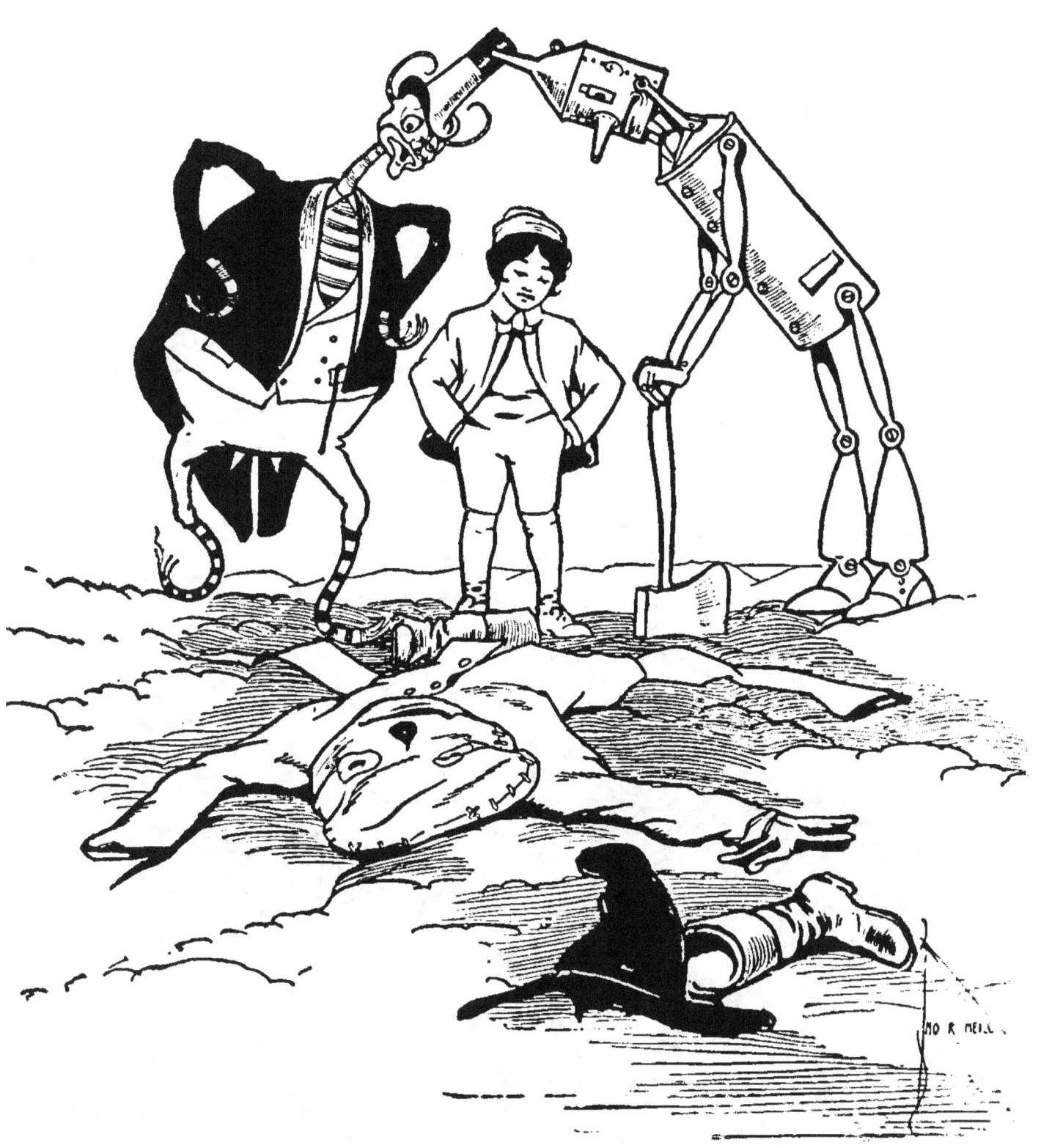

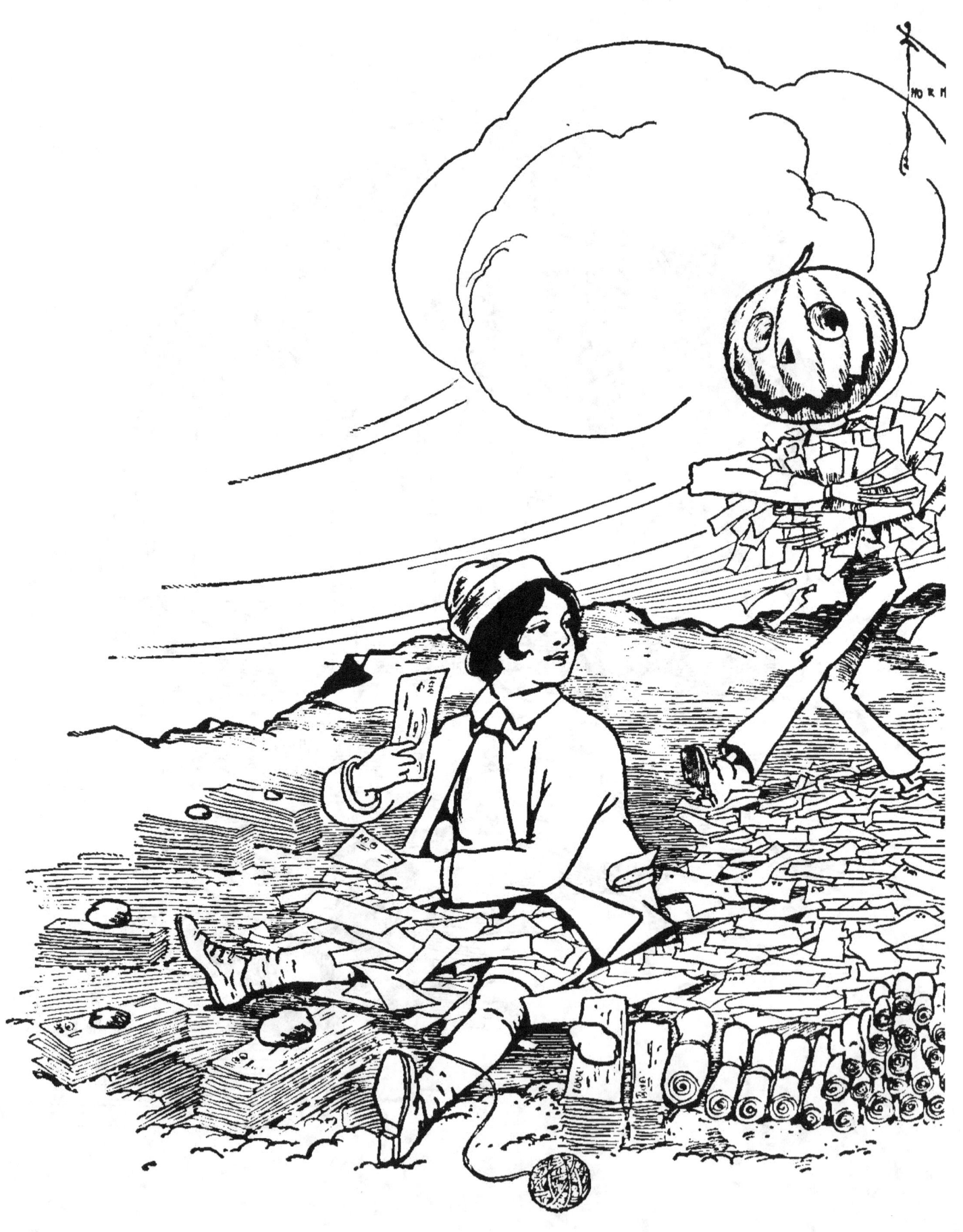

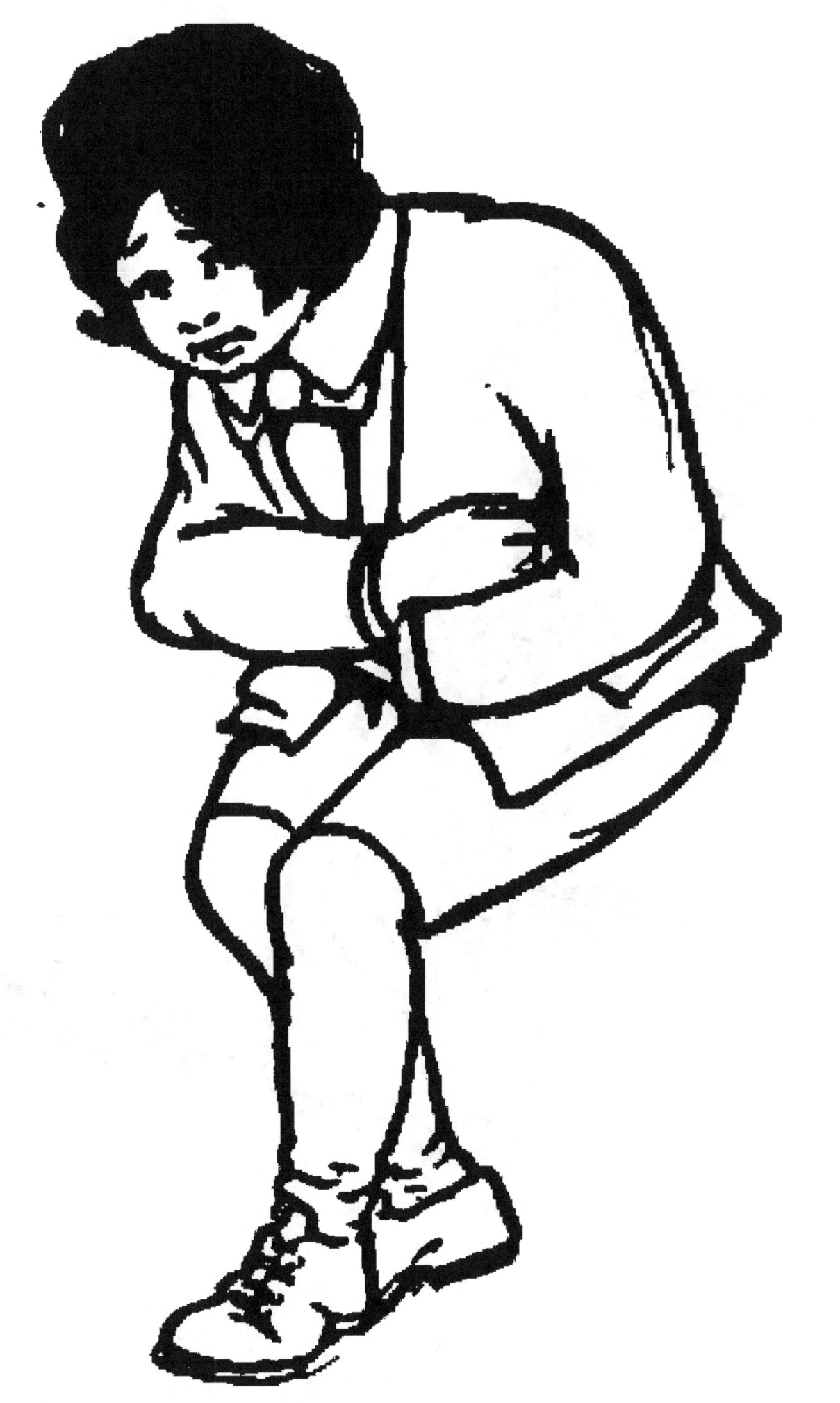

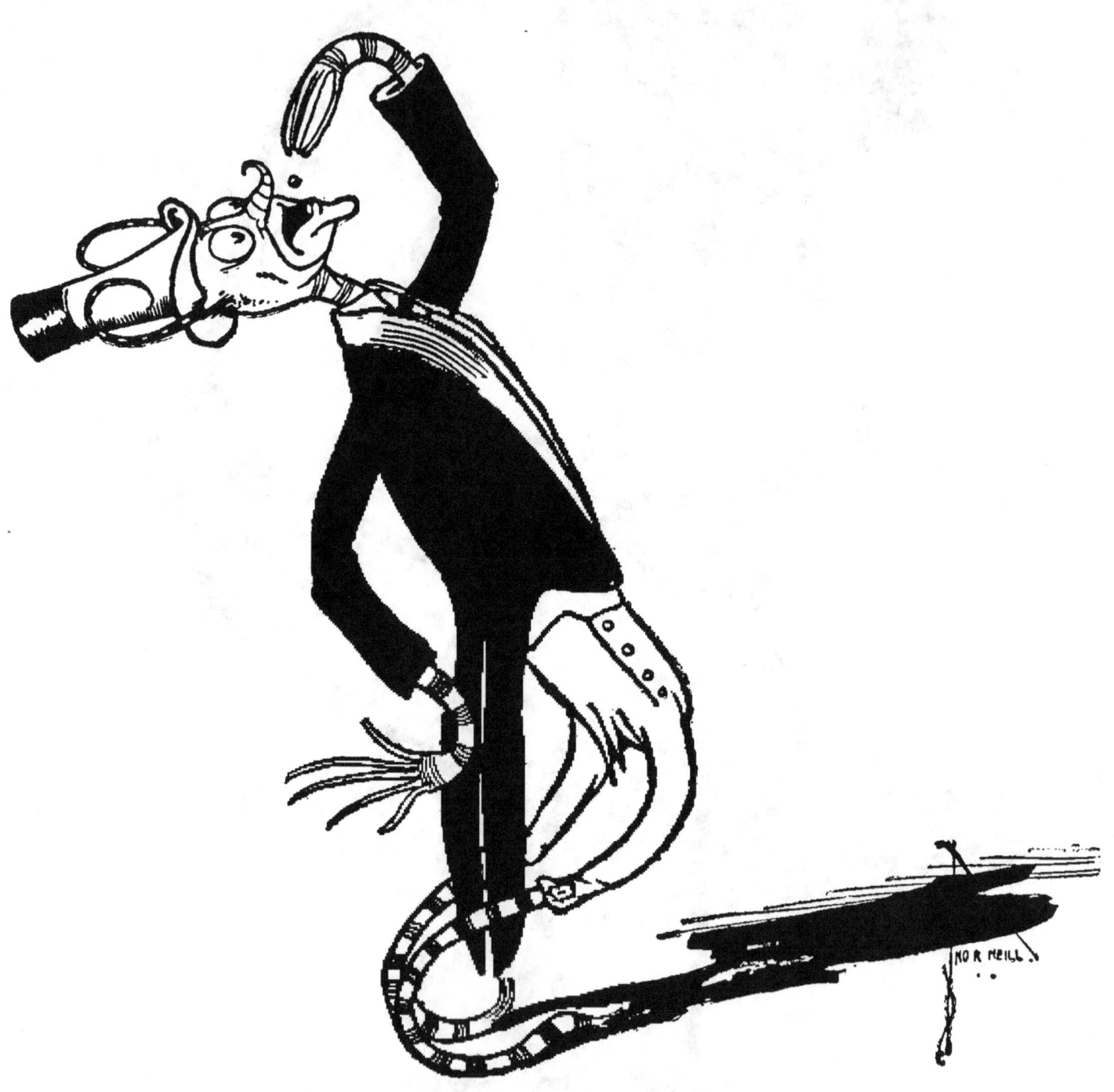

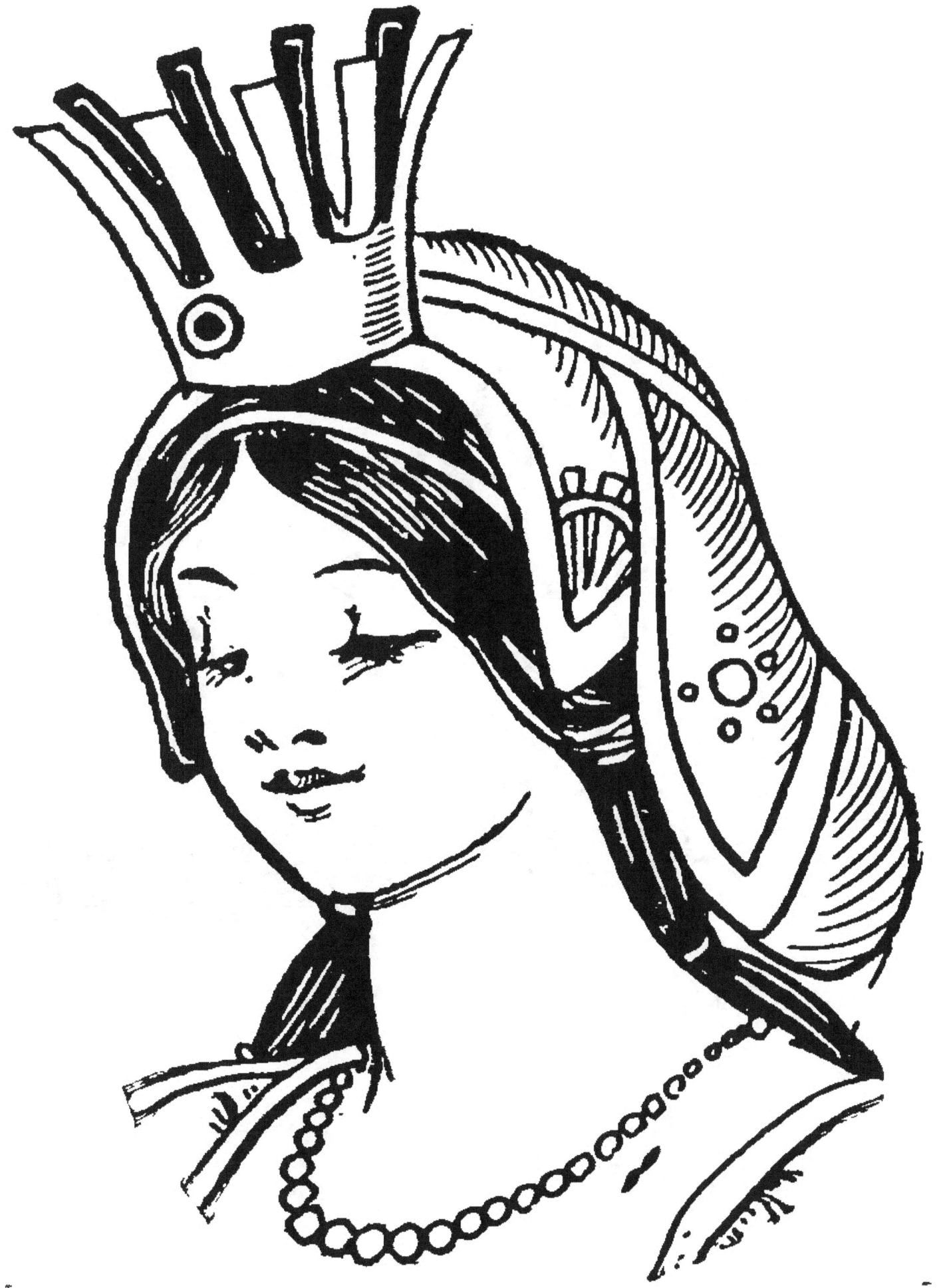

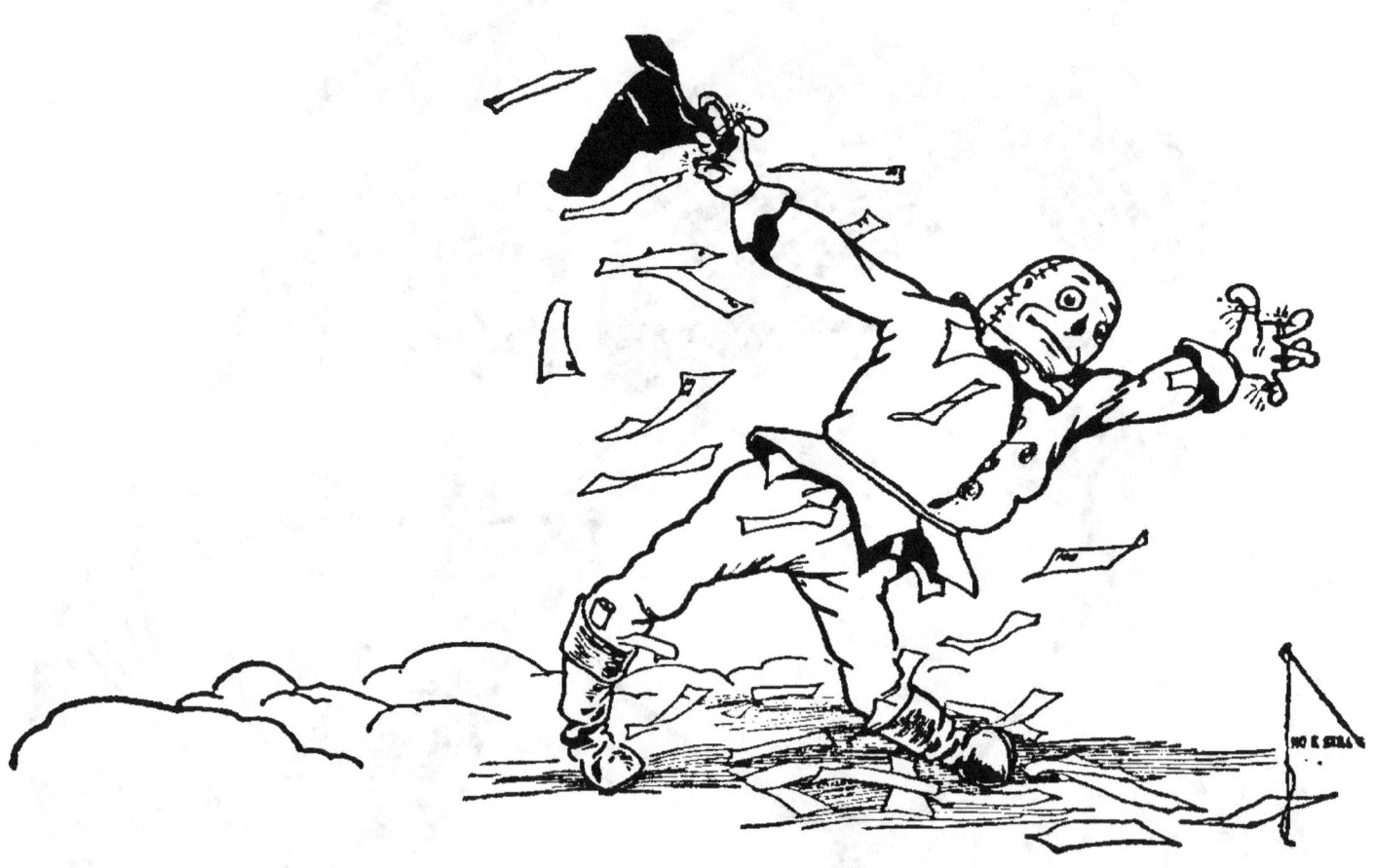

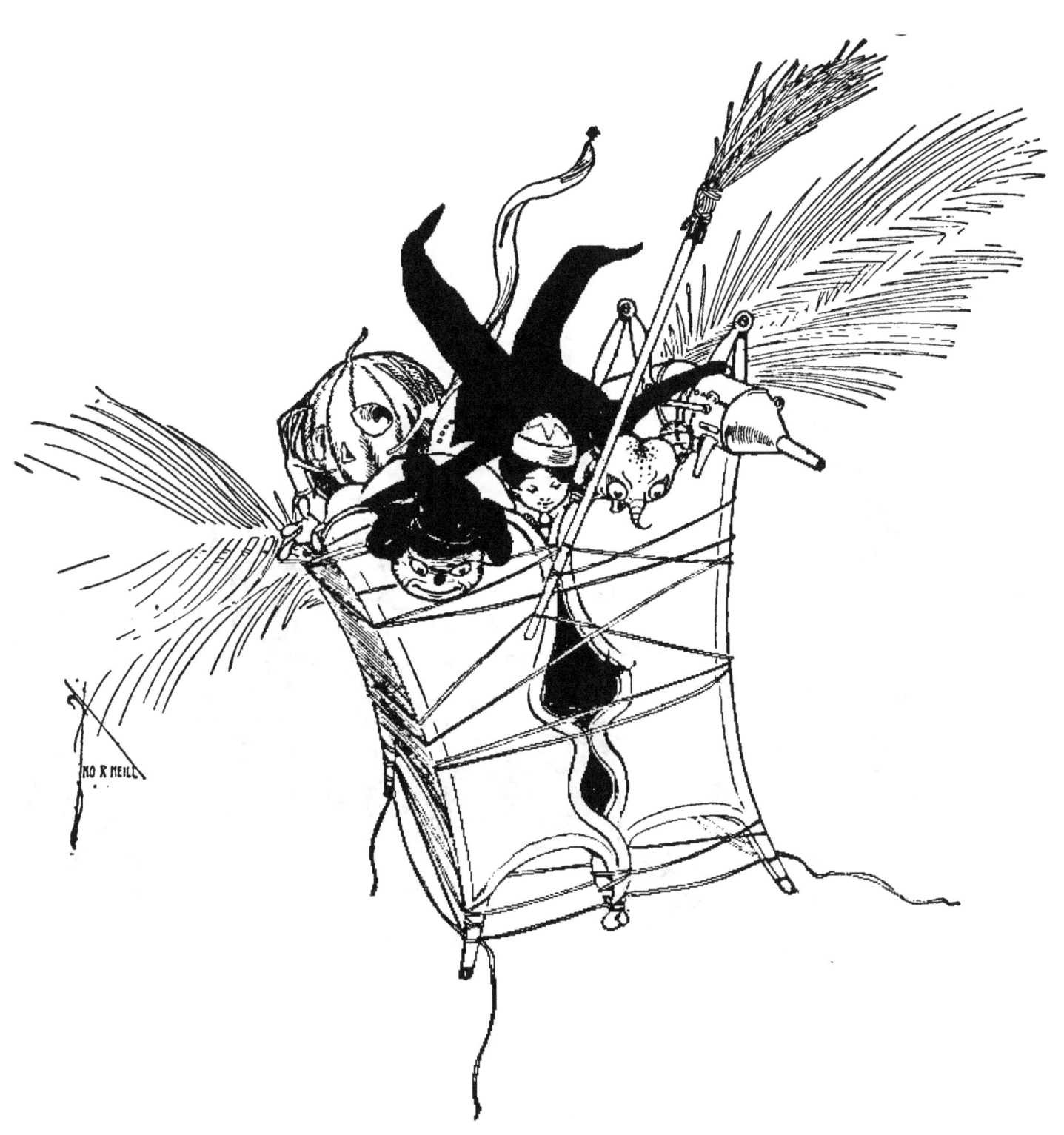

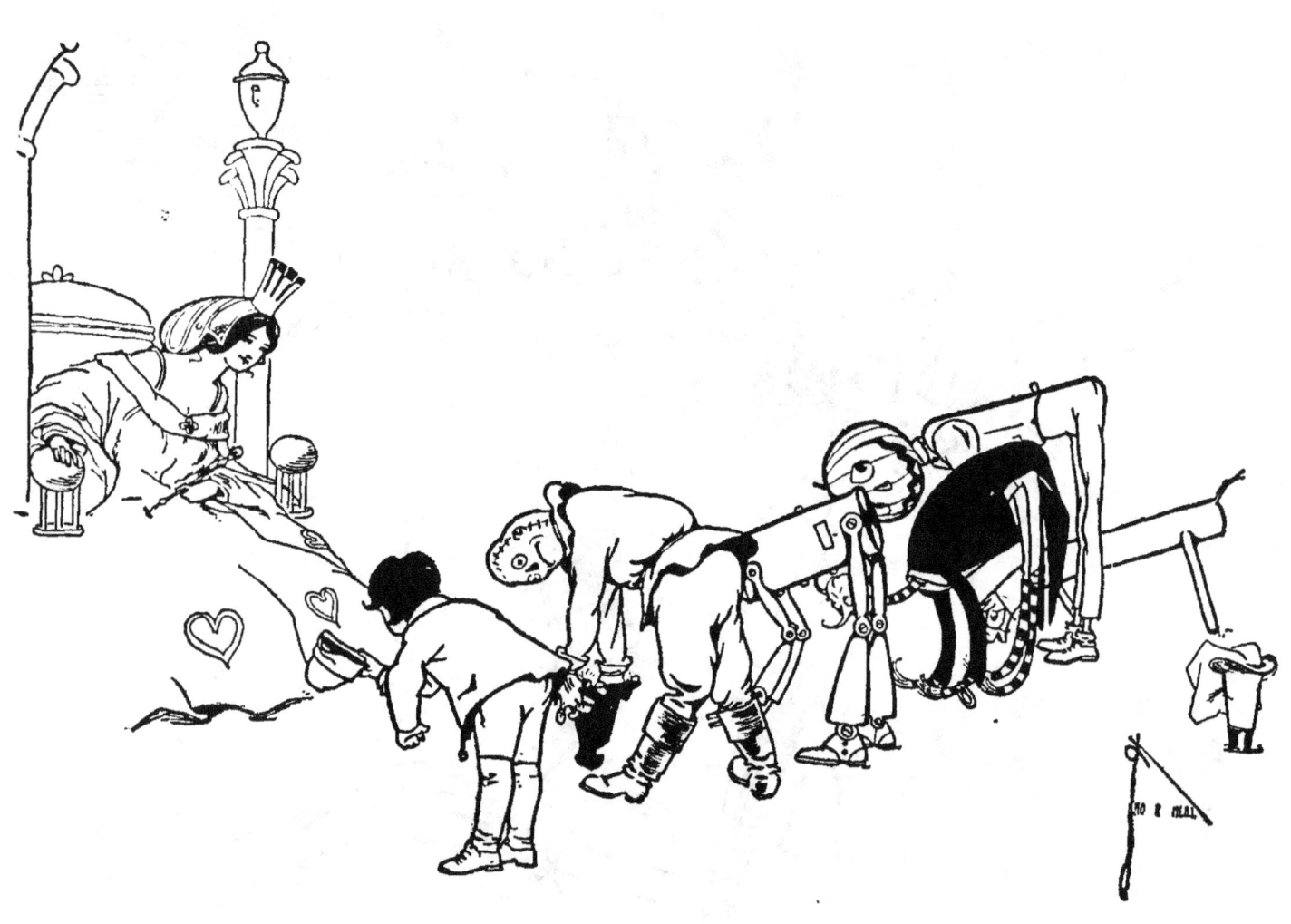

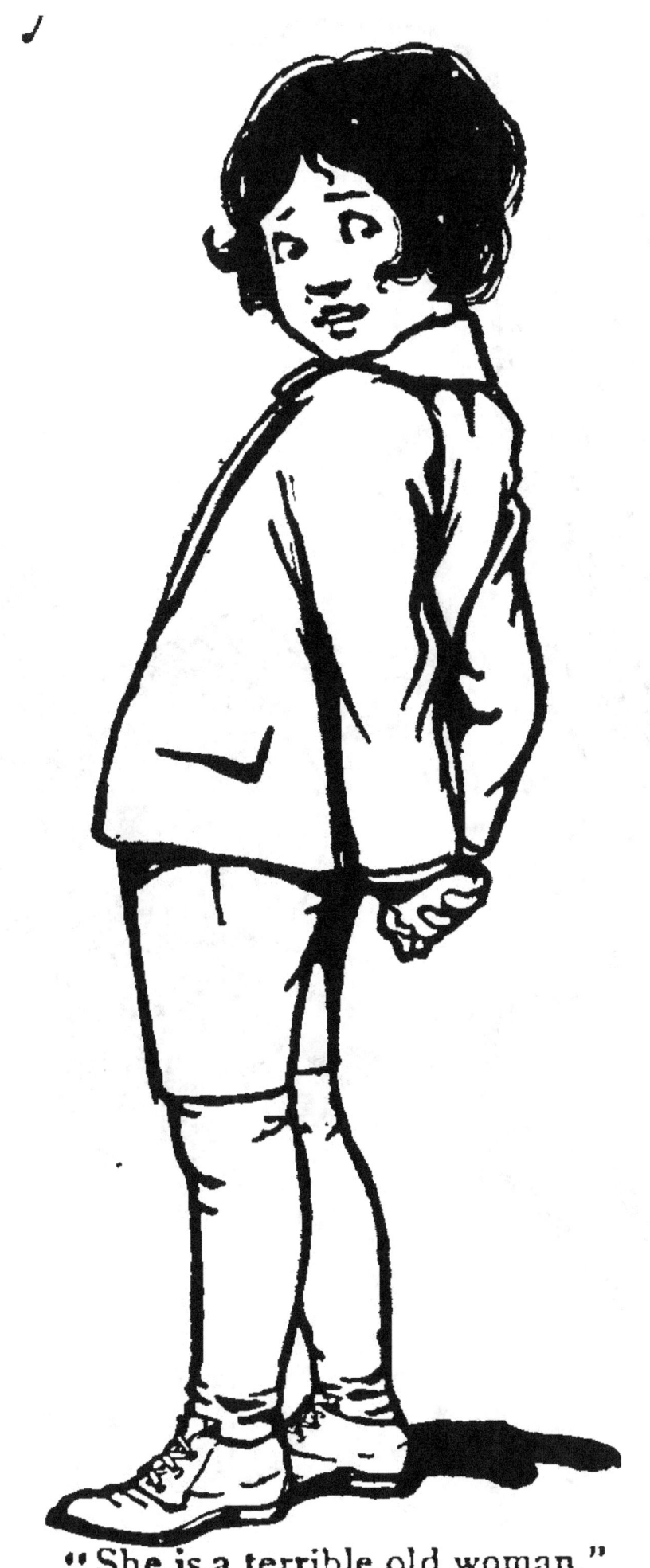

"She is a terrible old woman."

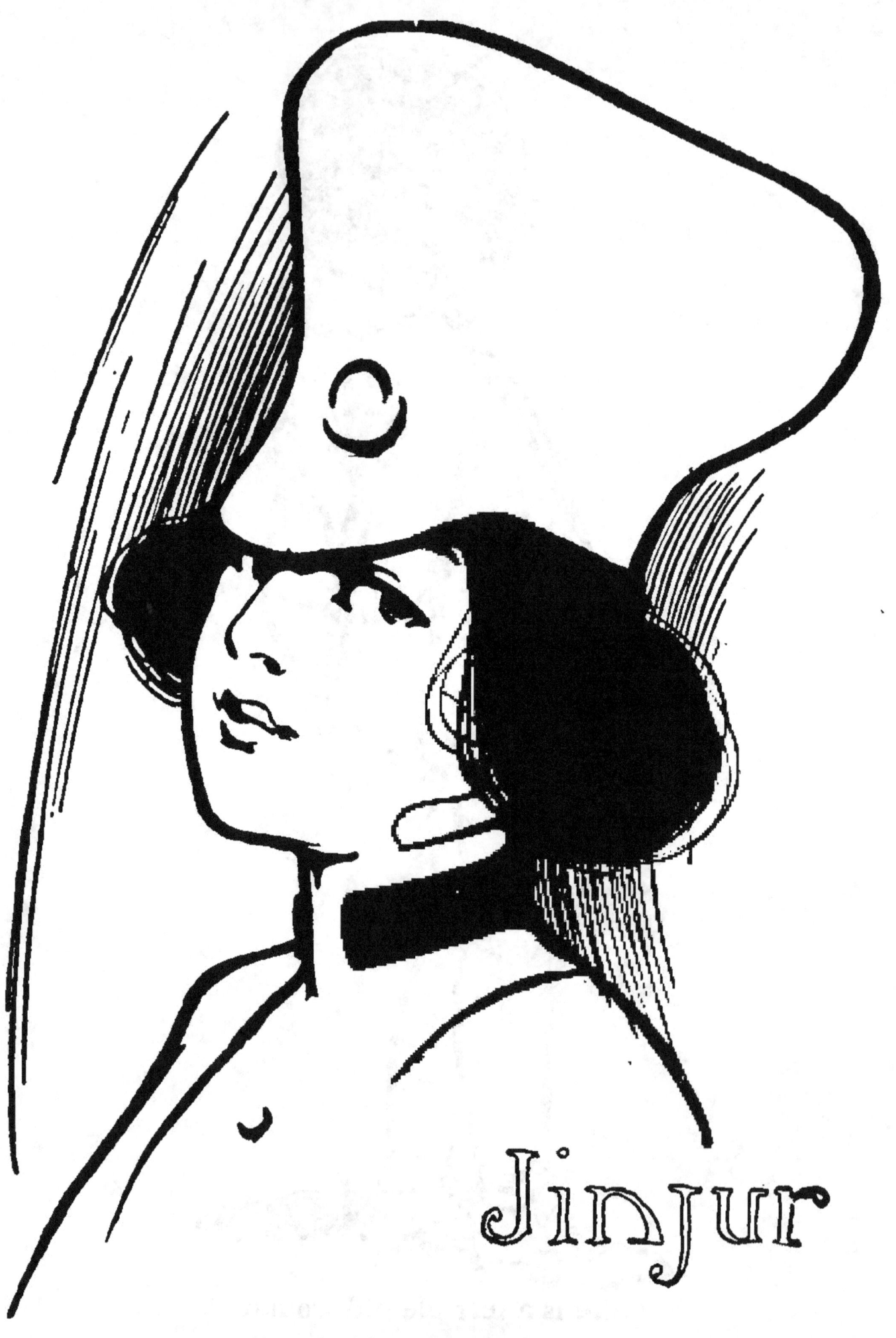

Jinjur

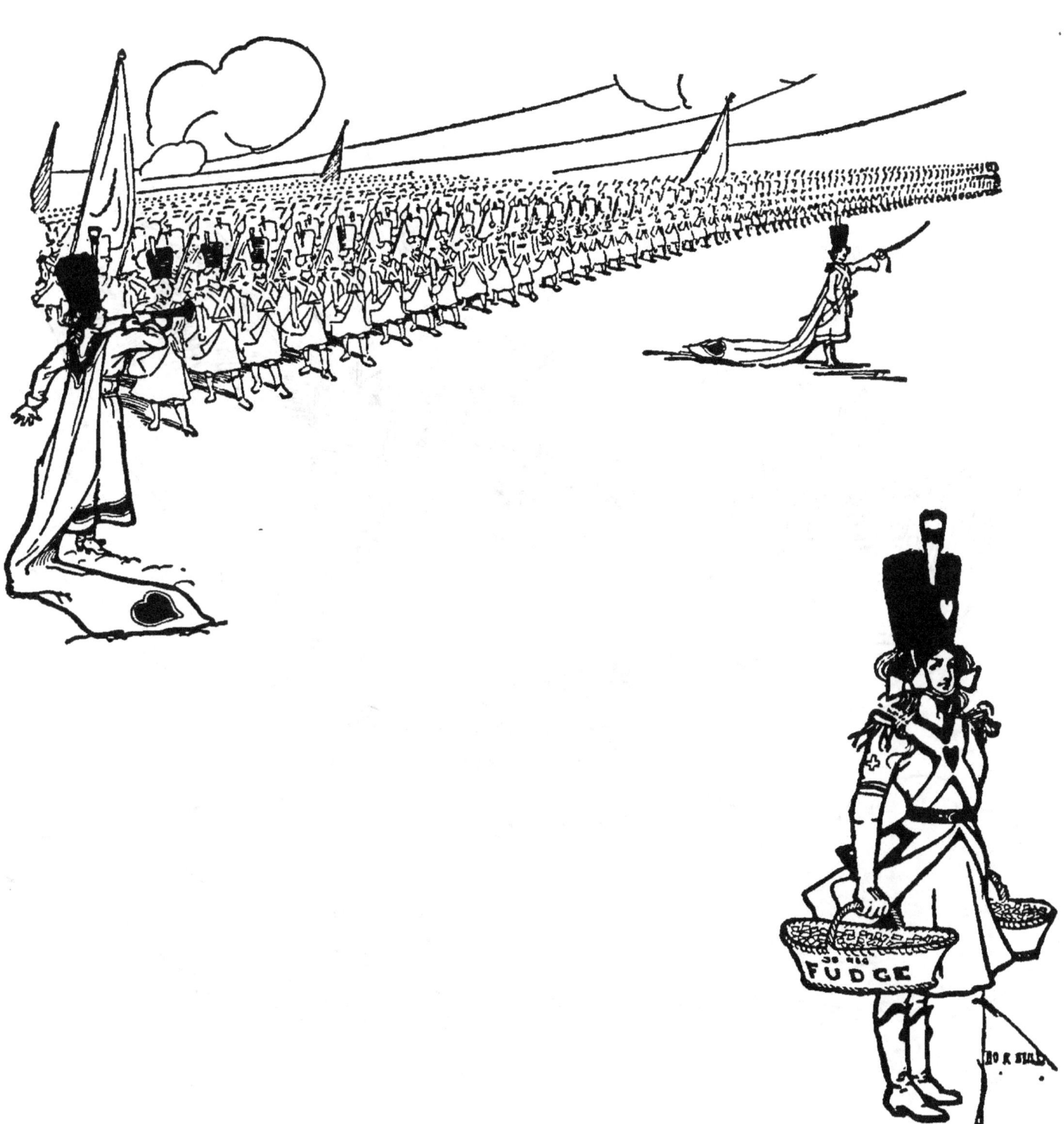

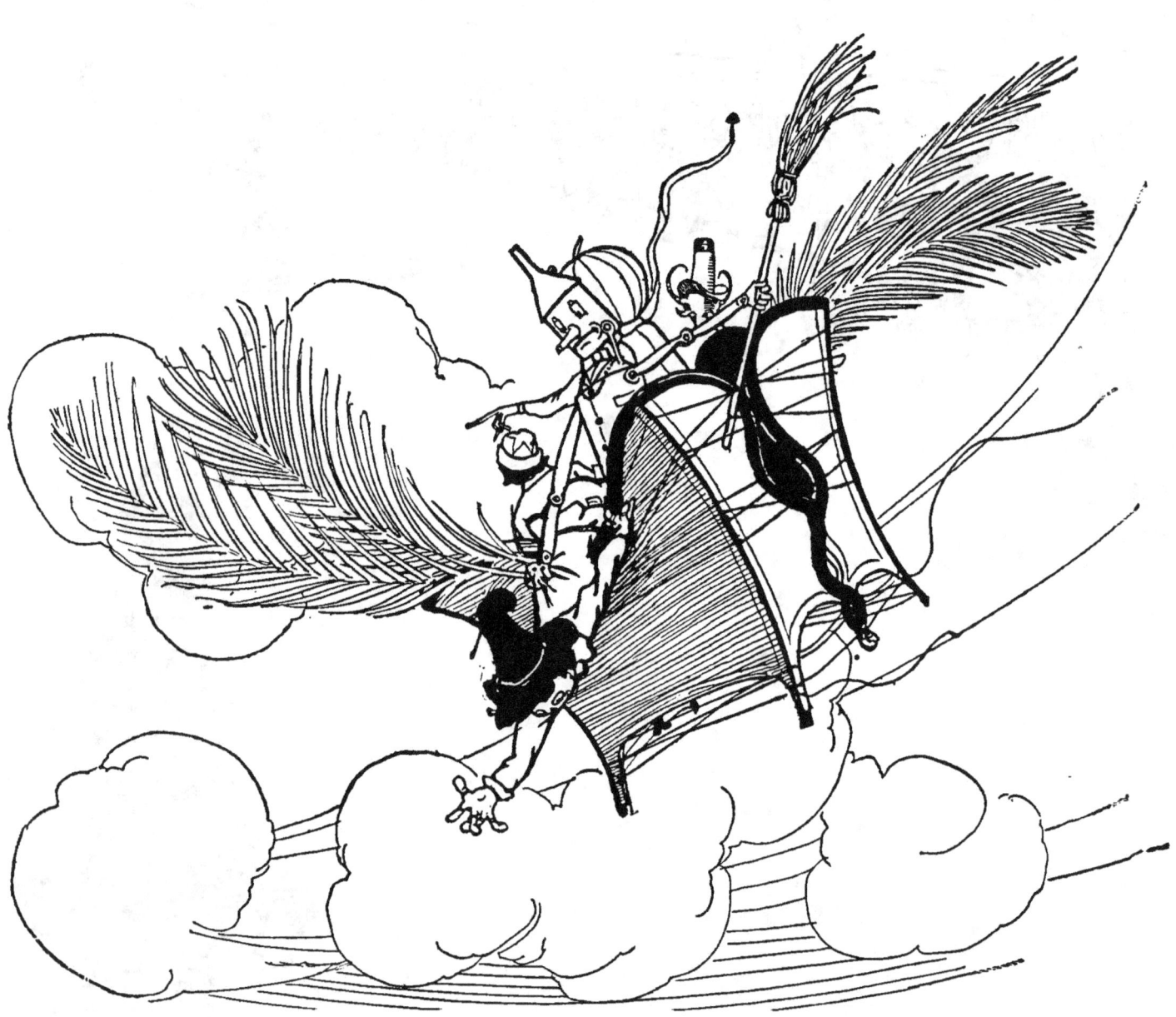

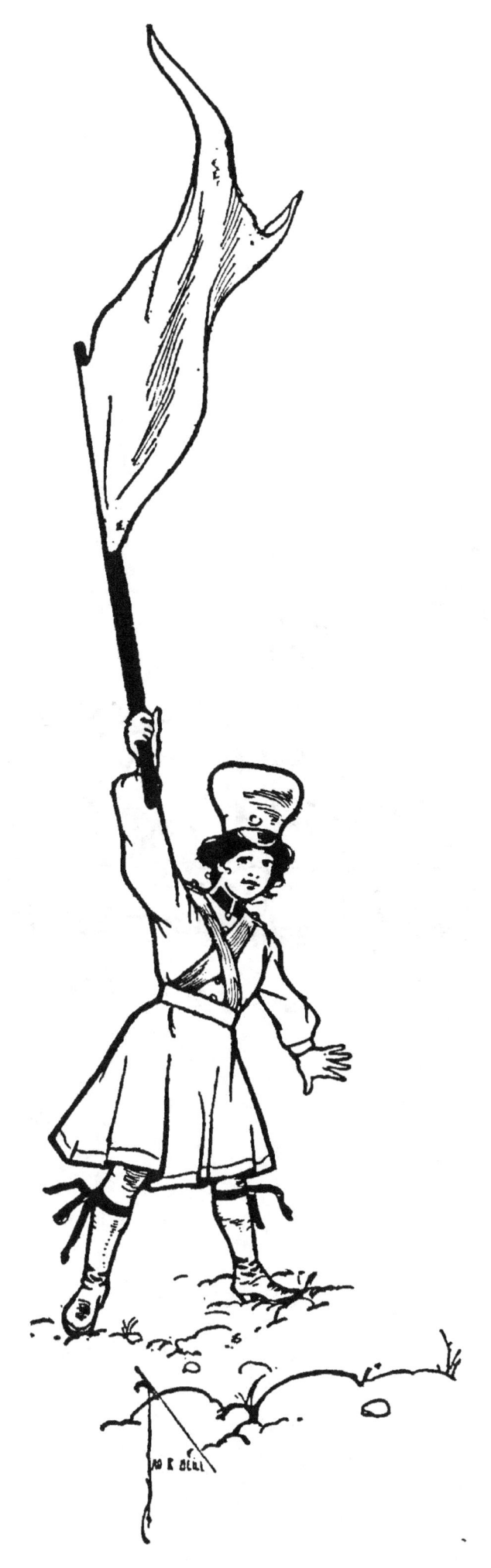

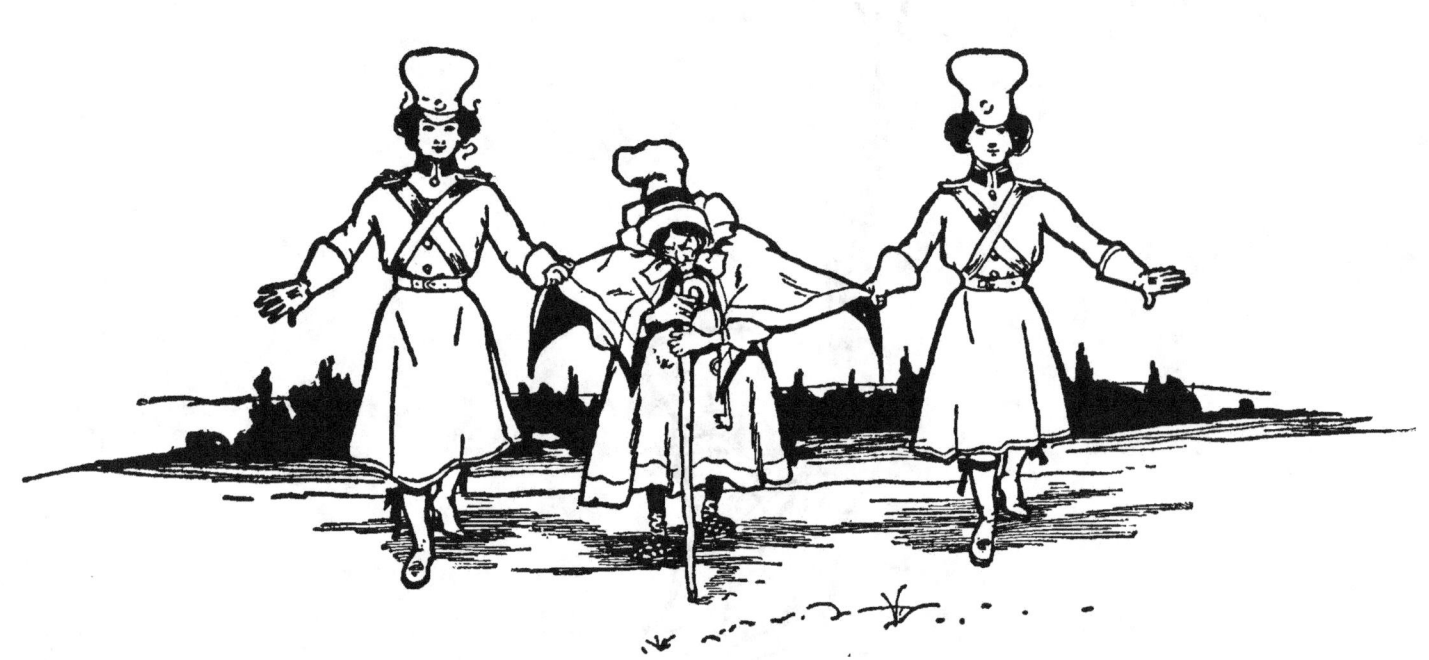

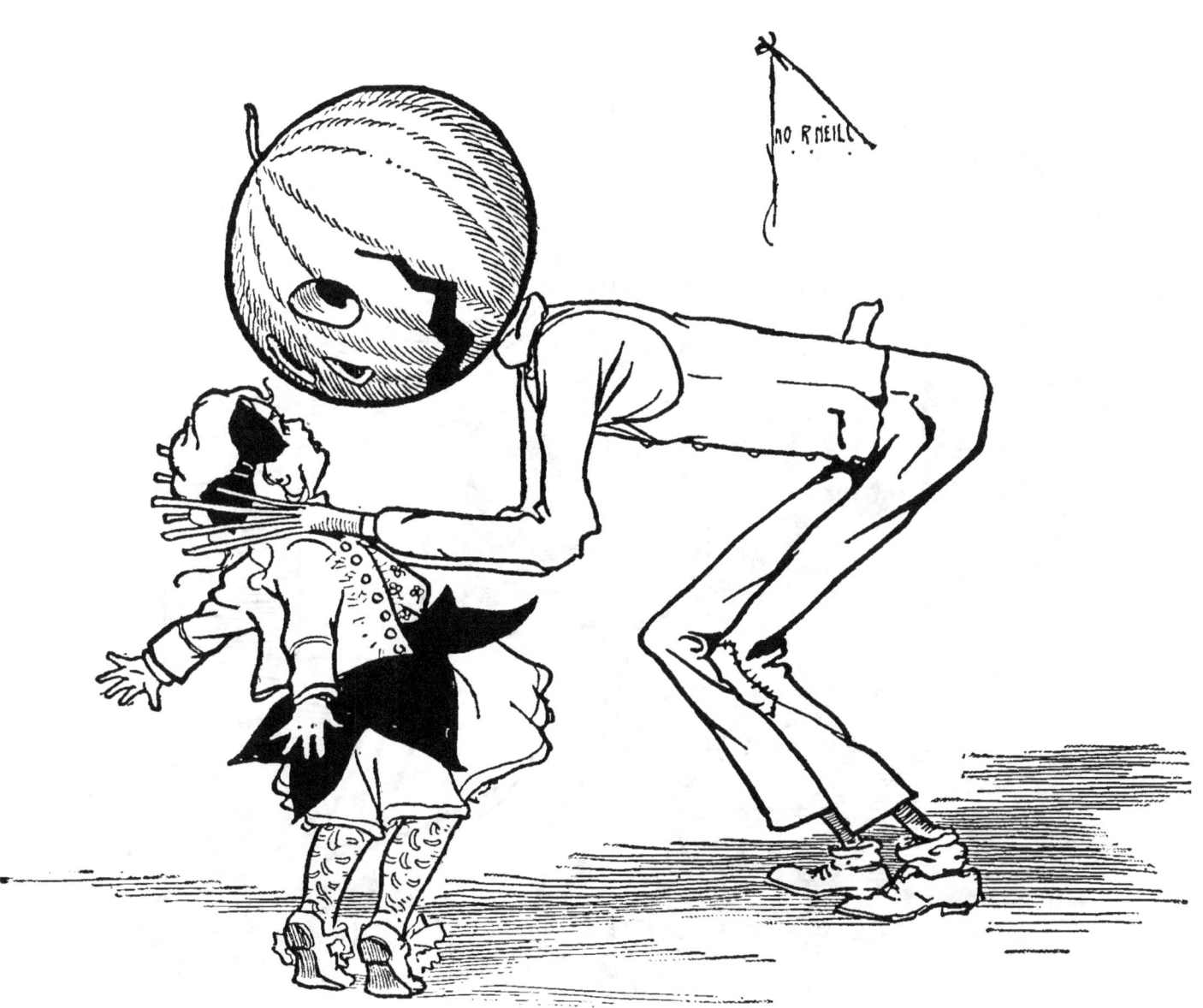

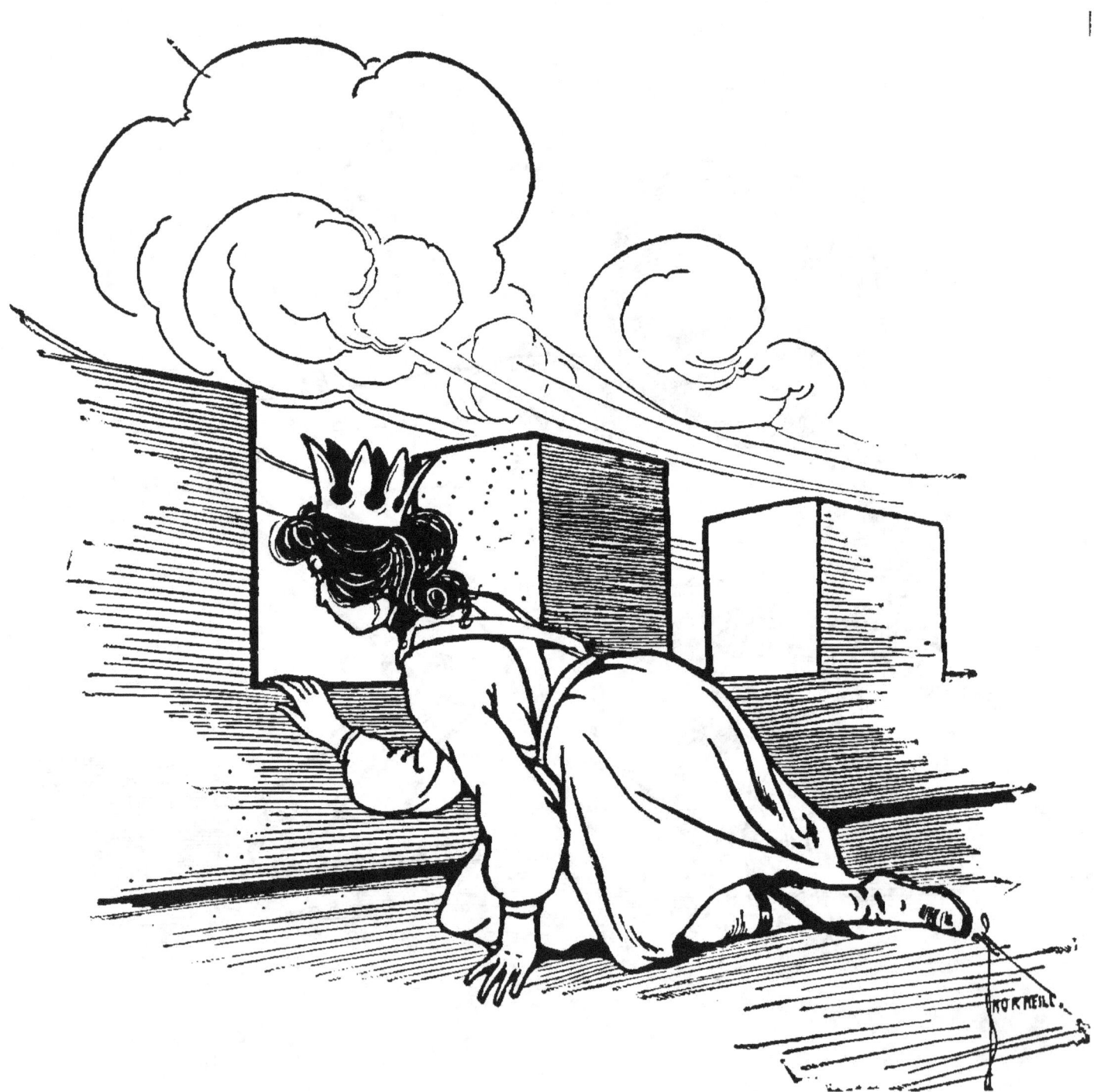

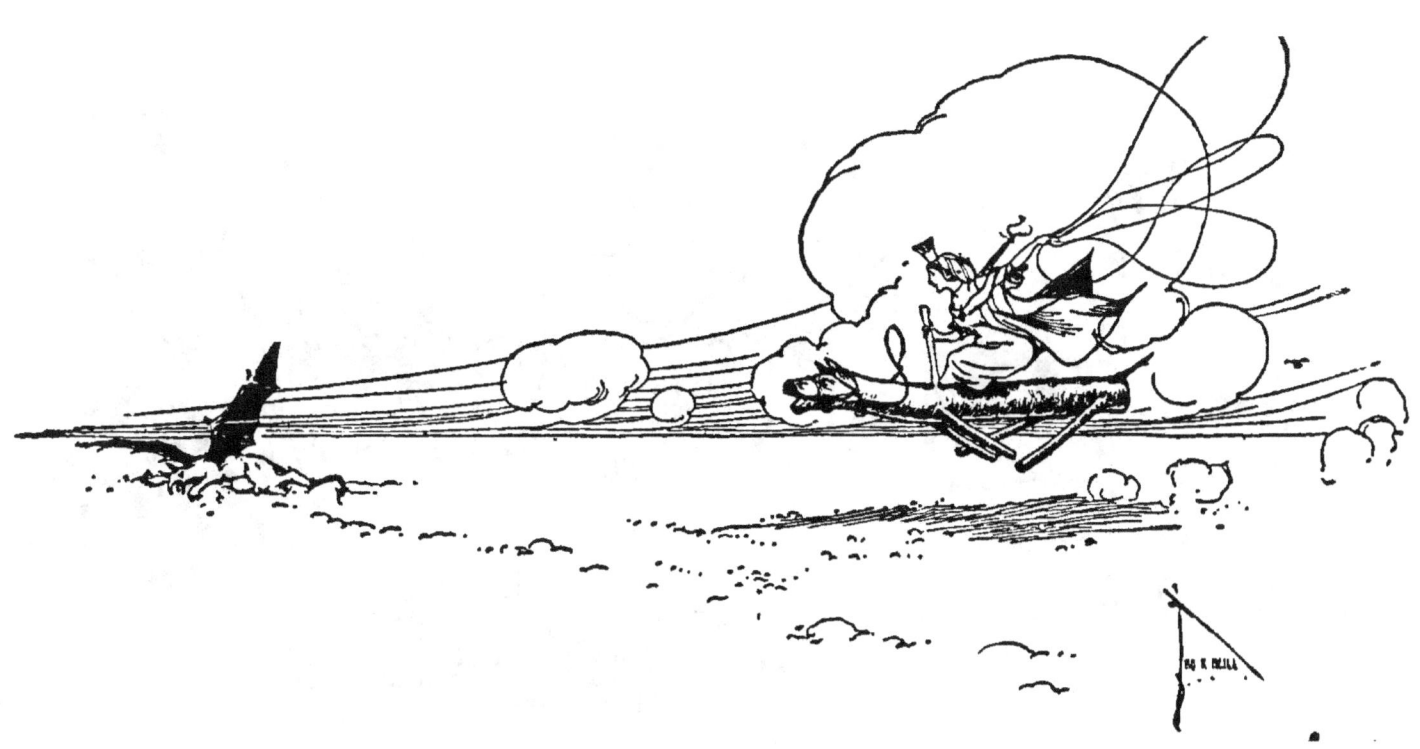

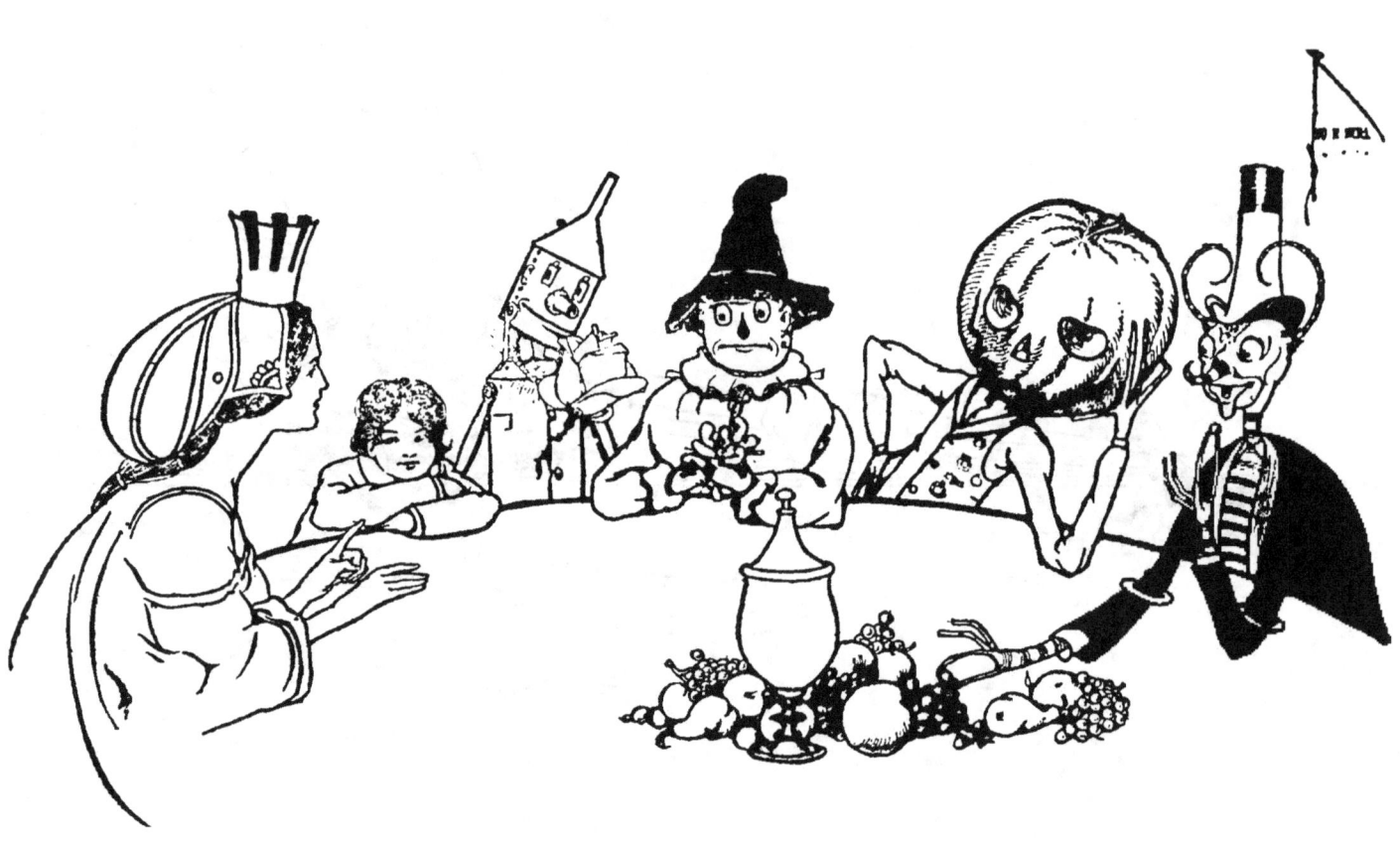

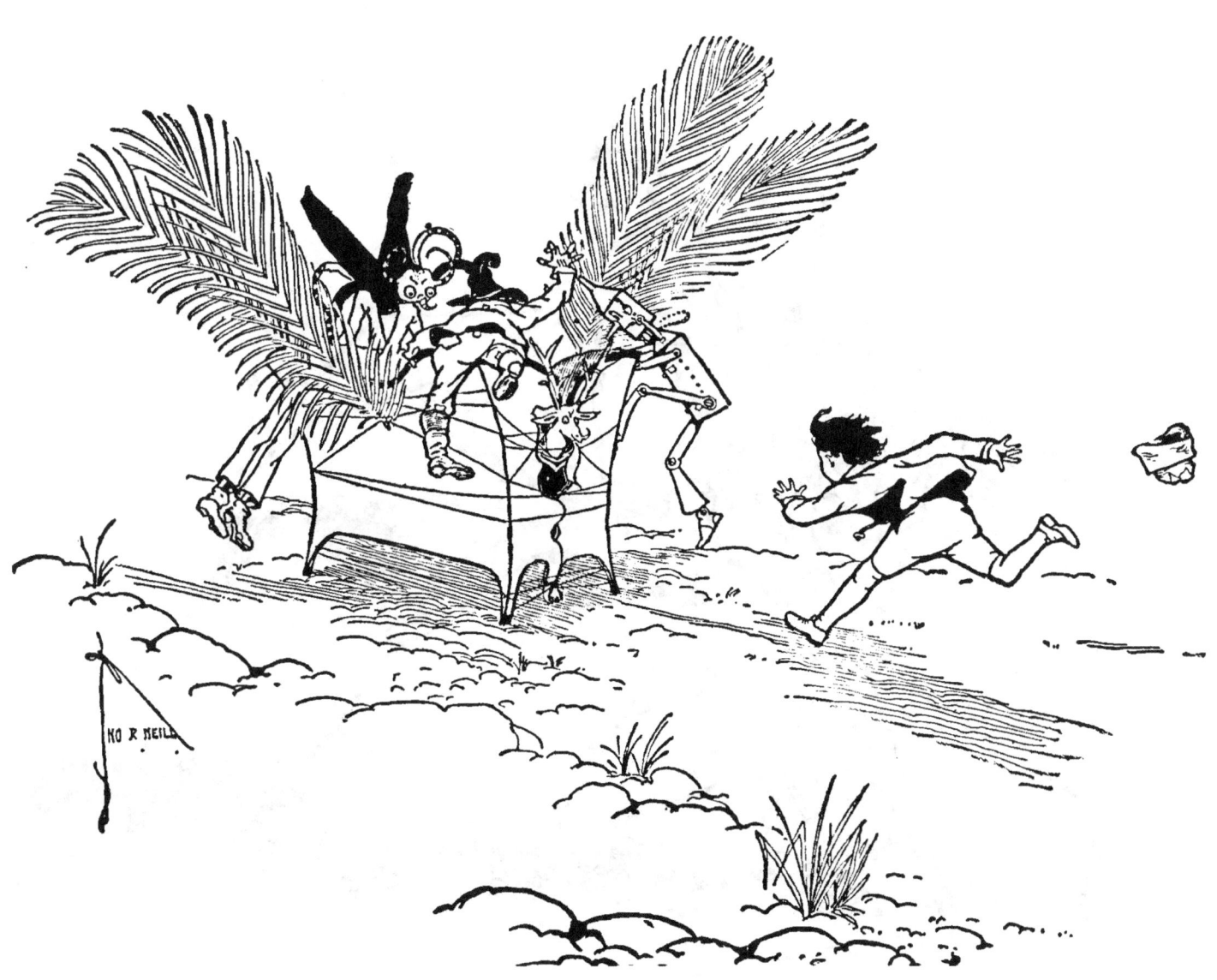

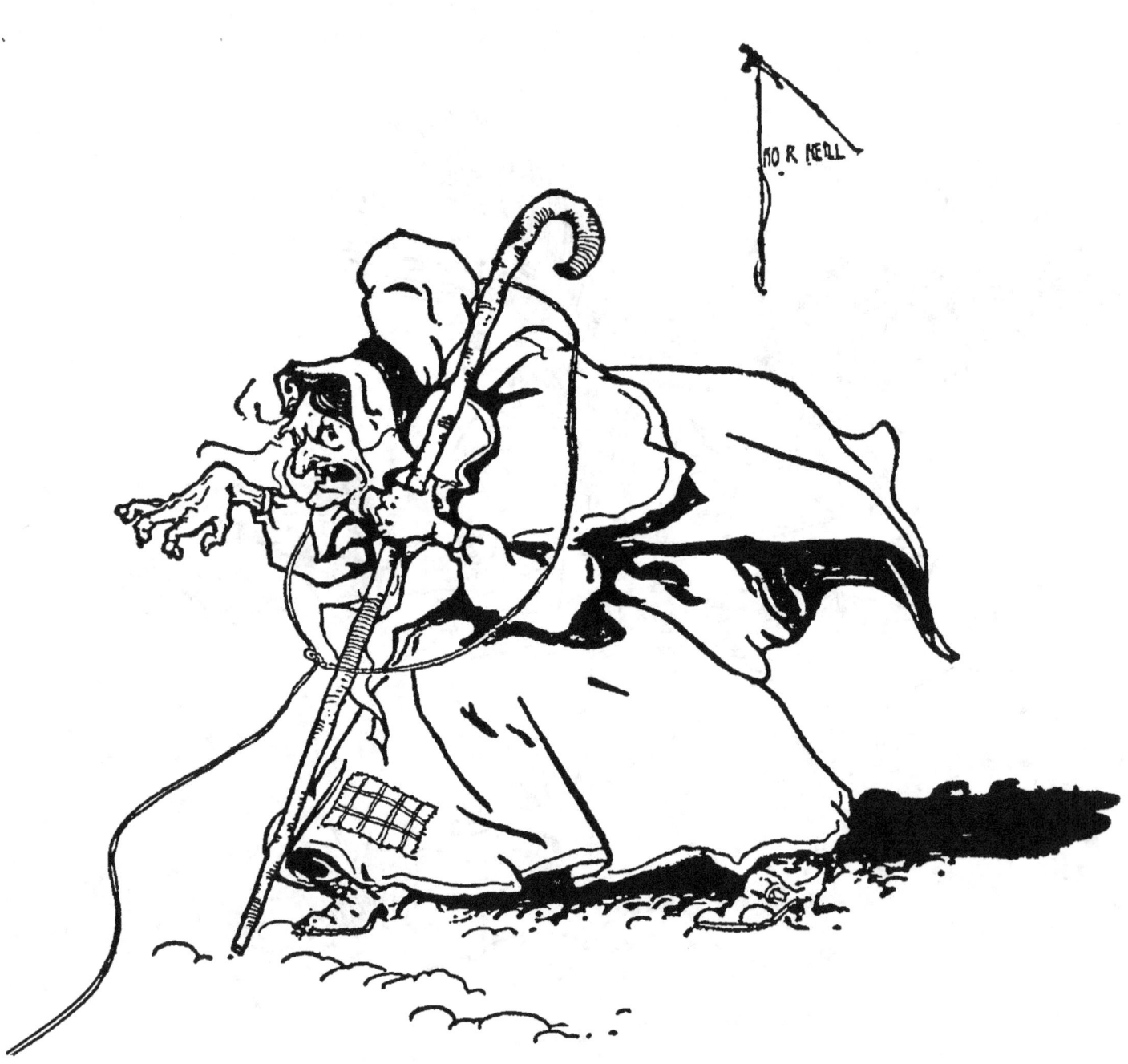

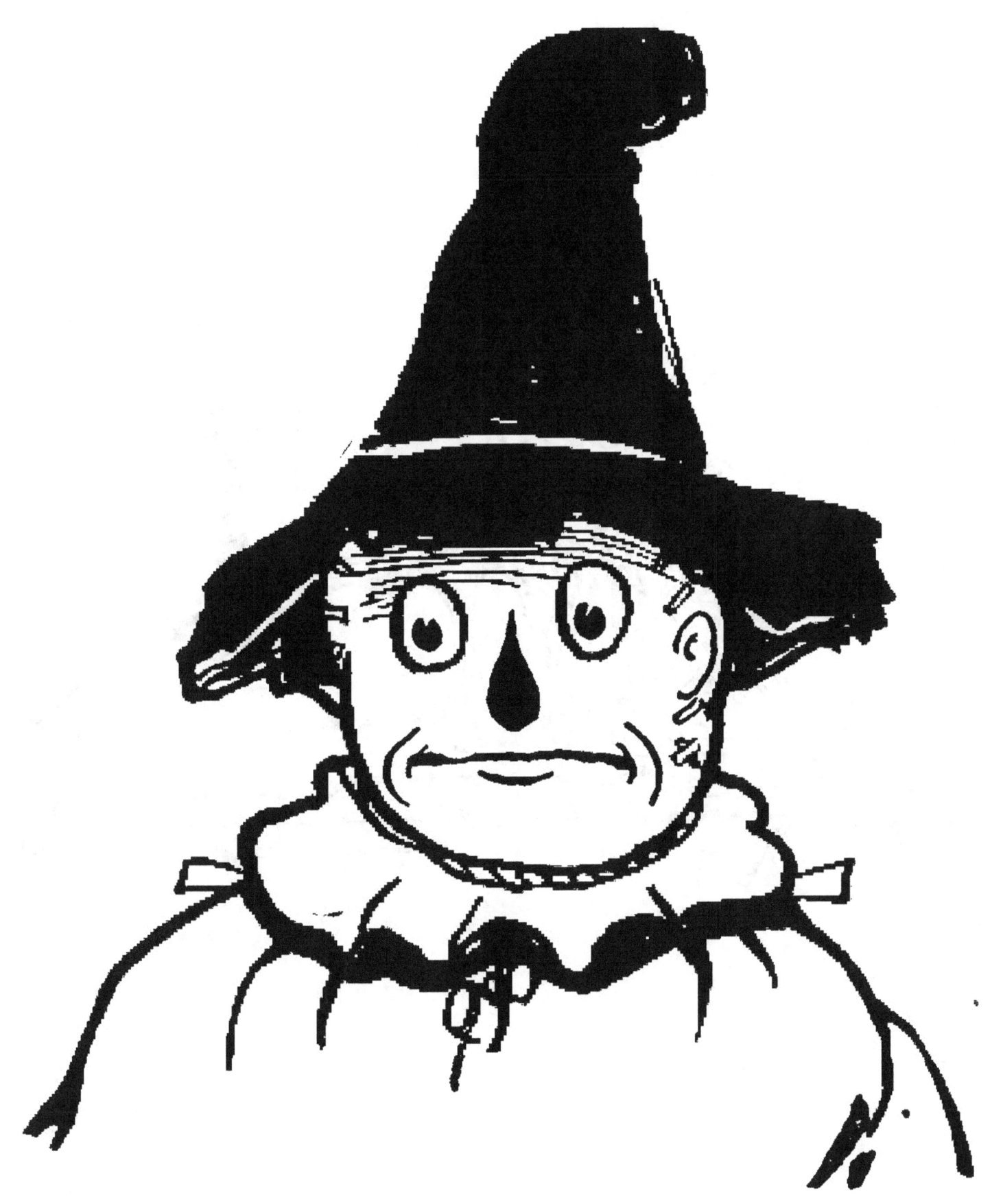

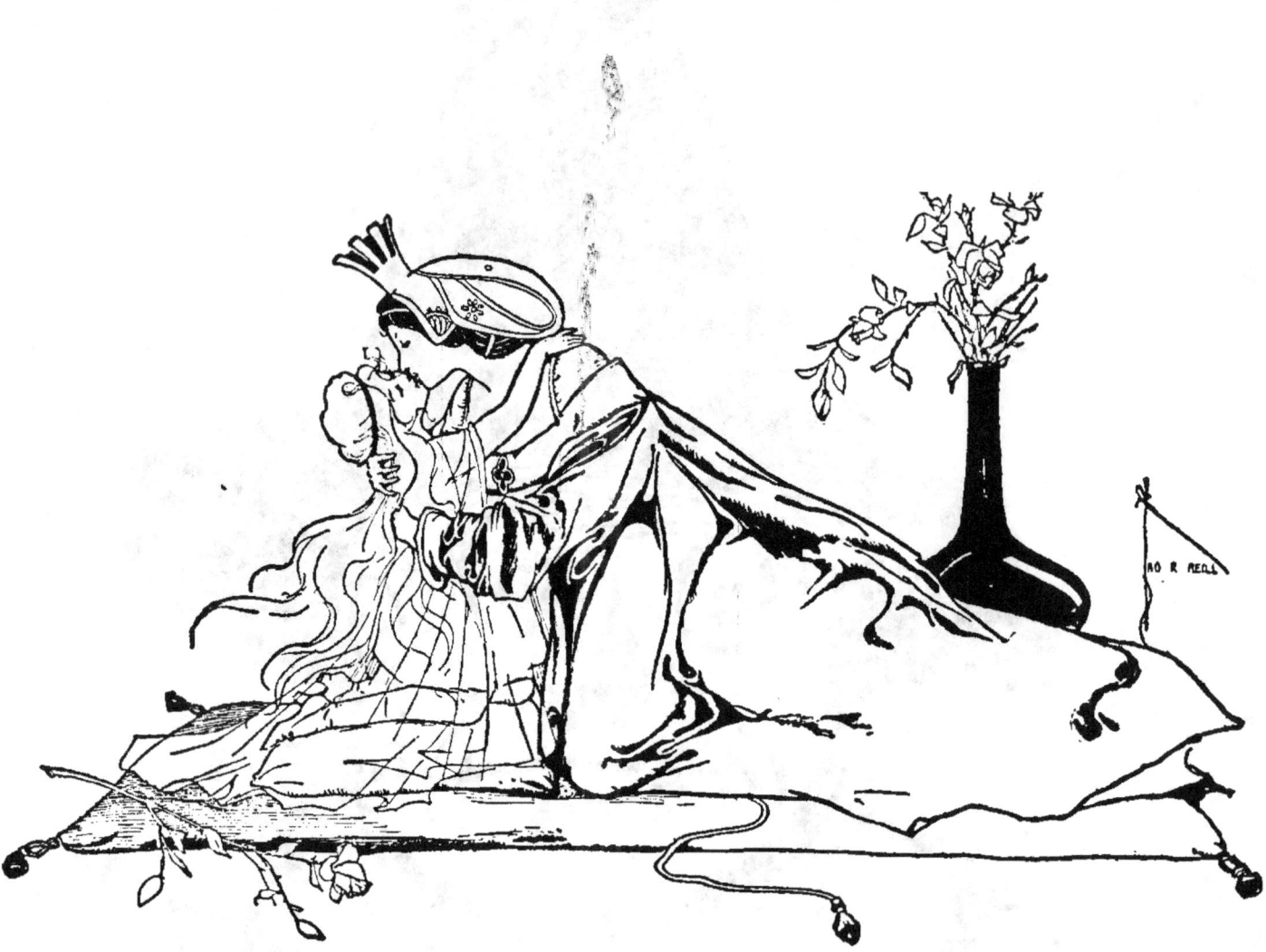

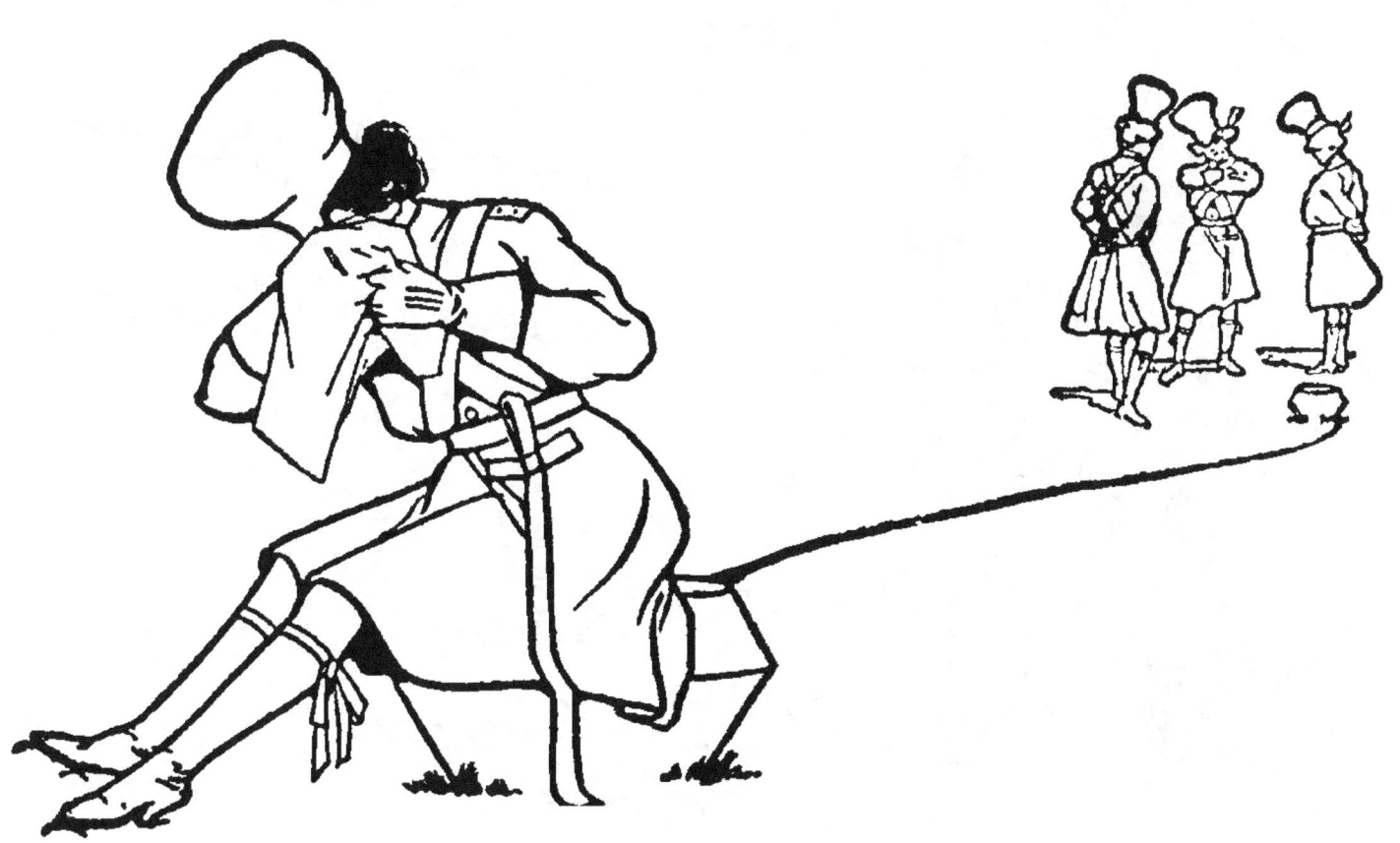

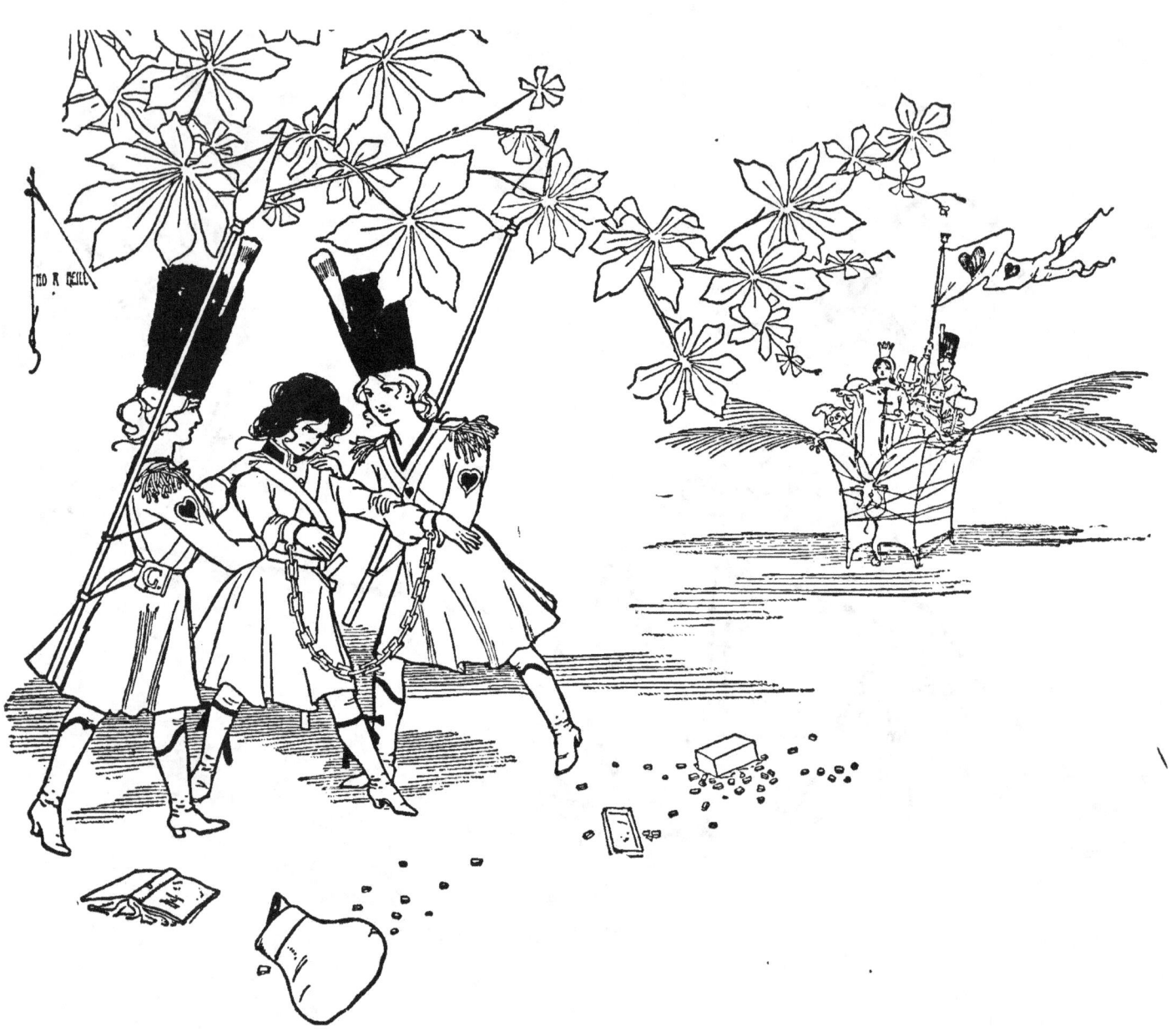

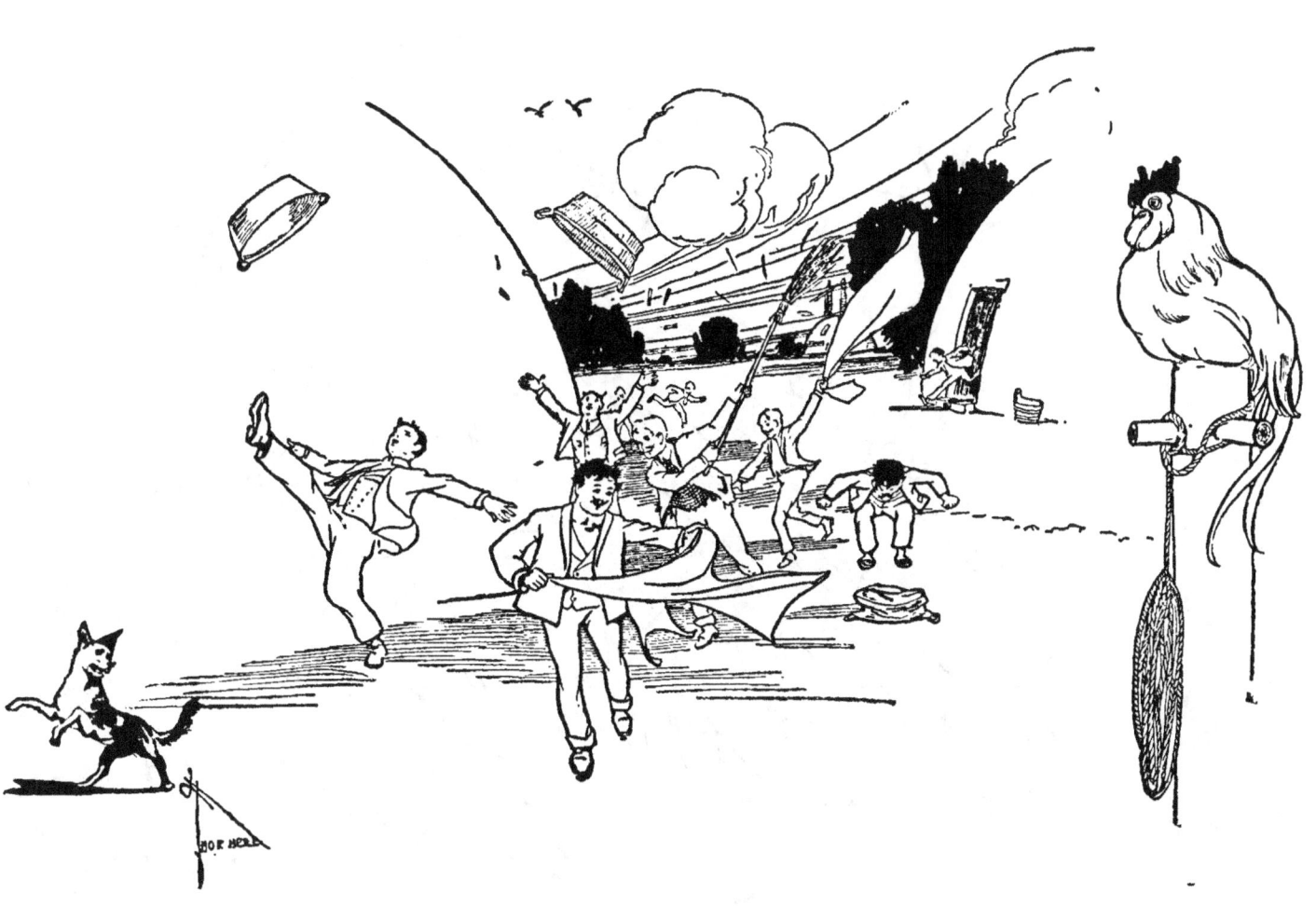

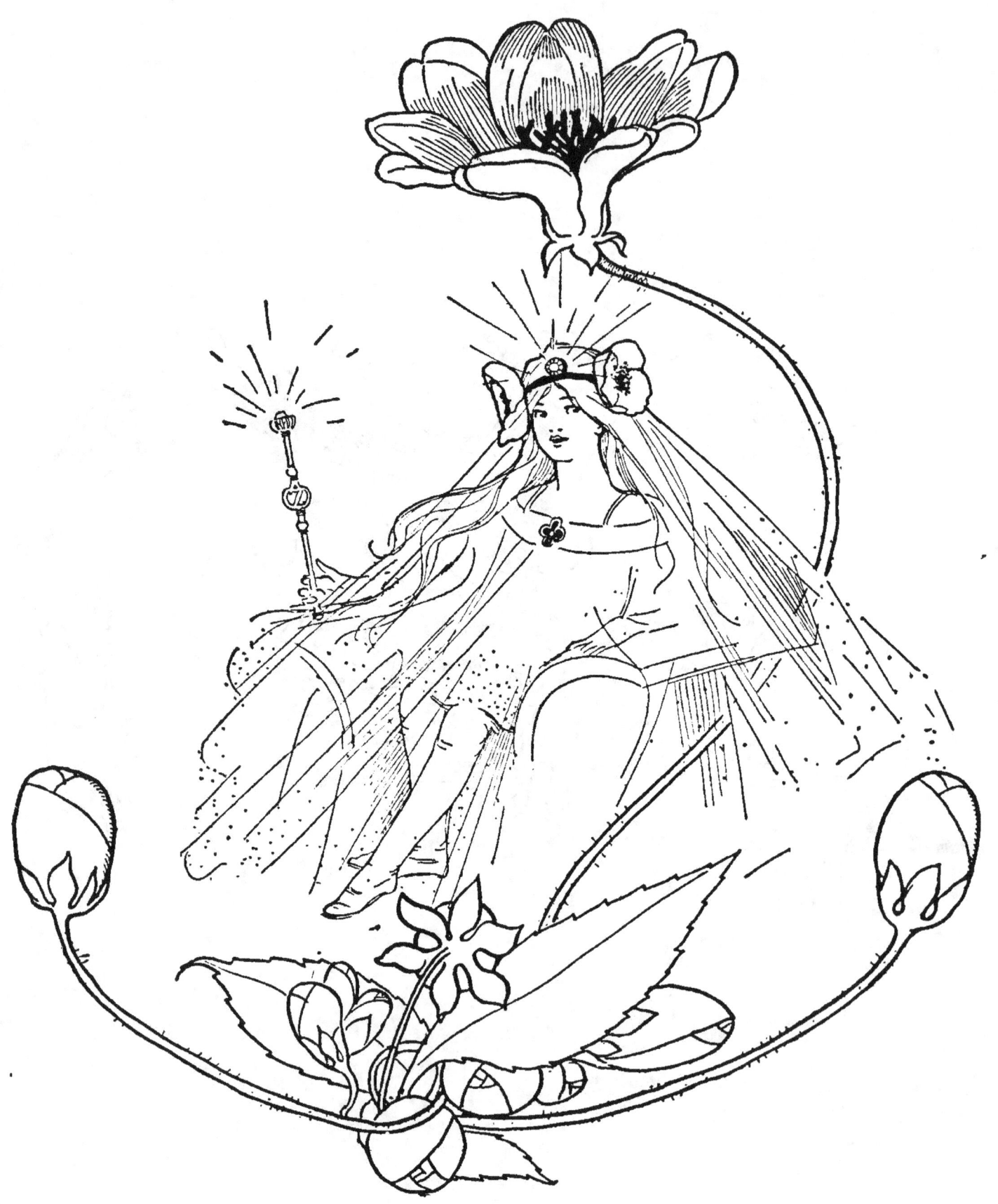